TO
COMFORT
THE
BEREAVED

Also by Aaron Levine

ZICHRON MEIR AL AVEILUS

HOW TO PERFORM THE GREAT MITZVAH OF BIKKUR CHOLIM

THE COMPLETE YIZKOR HANDBOOK

IN TIME OF NEED (revised edition)

THE NEW ROSH HASHANAH ANTHOLOGY

ROSH HASHANAH STORIES AND PARABLES

TO
COMFORT
THE
BEREAVED

A Guide for Mourners
and
Those Who Visit Them

ספר הלכות ניחום אבלים

Rabbi Aaron Levine

JASON ARONSON INC.
Northvale, New Jersey
London

First Jason Aronson Inc. softcover edition—1996

This book was set in 10 pt. Berkeley O.S. by Alpha Graphics of Pittsfield, New Hampshire.

10 9 8 7 6 5 4 3 2

Library of Congress Cataloging-in-Publication Data

Levine, Aaron, 1942-
    To comfort the bereaved : a guide for mourners and those who visit them / Aaron Levine.
      p. cm.
    Includes bibliographical references and index.
    ISBN 1-56821-109-0 (hardcover)
    ISBN 1-56821-966-0 (softcover)
    1. Mourning customs, Jewish. 2. Bereavement—Psychological
aspects. 3. Consolation. 4. Ethics, Jewish. I. Title.
    BM 712.L43 1994
    296.4'45—dc20

                                            93-39381

Manufactured in the United States of America. Jason Aronson Inc. offers books and cassettes. For information and catalog write to Jason Aronson Inc., 230 Livingston Street, Northvale, New Jersey 07647.

אֲנִי מַאֲמִין בֶּאֱמוּנָה שְׁלֵמָה, שֶׁתִּהְיֶה תְּחִיַת הַמֵּתִים בְּעֵת שֶׁיַּעֲלֶה רָצוֹן מֵאֵת הַבּוֹרֵא יִתְבָּרַךְ שְׁמוֹ וְיִתְעַלֶּה זִכְרוֹ לָעַד וּלְנֵצַח נְצָחִים

"I believe with complete faith that there will be a resurrection of the dead whenever the wish emanates from the Creator, blessed is His Name and exalted is His mention, forever and for all eternity."

Maimonides—Thirteenth Principle of Faith

"With faith
there are no questions.
Without it
there are no answers."

Rabbi Yisrael Meir HaKohen Kagan
The Chofetz Chaim

ה' נָתַן וַה' לָקָח יְהִי שֵׁם ה' מְבוֹרָךְ

"The Lord has given
and
The Lord has taken.
May the Name of the Lord
be blessed."

Job 1:21

וְהַמַּשְׂכִּלִים יַזְהִרוּ כְּזֹהַר הָרָקִיעַ
וּמַצְדִּיקֵי הָרַבִּים כַּכּוֹכָבִים לְעוֹלָם וָעֶד:
(דניאל יב ג)

This book is dedicated by the author to all of the generous sponsors whose magnanimous support has made possible its writing and publication.

May Hashem Yisborach bless them and their families with His bounty of blessings for long life, good health, much happiness and success.

May this book truly be a merit for all of their dearly beloved ones, to whom they have dedicated honor or memorial sponsorships.

נר תמיד

לזכר נשמת

רייחיאל ב"ר יצחק אייזיק ז"ל
נפטר כ"ח שבט תשמ"ה

האשה מרת פרומיט בת ר' שמואל הלוי ז"ל
נפטרה כ' מרחשון תשנ"ג

והבחור שמואל ע"ה ב"ר יחיאל ז"ל
נפטר ו' אדר תשל"ה

Dedicated in Loving Memory of

DR. JULIUS KUHL ז"ל

MRS. YVONNE F. KUHL ז"ל

SIDNEY KUHL ע"ה

תנצב"ה

by

The Kuhl Family

נר תמיד

לעילוי נשמות
אבי מורי
ר' **מאיר** ב"ר **אהרן** ז"ל **לעווין**
נפטר כ"א טבת תשמ"ג

בני
אפרים ע"ה ב"ר אהרן נ"י
הבן יקיר לי אפרים אם ילד שעשעים
כי מדי דברי בו זכר אזכרנו עוד על כן המו מעי לו,
רחם ארחמנו נאם ה'
נולד ב' תמוז תשל"ג ונפטר ביום הולדו ב' תמוז תשל"ה

<table>
<tr><td>אמי זקנתי מרת מירל בת ר' שמואל ע"ה
נפטרה ח' אייר תש"ה</td><td>אבי זקני ר' אהרן ב"ר מאיר לעווין ז"ל
נפטר ט' אדר ב' תרפ"ט</td></tr>
<tr><td>אמי זקנתי מרת חיה
בת ר' יהודה אריה ליב ע"ה
נפטרה ט"ז מנחם אב תשל"ד</td><td>אבי זקני ר' יצחק גרשון
ב"ר שמעון וואלף ז"ל
נפטר כ' אייר תשכ"ה</td></tr>
</table>

זקני אשתי

<table>
<tr><td>מרת רבקה בת ר' אשר אנשיל שניצער ע"ה
נפטרה ט"ו סיון תשכ"ב</td><td>ר' אפרים ב"ר ברוך נוסבוים ז"ל
נפטר י"א אייר תשכ"ד</td></tr>
<tr><td>מרת רחל לאה בת ר' אברהם סעגינער ע"ה
נפטרה ב' אלול</td><td>ר' חיים ב"ר יוסף מאיר בארנפרוינד ז"ל
נפטר ח' סיון</td></tr>
</table>

מורי ורבי הגאון מוה"ר **משה רפאל הכהן קפלן** זצ"ל
נפטר כ"א תמוז תשמ"ב

מורי ורבי הגאון מוה"ר **חיים מרדכי קטץ** זצ"ל
נפטר י"ב כסלו תשכ"ה

מורי ורבי הגאון מוה"ר **רפאל ברוך סורוצקין** זצ"ל
נפטר י"ג שבט תשל"ט

מורי ורבי הגאון מוה"ר **דוד קראנגלאס** זצ"ל
נפטר י"א טבת תשל"ג

מורי ורבי הגאון מוה"ר **יעקב יצחק הלוי רודרמן** זצ"ל
נפטר י"ד תמוז תשמ"ז

Contents

7 Visitation Obligations   61

Acknowledgments

I am eternally grateful, first and foremost, to the Almighty for His infinite kindness in allowing me to complete this, my sixth book. I pray for His continued guidance and blessings to allow me to publish my many unprinted manuscripts, especially the remaining volumes of my *Zichron Meir*, an encyclopedia of the laws of mourning. This book is based largely on one small section of that work.

It is my duty, but most certainly a very pleasant task, to express my appreciation to all the people who, in many ways, have contributed to making this book a reality.

To Mr. Arthur Kurzweil, who has been a source of encouragement from the moment he first saw the rough manuscript quite some time ago. He has headed the wonderful team at Jason Aronson Inc. who have enhanced this work immeasurably with their editorial and graphic expertise. No words can express adequately my sincere appreciation for all that they have done to assist me in bringing this work to fruition. A very special thanks to Muriel Jorgensen and Jean Pease, whose infinite patience and support kept me going through the difficult stages of production.

To the following publishers and authors who were so kind to grant me permission to quote from their works:

Rabbi I. Dvorkes and Feldheim Publishers for permission to excerpt stories from *A Tzaddik in Our Time* (Jerusalem, 1976) by Simcha Raz.

To Mr. Michael Benjamin and the Benjamin Family Foundation for permission to excerpt from their booklet *Nichum Aveilim* (Toronto, 1987) by Dr. Michelle Goodman, parts of my section on problematic grief in chapter 10; and from their pamphlet *Guidelines to Understanding the Tradition of Shiva* (Toronto, 1987) by Dr. Simcha Steven Paull.

To Dr. Michelle Goodman for providing me with the bibliography on Grief and Bereavement.

To Mr. Bernard Scharfstein of Ktav Publishing House, Inc., for permission to quote from *Understanding Bereavement and Grief* (New York, 1977), edited by Norman Linzer; from *The Holocaust and Halakhah* (New York, 1976) by Irving J. Rosenbaum; from *A Treasury of Sephardic Laws and Customs* (New York, 1986) by Rabbi Herbert C. Dobrinsky.

To Mr. Charles Bloch of Bloch Publishing Company for permission to quote from *A Time to Mourn* (New York, 1967, 1985) by Jack D. Spiro; from *The Authorized Daily Prayer Book* (New York, 1955) by Dr. Joseph H. Hertz.

To Mr. Jack Goldman of Soncino Press for permission to quote from *Horeb* (London, 1962) by Rabbi S. R. Hirsch, translated by Dayan Grunfeld.

To Rabbi Alfred J. Kolatch of Jonathan David Publishers, Inc., for permission to quote from *The Jewish Way in Death and Mourning* (New York, 1969) by Rabbi Maurice Lamm.

To Rabbi Yaacov Yisrael Byfus and Tashbar Horav for permission to quote from *Yalkut Lekach Tov* (Jerusalem, 5750) by Rabbi Byfus.

To Rabbi Shlomo Wolbe for very special permission to quote from *Alei Shur* (Be'er Yaakov, 1968), and to Rabbi Mendelson, who was most helpful in securing that permission.

To C. Christiansen of Bantam Doubleday and Dell for permission to quote from *When Sorrow Comes* (New York: Doubleday, 1950) by Grace Perkins Oursler and April Armstrong.

To Rabbi Abie Rotenberg for permission to quote the lyrics of *Conversation in the Womb* from *Journeys I* (1984), and *Neshamel'e* from *Journeys II* (1987).

To HaGaon Rabbi Chaim Pinchas Scheinberg, *shlita*, Rosh HaYeshivah of Torah-Ore, who took away from his precious time to peruse the manuscript and to grace it with his letter of blessing. His kindness and encouragement have been a great source of strength to me.

To the magnanimous sponsors whose generous tangible support afforded me the possibility of writing the main parts of this book during my two-year leave of absence from my educational duties, and to those who have additionally contributed more recently and enabled me to continue with my writing endeavors. May the Almighty bless each of them and their families with continued good health and success. May this book bring appropriate merit of memory and honor to the departed and to יב"לח"ם, the living, to whom they have dedicated their generous sponsorships.

To Rabbi Chaim Nussbaum, my esteemed uncle, may he live and be well for many years, for his constant guidance and encouragement and for the assistance provided through Moriah Foundation.

To my dear father, Mr. Myer Levine z"l, whose pride in my work always motivated me to forge ahead. May this book be a merit to his treasured memory.

To my dear mother, Mrs. Tina Levine, and to my dear parents-in-law, Mr. and Mrs. Moshe Nussbaum, whose constant interest and help have always been forthcoming. May the Almighty grant them length of days in good health, much *nachas*, and happiness.

Last, but certainly not least, to my dear wife, Chanie, and our dear children, Yitzchok Gershon, Chaim Ephraim, and Shneur Dovid, without whose constant tolerance, support, and encouragement my writing endeavors would be impossible. May the Almighty grant us many, many years of much *nachas* and many *simchas* in good health and prosperity.

I close with my humble thanks again to the Master of the World for all of His great kindnesses. May He continue to shower upon me good health and strength and a little wisdom, granting me the opportunity to complete many more projected works.

Rabbi Aaron Levine
Toronto, Canada
Completed with praise to the
Almighty, on the second day of
Tammuz (*yahrzeit* of my beloved
son Ephraim, ע"ה), 5753
June 21, 1993

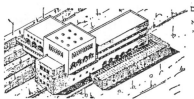

ישיבת .תורה־אור" בעיה"ק ירושלים

בנשיאות מרן הרב הגאון רבי חיים פנחס שיינברג שליט"א

"TORAH-ORE" SEMINARY

THE AMERICAN SEMINARY IN ISRAEL

Kiryat Mattersdorf — קרית מטרסדורף

ת.ד. ★ P.O.B. 6979   טל. ★ Tel. 373049

טל. תלמידים   Tel. Students 371400, 372200

JERUSALEM, 91150 ISRAEL

ב״ה ו׳ אייר תשנ״ג

מכתב תהלה

It is not my custom to write a letter of approbation on a halachic work. Nevertheless, it is indeed with great pleasure that I write this letter of commendation to Rabbi Aaron Levine, noted educator and author, upon the completion of his latest book, on the subject of *nichum aveilim,* comforting mourners.

In this book, the author expounds on the applicable halachic observances, and on related psychological and statistical data in the field of bereavement.

It is very evident that the production of this work entailed meticulous research. Its contents abide throughout with the letter and spirit of authentic halacha, and the author manifests a high level of compassion and empathy for those in grief.

Rabbi Levine himself experienced the anguish of losing a child, and several years later witnessed the terrible degenerating disease that took the life of his father, ע"ה. He also has written extensively on the subjects of sickness and mourning, and has published the first volume of a comprehensive compendium of codes and responsa on the laws of *aveilus.* He is thus in a unique position to write on the topic of comforting the bereaved.

I warmly welcome this valuable contribution to our storehouse of sacred literature. Bereavement is by its very nature a sensitive subject, and this book handles with deep understanding the task of offering guidance when it is most sorely needed.

I, too, add my blessings that the Almighty comfort the bereaved among the mourners of Zion and Jerusalem.

Rabbi Chaim P. Scheinberg
Dean, Torah-Ore Seminary

Introduction

I began writing on the subject of death, bereavement, and mourning over eighteen years ago when I was struck with the untimely death of my two-year-old son Ephraim ה"ע. Ten years ago I watched for six months how the illness of cancer slowly took away from me my beloved father, ז"ל.

Last year, before Rosh HaShanah, I was invited to speak to a support group in Toronto, Bereaved Jewish Parents. Generally, I believe in all types of support groups, certainly for those who find them necessary and helpful. But the idea of people who have been bereaved for many, many years getting together before each Jewish holiday to discuss how they were going to get through another difficult *Yom Tov* troubled me somewhat. It seemed to me that this was a way of perpetuating and adding to the grief rather than dealing with it, accepting it, and trying to get on with life. At the end of the evening a gentleman arose and said, "Remember, it is not *we* who have to ask *God* for forgiveness on Yom Kippur; it is *He* Who has to ask *us* for forgiveness."

I deeply sympathize with all bereaved and, having been an unfortunate member of this great family, I truly feel a deep empathy for them. I commend the support group for their wonderful intentions and no criticism is meant. One is not held accountable for statements such as the above remark when they are uttered out of the depths of anguish (see page 90). But throughout this book you will read of the Torah view that excessive grief is both untraditional and, more importantly, from a practical sense, actually harmful, both to the living and to the soul of the deceased. I tried to present this viewpoint that evening in the brief span of time that was allotted to me, as there were other speakers. Leaving the room that night I became more convinced that I must write a book to try to spread this lesson to the bereaved all over the world. It's not a popular stance, nor is it one that is immediately accepted. But the truth must be stated. The Torah view must be expressed.

There are appropriate times when we should remember: *Yahrzeit* and *Yizkor*, and other times when we visit the cemetery, such as on Tishah B'Av and *erev* Rosh HaShanah and *erev* Yom Kippur. But life must go on. Our dearly departed do not benefit in any way when we offer them, throughout our lifetime, testimonials of tears and sadness and monuments of unabated grief. Is it a tribute to the memory of our beloved departed that in mourning their death our grief causes us to die also while we are still living?

We may not castigate God and demand that He ask us for forgiveness. What we may do, however, will follow. But let me first tell you a story.

A little over thirty years ago, I was present at the *bar mitzvah* of the son of one of my great *roshei hayeshivah*, Rabbi Chaim Mordechai Katz, *ztz'l*, the former head of the Telshe Yeshivah in Wickliffe, Ohio. He began his speech as follows.

The great gaon, Rabbi Aryeh Leib Gunzberg, the Shaagas Aryeh (born 1695, died 1785) held his last rabbinic post in the city of Metz. All his life until that time he had suffered great poverty. When he first came to Metz he was shown his new home, a beautiful mansion compared to any in which he had lived previously. As he went from room to room admiring the comfortable and spacious living quarters, those around him detected some mumbling of Hebrew words but couldn't hear what the rabbi was saying. When they left the house, one of the more curious *baalei batim* asked the rabbi what it was he had been saying as he was inspecting the various rooms of the house.

"I'll tell you," said Reb Aryeh. "There is a verse in Psalms (90:15) that says: 'Make us happy [O, God] as the days You have afflicted us; we have seen bad years.' I interpret that to mean that we ask God to give us cause to rejoice according to the measure of affliction that He metes out to us. When I saw this beautiful mansion I repeated this verse over and over and said to God: Dear God, all my life You have afflicted me with poverty. Now I beseech You, corresponding to that measure of affliction, afford me a corresponding amount of rejoicing and allow me, with Your blessings, to live the rest of my life in comfort and tranquillity.

"In the Holocaust I lost a wife and ten children," continued Rabbi Katz. "My prayer to the *Ribbono Shel Olom* is that He will allow me to rejoice with this son and my other children in corresponding measure to the pain and affliction which He decreed upon me."

Since the loss of my beloved son, Ephraim, I have echoed these sentiments many times at family *simchas*. This we are permitted to say to the Almighty: "Dear God, I accept Your decrees, Your affliction, without questioning Your inscrutable ways. I do not murmur against the wisdom of Your secret ways. You are *Dayan HaEmes,* a true Judge. But please, I beg of You, corresponding to that measure of affliction, bless us with a full measure of joy and happiness with the rest of our loved ones, in health and happiness for length of days."

In May 1993 I had the good fortune of attending the Principals' Convention of Torah Umesorah, the National Society of Hebrew Day Schools, which was held in the company of many great *gedolim* (sages) of our time. I asked HaGaon Rabbi Shimon Schwab, *shlita,* to kindly tell me a "good word" that I could incorporate into this book. What follows is the incredible insight and explanation that he told me. In a way, it cancels out the title of this book, which was retained only because of the popular connotation of the words *nichum aveilim*—not because I disagree with the interpretation.

Rabbi Schwab, *shlita,* said to me, "*Nichum aveilim* does not mean 'to comfort mourners.' It means to 'change their minds.' I base this," he said, "on the following verse in the Torah in connection with the story of Joseph and his brothers after the death of Yaakov Avinu (Jacob): '. . .*Vayenachem osom vayedaber al libom*' (Genesis 50:21).[1] There we see clearly that the word *vayenachem* is not 'comforting,' because it is followed by the words *vayedaber al libom*, which means 'he comforted them'—he 'spoke to their hearts.' Joseph changed the minds of his brothers by convincing them that whatever they had thought to do, God had thought otherwise and planned it all for the good. They therefore had nothing to fear. The word *vayenachem* would be similar to the word in the verse at the end of Genesis 6:6: '*Vayinachem HaShem ki asah es ha'adam*'—'And *HaShem* regretted (changed His mind, *kivyachol*) that He had made man.'"[2]

This is also what is meant in the verse, "*Nachamu nachamu ami*" (Isaiah 40:1). God will ultimately change our minds about the tribulations of the *galus* (exile). We may have thought all along that they were bad for us. He will show us how they were all intended for good. And similarly the phrase, "*HaMokom yenachem eschem*" means the same thing. May *HaShem* change our minds about mourning by ultimately showing us how all was meant for the good, as He will show all the mourners of Zion and Jerusalem how the destruction of the Temples was all for the good.

Please refer to chapter 9, pp. 103-105, where I have elaborated on this concept and recorded the parable of the Dubno *Maggid*. How beautifully Rabbi Schwab has incorporated this lesson into the very word *nichum* of the Hebrew language.

It is in sincere attempt to clarify these truths and lessons that I present

this volume to all bereaved, with the prayers that many will be strengthened by the words of the Torah, the Talmud, the sages, and the lives of
our great *tzaddikim*, who bore grief uprightly and brought great merit in
doing so to themselves and the souls of their dearly departed.

I have also been asked many times about the proper procedures, customs, and origins for comforting the mourners, as well as what one should
say and do at the *shivah* house. To all those who share in this great *mitzvah*,
I pray that this work will help answer many of your questions.

Above all, may the time come when *HaShem*, in His infinite mercies,
"will destroy death forever and banish tears from all faces" (Isaiah 25:8).
Amein!

1

The Obligation to Perform Acts of Kindness

NICHUM AVEILIM—A COMPONENT OF THE MITZVAH OF CHESED

The *mitzvah* of *nichum aveilim* (comforting mourners), in addition to constituting an independent *mitzvah*, is also included in the general *mitzvah* of performing *chesed* (acts of kindness).

It is appropriate, therefore, to begin with a clarification of the obligation to perform the broader *mitzvah* of *gemillus chesed*.

MAN WAS CREATED ONLY BY MERIT OF DOING GOOD DEEDS

The *Midrash* states: "Rabbi Simon said: When the time came for God to create man, the ministering angels formed into groups. Some said man should not be created, and some said he should be created.... Kindness said: Let him be created since he will perform good deeds."[1]

From the above it is apparent that one of the justifications for the very creation of man was the fact that, once created, he would perform acts of kindness and good deeds.

THE TORAH BEGINS AND ENDS WITH CHESED

The Talmud points out that the Torah commences and also closes with narratives describing acts of *gemillus chesed* performed by the Almighty

Himself, *kivyachol*. The beginning of the Torah relates that *HaShem* made garments for Adam and Chavah (Eve), and the end relates that He buried Mosheh Rabbeinu.[2]

Not only are we obligated to emulate *HaShem*'s ways,[3] but we can furthermore deduce by *kal vechomer (a fortiori)*[4] that if *HaShem* Himself performs *chesed* for His creatures, certainly man should perform *chesed* for his fellow man.

LOVING YOUR FELLOW MAN AS YOURSELF

In addition, the obligation to perform *chesed* derives from the ever-present *mitzvah* of "*veohavta lerei'acha komocha*"—"You shall love your fellow man as [you love] yourself."[5] This *mitzvah* is regarded as such a fundamental principle of Judaism that Rabbi Akiva declared it to be the golden rule of the Torah.[6]

The Talmud also relates the story of the Gentile who wished to convert to Judaism on the condition that he be taught the whole Torah while standing on one foot. Hillel summed up the Torah by stating, "What is hateful to you do not do unto your fellow man. The rest is explanation; go study it."[7]

Conversely, loving one's fellow man means doing unto others that which we would want others to do unto us.[8]

IDENTIFYING TOTALLY WITH ANOTHER'S NEEDS

Real love of one's fellow man means a complete identification, understanding, and involvement with his needs and difficulties. Rabbi Moshe Leib of Sasov and Rabbi Dovid of Lelov told their disciples that a simple peasant had taught them the true extent of this. Each one once overheard the following similar conversation between two peasants.

"Do you love me?" asked the first.

"Of course I love you," responded his friend.

"Do you know what I need and what is troubling me?" asked the first.

"How can I know what you need and what is troubling you?" wondered the loving friend.

"Then you don't really love me," said the first peasant, "for if you did, you would surely know all my needs and all that troubles me."[9]

LOVING TO DO KINDNESS

The prophet Michah declares:

הִגִּיד לְךָ אָדָם מַה־טּוֹב וּמָה־ה' דּוֹרֵשׁ מִמְּךָ כִּי אִם־עֲשׂוֹת מִשְׁפָּט וְאַהֲבַת חֶסֶד וכו'

"Man, you have been told what is good and what *HaShem* requires from you; do justice, love kindness, and walk humbly with your God."[10]

Asks the saintly Chofetz Chaim: "Why does the above verse stress *love* kindness? Should it not merely have stated do justice, *do* kindness, and walk humbly?" Says the Chofetz Chaim:

> This teaches us an important lesson about our obligation to do kindness. Most of us, if not all, do perform kindnesses. But almost always our acts of kindness are reluctant responses to a request that we find difficult to refuse. A broken-hearted man may come to ask a favor. We are embarrassed to decline this request so we respond by helping him. But the situation had really left us with no choice, and the deed is not done with a real desire and a full heart, and often only in a manner that minimally satisfies the need.
>
> There is a great difference between this and one who performs *chesed* out of sheer love for the recipient of his *chesed*. The test for this is to compare how one acts toward his own family. When one feeds and clothes his own wife and children or performs a host of other kindnesses to them, out of a true love for them, he extends himself far beyond their minimum needs. He constantly seeks ways to do kindnesses to them even when not asked. And when he performs these kindnesses, he does them with a joyous heart, happy that he can do good to those whom he loves.
>
> Loving to do kindness means extending kindness to each and every one of our fellow men in the same manner that we would do so for our own families. It means searching eagerly for methods and ways, unsolicited, unapproached, performing beyond the call of duty with a fervor and joy that displays our enthusiasm for this *mitzvah*, responding so generously that we go even beyond the actual need.[11]

MORE PRECIOUS THAN SACRIFICES

Our *sifrei nevi'im* (writings of the prophets) are replete with verses that propound the significance of performing acts of kindness.

The prophet Hosheah exhorts in the name of the Almighty,

כִּי חֶסֶד חָפַצְתִּי וְלֹא־זָבַח, וְדַעַת אֱלֹקִים מֵעוֹלוֹת

"For it is *kindness* that I desire and not sacrifices."[12]

On this the *Yalkut* comments, "Says the *Ribbono Shel Olom*: 'The acts of *kindness* that you do unto each other are more precious to me than all the sacrifices offered to me by [King] Solomon.'"[13]

EQUIVALENT TO THE ATONING POWERS OF THE *BEIS HAMIKDASH*

The *Yalkut* there relates the following story:

"Rabban Yochanan ben Zakkai was once walking in Jerusalem accompanied by Rabbi Yehoshua. When he noticed the remains of the ruins of the *Beis HaMikdash* (the Holy Temple) Rabbi Yehoshua exclaimed, 'Alas, the place that possessed the virtue of atoning for our sins is now destroyed.' Said Rabban Yochanan ben Zakkai, 'My son, do not be distressed, for we have another means of atonement that is equally effective—acts of kindness. As it is written, "For it is kindness that I desire and not sacrifices." It is also written, "For I have said, the world will be built on kindness."'"[14]

GEMILLUS CHASADIM GREATER THAN TZEDAKAH

The prophet Hosheah proclaims,

זִרְעוּ לָכֶם לִצְדָקָה קִצְרוּ לְפִי־חֶסֶד וכו'

"Sow for yourselves charity and reap according to the kindnesses that you perform."[15] On this the Talmud comments: Rabbi Elazar said, "Acts of kindness are *greater* than *tzedakah*. When a man sows he does not yet know whether he will indeed eat the fruits of his sowing; but when he reaps, he shall certainly eat the fruits of his labor."[16]

The Talmud comments: Our Rabbis taught that in three ways acts of kindness are *greater* than *tzedakah*. Acts of kindness are accomplished not only by *monetary* means but also by one's physical body. *Tzedakah* is given only to the *poor*; acts of kindness are conferred upon both poor and rich. *Tzedakah* is given only to the *living*; acts of kindness are performed for both the living and the dead."[17]

ONE OF THE THREE PILLARS OF THE UNIVERSE

We are all familiar with the famous saying from *Ethics of the Fathers*,

עַל שְׁלשָׁה דְבָרִים הָעוֹלָם עוֹמֵד: עַל הַתּוֹרָה, וְעַל הָעֲבוֹדָה, וְעַל גְּמִילוּת
חֲסָדִים

"The world stands on three pillars—on Torah, on worship, and on acts of kindness."[18] The Talmud states: "There are three distinguishing characteristics of the nation of Israel—they are merciful, modest, and performers of kind deeds."[19] In yet another passage in the Talmud we are called גּוֹמְלֵי חֲסָדִים בְּנֵי גּוֹמְלֵי חֲסָדִים—"performers of kindness, children of performers of kindness."[20]

HOW OUR KINDNESS DIFFERS
FROM THAT OF OTHER NATIONS

Yet the question may be posed, "Is it only the nation of Israel who does kindness? Do not other nations also perform acts of kindness? In fact, one of the reasons we do not recite a blessing when we are about to do kindness is because this *mitzvah* is not exclusive to the nation of Israel.[21]

The answer to this can be found perhaps in a comment by the Ozerover *rebbe ztz'l*.[22] On the verse in the Torah, וכו' בָה יֵלְכוּ אֶת־הַדֶרֶךְ לָהֶם וְהוֹדַעְתָּ —"And you shall show them the way they should go,"[23] the Talmud states, "The *way*—this means *gemillus chasadim*, acts of kindness."[24]

> Asks the *rebbe*, "Does not another passage in the Talmud interpret this very same word, 'the way,' to mean *Talmud Torah*, the study and teaching of Torah?[25] Are these two passages thus not contradictory?"
>
> "No," answers the *rebbe*. "This teaches us that all the acts of kindness we do should not be performed merely out of common courtesy and pity, as is mostly the case with other nations. Rather they should be performed because of the Torah's command and in accordance with Torah guidelines. These very acts are thus transformed into Torah. Note that the *gematriya* (the numerical value) of the letters of the Hebrew word *Torah* equals the numerical value of the Hebrew words *gemillus chasadim* (611). This indicates that *chesed* is inseparable from Torah. Furthermore the Talmud points out that the very beginning and end of the Torah deal with acts of kindness."[26]

PERFORMING *CHESED* EACH AND
EVERY DAY OF ONE'S LIFE

The Chofetz Chaim writes the following:

> Some people mistakenly think that by performing one kind act for another person, they are freed of further obligation for several weeks, even if they could be doing the same for others also. I have elaborated on the trait of kindness to dispel this misconception. Every day of your life, whenever the opportunity arises to perform this *mitzvah*, you must perform it if you can, even many times in one day. . . .
>
> Just as a man must study Torah every day, so too must he be careful to show kindness every day of his life. As Rabbi Chaim Vital says in his *Sefer Shaar HaKedushah*, "A Jew should regret any day that has passed without Torah study or acts of kindness."[27]

Similarly the Shaloh HaKodosh writes: "Therefore, one should be extremely careful to observe the *mitzvah* of *gemillus chasadim* and should see to it that not a single day of the days of his life goes by without performing some deed of *gemillus chesed* with his body, his money, or his soul."[28]

REWARDS FOR THIS *MITZVAH*

Although our *mitzvos* should be performed *lishmah* (for their own sake) and not for the ulterior motive of receiving rewards, nevertheless the rewards vouchsafed by the Almighty for the fulfillment of this *mitzvah* are clear, as we shall also mention in the coming chapters.

We have also been taught that our conduct on earth brings a corresponding response from *HaShem* above. If a man acts kindly here on this earth, this arouses kindness above. The angels sing on that day, and the day is crowned because of him. If he acts mercifully on earth, mercy is aroused above upon that day, and the day is crowned in mercy because of him. Then that day stands ready to protect him in case of need. The rule is: However a man acts toward or judges others, in like manner he is treated and judged from above. He who does good deeds on this earth will gain merit, for arousing God's kindness depends entirely on one's earthly conduct.[29]

Rabbi Shimon ben Elazar taught: The verse states, "You shall love your fellow man as yourself, I am *HaShem*. I, *HaShem*, have created him. If you will love him you can trust Me to surely repay you with great reward; if not, I am also the Judge who exacts retribution."[30]

In *Pirkei d'Rabbi Eliezer* the following is written:

King Solomon saw how the trait of performing good deeds was so great in the eyes of the Almighty. Therefore when he built the Temple he built two gates—one for bridegrooms and one for mourners. . . . Those who entered through the gate of the mourners would say upon seeing a mourner: "May He Who dwells in this House comfort you." . . . When the Temple was destroyed it was instituted that bridegrooms and mourners should go to the synagogues and houses of learning. People who saw . . . the mourners would sit on the ground next to them [to comfort them] . . . in order that Israel would meet their obligation to fulfill the *mitzvah* of *gemillus chasadim*. And upon them it is said: "Blessed are You, *HaShem*, Who pays a great reward to those who perform kind deeds."[31]

WHAT WE SHOULD ASK OURSELVES

In keeping with the lessons taught to the rabbis of Sassov and Lelov by the simple peasants, perhaps each of us should ask ourselves: "Do I really know and appreciate how much my friend may need me in this difficult time? Am I truly concerned for his or her welfare? If I were in mourning, sitting *shivah*, God forbid, in what manner would I want others to visit me, to care for me and comfort me? How do the Torah, Talmud, and *Shulchan Aruch* instruct me and help me in the performance of this *mitzvah* to its fullest extent in accordance with their guidelines and ideals?"

The following chapters will answer most of these questions. Let us study them and resolve to strengthen our commitment to the *mitzvah* of *nichum aveilim*.

2

The Obligation to Comfort
the Mourner

A *MITZVAH* FROM THE TORAH

There are opinions that the *mitzvah* of *nichum aveilim* is an ordinance
established by rabbinical legislation [*d'Rabbanan*].[1] Most halachic codifiers,
however, classify this *mitzvah* as a biblical precept [*d'Oraisa*].[2] In fact, this
mitzvah may constitute the fulfillment of *several* Torah precepts.

EMULATING THE ALMIGHTY

One of these precepts is the essential principle of the Torah that one should
"walk in the ways of the Almighty" by emulating His deeds.[3] The Torah records
that *HaShem* Himself, *kivyachol*, performed this *mitzvah* by visiting our patriarchs Isaac[4] and Jacob[5] to comfort them after the loss of their loved ones.

LOVING ONE'S FELLOW MAN

A second precept that *nichum aveilim* directly fulfills is the *mitzvah* of "You
shall love your fellow man as [you love] yourself." This has been discussed in
the first chapter.

GEMILLUS CHASADIM

The Torah states: "And you shall show them the *way* on which they should
go."[6] From the word *haderech*—the way—the Talmud deduces a direct ref-

9

erence to the *mitzvah* of *gemillus chasadim*.[7] Certainly the *mitzvah* of *nichum aveilim* is included in the all-encompassing *mitzvah* of performing kindness.[8] This has also been discussed at length in the first chapter.

GLADDENING THE HEART OF THE DEPRESSED

There is generally a *mitzvah* of cheering anyone, even a person who is in the best of physical health, when we notice that he or she is despondent.[9] The following incident is related about Rabbi Yisroel of Salant.

A student of Rabbi Salanter once noticed him standing on a street corner, seemingly engaged in idle chatter and joking with a stranger. The student who was accustomed to Rabbi Salanter's serious demeanor and behavior was puzzled by this totally uncharacteristic levity. When he later questioned his mentor concerning the incident, Rabbi Salanter explained his conduct as follows: "That man had personal problems that were causing him much despondency; all I was trying to do was to cheer him out of his depression."[10]

The Talmud also relates the following story:

Rabbi Beroka the Seer frequently went to the marketplace of Bei Lapat, where Elijah the prophet often appeared to him. Once, Rabbi Beroka asked him, "Is there anyone in this place who has a share in the World to Come?"

Elijah replied, "No." While they were conversing two men passed by and Elijah remarked, "*These* two have a share in the World to Come."

Rabbi Beroka approached the two men and asked them what their occupation was. They replied, "We are jesters. When we notice people who are depressed we cheer them; when we see two people quarreling we strive hard to make peace between them."[11]

Certainly this *mitzvah* applies to a mourner whose heart is burdened and despondent over his great loss and who needs words of comfort to cheer him and raise his failing spirits.[12]

RESTORING A LOST OBJECT TO ITS OWNER

Another precept that *nichum aveilim* fulfills is that of *hashavas aveidah*— restoring a lost object to its rightful owner.[13] If one is required to return a lost monetary object, how much more so is one required to restore and return health and life itself to its rightful owner.[14]

Often a mourner can be so overcome by grief that his very physical and mental state of health can be in jeopardy. A visit to comfort him and to raise his spirits can be vital in restoring sound health to him. Similarly, his faith in God may be shaken a little through the tragedy that may have occurred. A visit to him at this time can bring about some restrengthening of faith, which is as important as restoring to him physical health.[15]

NO LIMIT

The *mitzvah* of *nichum aveilim* being part of *gemillus chasadim* is enumerated among those *mitzvos* that have no limit,[16] and the more one visits even the same mourner, the more praiseworthy he is.[17] Obviously, this is true only when his multiple visits are appreciated and wanted by the mourners and do not, on the contrary, become burdensome to them.[18]

NO *BRACHAH*

The *mitzvah* of *nichum aveilim* does not call for the customary recitation of a *brachah* (blessing), as is the case upon performance of many other *mitzvos*. This in no way reflects upon the significance of the *mitzvah*. Among the reasons offered are the following:

1. One recites a *brachah* only for a *mitzvah* that is totally within his own power to fulfill, but not when its fulfillment also depends on others. It is possible that the mourner may not appreciate or even want the visit. Thus the fulfillment of this *mitzvah* is no longer totally within one's power alone to achieve.[19]

2. One recites a *brachah* only for *mitzvos* that are exclusive to the Jewish people. Comforting mourners is among those deeds that are performed by other nations as well.[20]

3. One recites a *brachah* only for *mitzvos* that are not constant. The *mitzvah* of *nichum aveilim* is constant, that is to say, there is no time when one is exempt from fulfilling it.[21]

4. One does not recite a *brachah* where pain of others in involved.[22]

PRECEDENCE OVER OTHER *MITZVOS*

The *mitzvah* of *nichum aveilim* takes precedence over the *mitzvah* of *bikkur cholim*, visiting the sick, if it is impossible to do both. The former is an act of kindness to both the living and the dead.[23] Similarly it takes precedence over the *mitzvah* of rejoicing the bride and groom.[24]

THE REWARDS

The *mitzvah* of *nichum aveilim*, being part of the general *mitzvah* of *gemillus chasadim*, is enumerated among those *mitzvos* the fruits of which are enjoyed in this world, while the principal remains for the performer in the World to Come.[25]

In the first chapter we pointed out how *gemillus chasadim* is *greater* in three ways than the regular giving of charity. If so, we need merely look at some of the great rewards vouchsafed to the donor of charity to gain an insight into the great reward promised to one who performs kind deeds. Following are just a few of the famous quotes in this respect:

• "There is no greater antidote to the Angel of Death than the giving of charity."[26]
• "Great is charity for it reaches the very throne of Glory itself."[27]
• "Rabbi Yehoshua ben Korcha said, 'From the power of charity the dead will be resurrected.'"[28]
• "Even if the angels of punishment will be given permission to extract their due from a person, the angel appointed over charity will not let them do so."[29]
• "Charity pushes away evil happenings that are decreed upon a person . . . and more, it adds length of days to a person's life."[30]
• "Never allow the *mitzvah* of charity to be slighted in your eyes, for not giving it results in twenty-four curses, and the reward for giving brings twenty-four blessings."[31]

If these are the rewards for regular charity, how much more so are the rewards promised to those who perform acts of kindness. Specifically in reference to the *mitzvah* of comforting the mourners it is said: "Blessed are You, *HaShem*, Who pays a great reward to those who perform kind deeds."[32]

We also find in the *Midrash*, specifically in reference to the *mitzvah* of *nichum aveilim*, that one is saved from the punishment of *Gehinnom* and that the spirit of *ruach hakodesh* descended upon the friends of Job who visited him while he was mourning.[33]

In the same *Midrash*, on the verse referring to comforting the mourner, on the words וְהַחַי יִתֵּן אֶל־לִבּוֹ —"and the living shall impress it upon his heart" (Ecclesiastes 7:2) the *Midrash* says: "This [the word *chai*] refers to the *Chai HaOlomim*, the Eternal Living One, Who will repay man for every step that he takes performing acts of kindness."[34]

Sefer HaChayim writes the following:

[Regarding] anyone who comforts mourners, at the time of his death, the Almighty instructs the angels who are in charge of "comfort" to take his soul to the section of "rejoicing" in the Garden of Eden, to comfort it there. This is reward measure for measure—since he comforted others during his lifetime, God rewards him appropriately, since he grasped on to the Almighty's trait of comforting, as it is written, "I am the One Who shall comfort you." Therefore it also states, "Take comfort, take comfort, My people, says *HaShem* your God"—meaning "to whom shall one comfort? To those who comfort my people."[35]

May we merit to have a share in this great *mitzvah*!

3

Our Rationalizations for Avoiding the *Mitzvah* of *Nichum Aveilim*

LAZINESS, APATHY

In the performance of some *mitzvos* of *gemillus chesed*, excuses can easily be found to avoid doing the *mitzvah*. Most of these are due to laziness or to a general apathy toward helping others.

Where *nichum aveilim* is concerned, almost everyone who knew the deceased or who knows a member of the bereaved family is generally touched by either the death of their acquaintance or their friend's loved one, or by the grief that is sustained by the family at their great loss.

Thus, laziness and apathy are really not relevant to our *mitzvah*. One genuinely wants to do what can be done to offer support and comfort to the mourners.

DISCOMFORT, FEAR

But facing a bereaved person is often somewhat uncomfortable. Confronting death in any form, even by merely entering the deceased's house or the mourner's home, strengthens one's own apprehensions of death and causes discomfort. We live in a death-denying society and have been raised among those who maintain that the notion of death or any discussion of death is taboo.

The subconscious comes to the fore and many rationalizations set in to cause an avoidance of performing our duty. Sometimes even well-meant feelings win out and convince us that it would be better if we did not visit the mourners at this period of time. In addition to the aforementioned apprehensions, we may think any of the following:

> "I'm afraid I might lose control of my emotions in front of the bereaved and may only add to their sorrow rather than lighten their burden or comfort them."
>
> "I might say the wrong thing to the mourners and could possibly even worsen an already trying and difficult situation."
>
> "I'm unfamiliar with death, having, thank God, never experienced the death of a close relative or friend. I wouldn't know what to say or do in a house of mourning!"
>
> "I have unresolved feelings of grief from the deaths of my own loved ones and I'm afraid that the wounds may be reopened and cause me renewed pain."

There may be many other reasons that we proffer to ourselves in this regard. How are we to overcome these sentiments and banish these thoughts? How are we to realize that nothing should stand in the way of performing this great *mitzvah*?

THE WISDOM OF KING SOLOMON

King Solomon taught us: טוֹב לָלֶכֶת אֶל בֵּית אֵבֶל מִלֶּכֶת אֶל בֵּית מִשְׁתֶּה בַּאֲשֶׁר הוּא סוֹף כָּל הָאָדָם וְהַחַי יִתֵּן אֶל לִבּוֹ.

"It is better to go to the house of mourning than to go to the house of partying, for it [death] is the end of all mankind, and the living will attend their hearts [to it]."[1]

Two verses later he teaches us: לֵב חֲכָמִים בְּבֵית אֵבֶל וְלֵב כְּסִלִים בְּבֵית שִׂמְחָה.

"The heart of the wise is in the house of mourning; the heart of the fool is in the house of rejoicing."[2]

The wisdom of Solomon applies to *all* people. It takes into consideration any and every one. It takes into account all of the reasons and rationalizations for avoiding a visit to the house of mourning. The statements are clear. It is wise and proper for anyone to pay a condolence call. Let us examine briefly this wisdom and learn why we should not allow any reason to deter us from this *mitzvah*.

The story is told of the great chassidic master Reb Simchah Bunem of Przysucha. During the final moments of his life, as he lay on his death-bed, his wife, seeing the end drawing near and unable to control her grief, burst into tears. Immediately he turned to her and said, "Why are you crying? All my life was only that I should learn how to die!" And with these words, with a radiant smile upon his face, he returned his soul peacefully to his Maker.[3]

It is true that the *Zohar* tells us that no one can ever contemplate his own death. "Rabbi Elazar said: Even were a man to live a thousand years, on the day that he departs from this world it seems to him as though he had only existed for one day."[4] As long as the soul is joined to the body, as long as we live on this earth, the urge to live is so powerful that we cannot come to grips with our own death, our separation from the life of the body. "Against your wish shall you die," teaches the *Mishnah*.[5] No one wants to die. But it is the inescapable eventuality of every human being. As the Talmud says: "Our brethren who are worn out and crushed by this bereavement, set your heart to consider this: This [death] stands forever; it is a path from the six days of Creation. Many have drunk, many will drink [from the cup of sorrow]. . . . Our brethren, the Master of consolation should comfort you."[6] From dust we came and to dust we shall return.[7]

Life on this earth is transient; it is only the corridor to a greater life in the World to Come. "Prepare yourself in the anteroom so that you can enter the palatial halls of the World to Come."[8]

THE PARABLE OF THE TWINS

Although all notion of life in the World to Come is foreign to us, the great scholar Rabbi Yechiel Michel Tuchachinsky offered us a parable that draws us closer to an understanding of the reality of life in the World to Come. His analogy is starkly dramatic, conveying the belief in the reality of the Afterlife even though this must be refracted through the prism of death. What follows is an adaptation of the parable as developed by Rabbi Maurice Lamm.

> Imagine twins growing peacefully in the warmth and safety of their mother's womb. Their lives are secure and all their needs are met. Their whole world is the interior of that womb. They cannot conceive of another world—one larger, better, and more comfortable than the one in which they presently live. As they drop lower and lower down the birth canal, they begin to wonder, "Surely if this continues we will one day cease to exist here. Then what will happen to us?"
>
> Now the first infant is a believer. He is heir to a tradition that tells him there will be a "new life" after this wet, warm existence of the womb—a strange belief, seemingly without foundation, but one to which he clings steadfastly. The second infant is a complete skeptic. Mere stories do not convince him. He believes only in that which can be clearly demonstrated. He is enlightened and tolerates no idle conjecture. What is not within one's experience can have no basis in one's imagination.

Says the believer, "After our 'death' here, there will be a great, new world. We will eat through our mouths; we will see great distances; we will hear through our ears; our feet will be straightened; our heads up and free, rather than down and bent over."

"Nonsense," replies the skeptic. "You're straining your imagination again. There is absolutely no foundation for this belief. It is a historically conditioned subterfuge, an elaborate defense mechanism designed to calm your fear of 'death.' There is only this world. There is no world to come!"

"Well, then," asks the first, "what do you think it will be like?"

The second brother snappily replies with all the assurance of the slightly knowledgeable, "We will go with a bang. Our world will collapse and we will sink into oblivion. No more. Nothing. Black void. An end to consciousness. Forgotten." These may not be comforting thoughts, but they are reasonable ones.

Suddenly the water inside the womb bursts and the womb convulses. Upheaval, turmoil, writhing—everything lets loose. Then a mysterious pounding—faster, faster, lower, lower. The believing brother, tearing himself from the womb, exits and falls outward. The skeptic in the womb hears an ear-splitting cry and a great tumult from the black abyss. He shrieks, startled by the "accident" that befell his brother. He bewails the tragedy, the 'death' of his previously perfectly healthy brother. "Why didn't he take better care of himself; why did he fall into that terrible abyss? Oh, what a horrible end, just as I had predicted!"

Meanwhile, as the skeptical brother mourns, his "dead" brother has been born into the "new world." The ear-splitting cry is a sign of health and vigor, and the tumult is a chorus of *mazel tovs* sounded by the waiting family, thanking God for the birth of a healthy son.

Says Rabbi Tuchachinsky: "Just as we separate and 'die' from the womb, only to be born to a better life, so, too, we separate and die from our earthly world, only to be reborn to a better life of eternity. The exit from the womb is the birth of the baby. The exit from the body is the re-emergence of the soul at a higher level. Just as the womb requires a gestation period of nine months, so, too, this world requires a residence period of seventy or eighty years. As the womb is a corridor to life in this world, this world is a corridor to eternal life in the World to Come."[9]

In the tape recording, *Journeys I (Conversation in the Womb)*, Rabbi Abie Rotenberg has captured this parable in song.

My dear brother, look around and tell me what your eyes behold.
Don't deny that you see, it's only you and me, and our existence
It is empty, it is cold; our existence it is empty, it is cold.
But dear brother, you must have faith that we are not the only ones
Because in the distance there is a place, where we'll stand up tall and straight.
Oh, I believe that there is a world to come, yes I believe that there is a world
    to come.

My dear brother, don't be blind, don't be stubborn, don't be set.
Imagination, it's all right but it won't light up the night.
What you see is exactly what you get; what you see is exactly what you
   get.
But dear brother, you will surely find when all is said and done
That the future it will show there is so much we don't know.
Oh I believe that there is a world to come, yes I believe that there is a world
   to come.

My dear brother, where have you gone, is this the moment I have known?
I can faintly hear the cry, my dear brother must have died, it's all over
Now forever I'm alone, it's all over now forever I'm alone.
But dear brother, please don't mourn me when my life has just begun.
What you hear are sounds of joy, congratulations it's a boy.
Oh I believe that there is a world to come, yes I believe that there is a world
   to come;
What you hear are sounds of joy, congratulations it's a boy.
Soon you'll be here with me in this world to come, soon you'll be here with
   me in this world to come.

It is possible that Rabbi Tuchachinsky had in mind the following incredible *midrash* when he prepared his famous parable (naturally, part of
this *midrash* must be understood in kabbalistic terms):

Rabbi Yochanan said, that which it is written (Job 9:10), "[God] Who
performs great deeds that are unfathomable, and limitless wonders."
Know that all the souls that were since Adam, the first man, and that
will be till the end of the world, all of them were created during the six
days of Creation. All of them were in the Garden of Eden; all of them
were at the giving of the Torah. As it says (Deuteronomy 29:14), "Those
who are standing with us here today and those who are not with us here
today." And that which it says, "Who performs deeds that are unfathomable"—these refer to the great deeds that God does when forming the
fetus. For when man comes to cohabit with his wife, God signals to the
angel in charge of conception and says: "Know that tonight a person
will be formed from the seed of that certain man. Guard the seminal
drop, take it, and implant it in the storage for 365 parts." The angel then
brings the seed before God and says to Him: "I have done all that You
have commanded me. What will now be decreed on this drop?" Immediately the Almighty decrees what will be the end of this drop—whether
male or female, weak or strong, poor or rich, short or tall, ugly or hand-
some, fat or thin, timid or outgoing. And so He decrees all that will
happen to him, all except whether he will be righteous or wicked. That
He hands over into the hands of man himself as it says: "See, I have set
before you today life and good, death and evil."
   Then God signals the angel who is in charge of the souls and says
to it: "Bring me that certain soul that resides in *Gan Eden*, whose name

is such, and whose appearance is such," for all the souls that are destined to be born were all created from the day the world was created, and until the world will end they are all prepared to enter a person. . . .

Immediately the angel goes and brings the soul before God. When it appears, it bows and postrates itself before the King of Kings, the Holy One, blessed is He. At this time God commands the spirit to enter that certain seminal drop. The spirit responds: "Master of the Universe, I am satisfied with the world in which I have lived from the day You created me. Why do You wish that I should enter that fetid drop, I who am holy and pure, created from Your glory?" At once the Almighty says to the soul: "The world into which I want you to enter will be better for you than the one in which you have lived, and from the time that I formed you, I formed you only with the intent that you should enter this drop."

Immediately God forces the soul to enter. After this the angel replants the soul in the mother's womb and prepares two angels that will guard it and prevent it from exiting or falling, and kindles a light above his head. This is what it says in the verse (Job 29:2-3), "Would that I were in my early months, as the days when God watched over me. When He lit His candle over my head, etc." And the soul can see from one end of the world to the other.

The angel takes the soul from there and leads it to *Gan Eden* and shows it the righteous who are sitting in honor, with their crowns upon their heads. The angel says to the soul, "Do you know who these are?" The soul responds, "No, my master." The angel says, "These were formed as you were in the wombs of their mothers. They went out into the world and kept the Torah and the *mitzvos*. Therefore they merited all of this good that you see. Know that you, too, will exit into the world, and if you will merit to keep God's Torah, you will merit this reward, and the honored place that these merited. But if you do not obey the Torah, you will acquire another place."

That night the angel takes the soul to *Gehinnom* and shows it the wicked who are being beaten by angels of destruction with fiery sticks. Those souls scream, "Woe, woe," but they receive no pity. Then the angel says to the soul, "Do you know who these are?" And the soul responds, "No, my master." The angel says, "Those being burned were created as you were, exited into the world, but did not keep the Almighty's Torah or His statutes. Therefore they were subjected to the shame that you observed. Know that you, too, will exit into the world. Be righteous, do not be wicked. Then you will merit to live in the World to Come."

Therefore God warns him about everything, and the angel accompanies him from morning to night. He shows him the spot where he will die and the place where he will be buried. Then he takes him for a tour of the whole world, showing him the righteous and the wicked—everything.

In the evening he returns him to his mother's womb. God makes a barrier, and he dwells in the womb for nine months. During the first three, in the lower chamber; during the next three, in the middle one;

and during the last three, in the upper one. When the time comes for him to exit into the air of the world, he rolls and descends in one second from the upper to the middle, and from the middle to the lower. Until that time he eats and drinks from whatever his mother ate and drank and does not bring forth any excrement. . . .

At the end, his time comes to exit into the world. The angel appears and says to him, "The time has come for you to exit." The soul responds, "Why do you wish to take me out to the world outside?" Says the angel to him, "My son, know that you are formed against your will, and now you shall be born against your will. You shall be forced to die, and you shall be forced to give a reckoning and account of your actions before the King of Kings, the Holy One, blessed is He."

He does not wish to exit until the angel strikes him, extinguishes the light above his head, and escorts him out into the world by force. Immediately, the baby forgets all that he saw and knew before he exited. Why does the child cry as it exits? Because he has lost his place of rest and respite, the world from which he exited.

At this time, seven worlds and stages of time descend upon him. In the first he is likened to a king; all enquire about his welfare and wish to see him. Everyone wants to hug and kiss him during the first year. In the second, he is likened to a swine who wallows in the filth. So is the two-year-old who dirties himself with excrement. In the third, he is likened to a goat who jumps from here to there in the good pastures before his mother. So the child gives pleasure to his mother and father, jumping from here to there, playing, and all delight in him. In the fourth he is likened to a horse that prances in the streets until he reaches maturity at the age of eighteen. Then, just as the horse runs and takes pride in itself, so, too, the young man prides himself with his youthful strength. In the fifth he is likened to a mule upon which they place a saddle. So, too, with man. They place a burden on him. He marries, bears sons and daughters, goes to and fro in search of his livelihood—until he reaches his fortieth year. In the sixth he is likened to a brazen dog taking from here and there and not feeling any shame. In the seventh (if he reaches senility) he is likened to a monkey, whose countenance is different from all other creatures. He asks constantly for things, eats and drinks like a child, plays like a baby, and reverts to his youth as far as his mental capacities. Even his children and family members laugh at him. When he speaks, they say to others, "Leave him. He is old, likened to a monkey in all his ways." Even children laugh at him and play with him. Even a free bird will arouse him from his sleep.

When in the end his time comes, the angel comes and says to him, "Do you recognize me?" He responds, "Yes." Then he asks, "Why do you come to me today of all days?" The angel replies, "In order to take you from this world, for the time has come for you to die." Immediately he begins to cry and lets his voice be heard from one end of the world to the other. No creature, however, is able to hear or recognize his voice except for the rooster alone. He then says to the angel, "But you have

already taken me out from two worlds and brought me to this world."
The angel responds, "Did I not already tell you that you were formed
against your will, and you were born against your will? You were forced
to live, you are forced to die, and you are forced to give a reckoning and
accounting of your deeds before the Holy One, blessed is He."[10]

Again, Rabbi Abie Rotenberg has beautifully recorded the message of
this *midrash*, in his *Journeys, II* tape (*Neshomele*):

Come with me, little *neshomele,* let me hold you in my hand,
And we'll fly away, you and I together, to a place down on the land.
Come with me little *neshomele;* don't shy away . . . do as you're told.
There's a little child waiting to be born today. You're to be his spark,
    his soul.
But dear Malachel, *no, I don't want to go.*
There is so much pain and evil upon the Earth below.
Let me stay up here in Heaven where it's safe and I'll be pure.
Please don't make me go away. Can't you see I'm so afraid?

Come with me little *neshomele,* it's time you faced your destiny.
And as we fly beneath the clouds now I will show you
There is so much you can be.
Yes, dear Malachel, *I can see* kedushah *[holiness] over there.*
Look, someone's learning Torah; there's another deep in prayer.
I will stay here if you answer me, it's all I need to know.
You must promise me, dear friend, that I too will be like them.

Come with me, little *neshomele,* oh it's a task that I must do.
As I tap you on the lip you will forget me.
You're on your own; it's up to you.

[MUSIC / PASSAGE OF TIME]

Come with me, little *neshomele,* let me hold you in my hand,
And we'll fly away, you and I together, to a place above the land.
But dear Malachel, *no, I don't want to go.*
I'm not ready to go with you. Where you take me I don't know.
Let me stay right where I am. There's so much more I need to do.
Please don't make me go away. Can't you see I'm so afraid?

Come with me, little *neshomele,* I've only come to take you home.
There is no need to fear your destination.
You've earned a place right by the Throne . . .
A place right by the Throne.

The essence of Rabbi Tuchachinsky's parable is beautifully stated in
the following passage:

I am standing on the seashore. A ship at my side spreads her white sails to the morning breeze and starts for the blue ocean. She is an object of beauty and strength, and I stand and watch her until at length she is only a ribbon of white cloud just where the sea and sky come to join each other. Then someone at my side says: "There! She's gone!" Gone where? Gone from *my* sight—that is all. She is just as large in mast and hull and spar as she was when she left my side and just as able to bear her load of living freight to their destination. Her diminished size is in *me*, not in her, for just at the moment when someone at my side says, "There! She's gone!" there are other voices ready to take up the glad shout, "There! She comes!" And that is dying.[11]

Contemplating and preparing for death, not in an ever-brooding or morbid manner, but in a manner that infuses our lives with a goal and purpose, with a *raison d'être* for living, changes the very essence of life itself. It keeps us focused on the right path of living, which is to prepare us for life eternal.

TWO OF LIFE'S MOST IMPORTANT LESSONS

Visiting a house of mourning pounds home to us two of life's most vital lessons. One is that none of us will live forever; therefore we should be constantly preparing ourselves for the World beyond. The other is that we are presently alive, thank God, and still have, hopefully, many years ahead of us in which to make our mark in this world, simultaneously gathering the wherewithal to prepare for the eventuality of life after death. Each moment of life is too precious to be wasted or squandered. We must ensure that we infuse the time still allotted to us with the true essence of life itself.

ADDITIONAL REFLECTIONS

In addition we learn the following:

1. To appreciate life itself and the lives of the loved ones we are still fortunate enough to have with us. Too often, we take both for granted!

2. To realize that as the people of God we are never alone. We are not single units living in isolation one from another. Rather, we are part of an enduring and everlasting community both in life and in death. Accordingly, we must fulfill our obligations to other members of our community who need us in their time of sorrow.

3. To recognize that giving of ourselves to others who are in mourning is a deeply human and sharing experience. The bonds of friendship are strengthened not only by participating in another's joys, but perhaps

even more so by empathizing with them and caring for them in times of sorrow.

4. To recognize that God Almighty is the Author of life and death. As we recite on Yom Kippur night:

> We are as clay in the hands of the potter, who expands or contracts it at will;
>
> We are as stone in the hands of the mason, who preserves or smashes it at will;
>
> We are as the helm in the hands of the seaman who handles or abandons it at will;
>
> We are as glass in the hands of the glazier who shapes or dissolves it at will;
>
> We are as cloth in the hands of the draper who drapes it straight or crooked at will;
>
> We are as silver in the hands of the smith who makes it pure or impure at will.[12]

As the Torah states: "See now, it is I. I am the [only] One. There are no other gods with Me. I cause to die and I give life; I crush and I heal, and no one can save [another] from My hand."[13]

As the Author of death, it is God Who can advise us what we should do when others are confronted with death. The Torah, the Talmud, and the *Shulchan Aruch* (the Jewish Code of Law), when studied properly, afford us the guidance we need in dealing with the mourners. In His inscrutable and indiscernible wisdom, God has decreed death. "But there is none more merciful than I," says God.[14]

He, too, is the Author of grief and of the apparatus that makes up all of man. The philosophical thoughts, the psychological feelings, the emotional sentiments, the spiritual sensations, the metaphysical truths—all emanate from the Creator of man.

And in His handbook He teaches us how to address all of these. We need but follow His commandments and we know that by so doing, we will gain His help in all that we do.

In the coming chapter we will discuss some of the natural truths of grief and of those who grieve. We will see how the wise dictates of the laws of *nichum aveilim* take into account all of these truths. This alone should suffice to help us overcome any deterrents to perform this *mitzvah*.

THE ALMIGHTY HELPS IN THE OUTCOME OF A *MITZVAH*

But before we proceed to the next chapter, it would serve us well to reflect on the words of Rabbi Aaron Berechiah of Modena, the author of the great work *Maavor Yabok*, the classic source of many of our mourning customs.

It is inappropriate for the nation of Israel, the performers of kind deeds, who involve themselves with the needs of the dead, to wonder to themselves and say, "How can we properly say and concentrate on the verses recited during the handling and purification of the dead?" For all will properly follow the right intentions. Man merely has to perform a little, and the Almighty will help and support him in great measure. Man begins, and doesn't know how to end, but Godly assistance upholds him and guides him. This is what is meant by "the Divine Omnipresence resting on the actions of man" as is explained in the *Zohar*. Similarly it says, "Just open for me an opening the size of a pinhead and I shall open for you an opening as large as a palatial hall." All holy work is accomplished by itself. It is sufficient that man just begin it. Then *HaShem* will see to its completion.[15]

Surely the same applies to the honor of the living, for it is an established axiom that the honor of the *living* takes precedence over the honor due to the dead.[16]

We should therefore not concern ourselves with any excuses that would deter us from making a *shivah* call. We must go with the sincere and pure intent to emulate God's merciful ways and to perform a great *mitzvah* of *chesed*. God will allow His *Shechinah* to rest upon our actions and crown our efforts with fulfillment.

Certainly we should all pray that the time will come when

בִּלַּע הַמָּוֶת לָנֶצַח וּמָחָה ה' אֱלֹקִים דִּמְעָה מֵעַל כָּל פָּנִים וכו'

"God will destroy death forever and will banish tears from all faces"[17] and no condolence calls will be necessary.

But until then, let us study the appropriate ways to perform this *mitzvah* so we can provide our grieving brothers and sisters with the solace and consolation they so sorely need.

4

Understanding the Nature of Bereavement, Grief, and Mourning

THE STUDIES

Many studies have been made in the non-Torah world, *lehavdil*, on the subject of bereavement, grief, and mourning.[1] It is certainly true that our Torah is all-embracive and the dictum, "Turn it over and turn it over [again] for all is in it,"[2] is not just a religious pronouncement but a fact. Nevertheless, in the spirit of "There is wisdom among the nations,"[3] it is worthwhile to consider some aspects of these studies to see how they relate to the eternal truths of the Torah. Familiarizing oneself with them will certainly help one to understand the nature of mourning and the significance of the condolence call. But even more, it will in fact highlight the wisdom of our traditions and show how *halachah* and our *minhagim* (customs) address themselves not only to the spiritual aspects of mourning and the *shivah* call but to their very practical aspects as well.

There is an underlying assumption in these studies that "normal" people under "normal" circumstances experience a "normal" grief reaction and ultimately return to a "normal" state of well-being.

If this is true in a general sense, then, unquestionably, one bound up with faith in God, one who has the stability of religious beliefs, and one who adheres to the wisdom of the traditions of our Torah and the sages will certainly be enabled to cope with the complexities of the grief process. For it is certainly true that many of the problems encountered—be

25

they physical or emotional, physiological or social—that are symptomatic of grief responses as seen in these studies, result from the many factors that are absent in a nonreligious framework.

In parts of the secular world, on a public level, there exist a denigration and a stigmatization of grief. This is inextricably bound to the public callousness and attitude toward death in general. When death and burial are merely the ends and the means of *disposing of the body,* then grief and mourning have no proper place, and the concomitant problems of pathological and unnatural grief result.

In one enquiry in Britain the following conclusion was made:

> The most typical reaction of the majority in Britain today (and, as far as my evidence goes, in all English-speaking countries with a Protestant tradition) is the denial of mourning, in a period after the funeral. Certainly, social recognition of mourning has virtually disappeared. . . . Giving way to grief is stigmatized as morbid, unhealthy, demoralising— very much the same words are used to reprobate mourning as were used to reprobate sex; and the proper action of a friend or well-wisher is felt to be distraction of a mourner from his or her grief; taking them "out of themselves" by diversions, encouraging them to seek new scenes and experiences, preventing them "living the past." Mourning is treated as if it were a weakness, a self-indulgence, a reprehensible bad habit instead of a psychological necessity.[4]

As an American writer puts it:

> There is a disturbingly growing tendency in modern American Jewish life to ignore the reality of death and the basic needs of the bereaved and conform increasingly to the general attitude of the majority culture.
>
> Modern American society has also turned the funeral into something "lovely" and unreal, conducted with soft music, perfumed flowers, honeyed circumlocutions, as "live" a corpse as the cosmetic arts can simulate, and a synthetic disguised burial. The whole purpose of the modern funeral is to mask the idea of death and the dead. The atmosphere of the funeral, totally unreal, must wind up being emotionally unsatisfying and psychologically frustrating. Instead of affording an opportunity to give vent to genuine feelings, to face the reality of death bravely, and to seek the support of others, it encourages all of the unwholesome mental mechanisms described earlier and fosters confusion and conflict. Its therapeutic value, therefore, is greatly diminished. Grief must be expressed in some way since the feelings engendered by bereavement are too strong to suppress. They may remain dormant for a while, but sooner or later they must come to the surface. The tensions and conflicts created by the death of a loved one can only be relieved through expression.
>
> The absence of definite rituals and customs to guide the bereaved through the period of mourning, which comes after the funeral, is an-

other serious lack in our American sociocultural system. In contemporary society there are no definite mourning patterns and few expecta-
tions of the mourner. He does not know what is expected of him, and
consequently the therapeutic effect of the work of mourning is tragi-
cally lost. The unrelieved frustration of the love impulses toward the
deceased and the intensification of feelings of guilt can create a situation where grief is distorted pathologically instead of assuaged, engen-
dering ambiguity and confusion. Too much is left to the individual at a
time when his helplessness and weakness are critical.

Our American culture does not meet the needs of the mourner.
The threatened collapse of the traditional Jewish sociocultural system,
depriving the Jew of the shelter of his self-contained Jewish community, would leave him just as bewildered in his grief as the non-Jew.[5]

When death, the funeral, burial, and mourning, however, are elevated
to the status of *yakra deshechiva* and *yakra dechaya*—the honor and respect
due both to the deceased and to the living[6]—then the noble purposes of
our traditions in handling the tragedy of death are clearly manifested by
the way they aid in the entire healing therapy of the mourning process.
And as part of this process, the *mitzvah* of *nichum aveilim*, comforting the
mourners, is directly intertwined with the support that helps the bereaved
in their understanding of death and in reorienting themselves to normalcy
following the shock of the death of their loved one.

THE PHASES OF BEREAVEMENT, GRIEF, AND MOURNING

Although the studies express themselves in slightly different terms and
groupings of reactions, one may combine them and emerge with the following basic components and descriptions of the different phases involved
in the totality of the mourning process.

It must be stressed, however, that *no two mourners undergo identical
grief and mourning experiences*. How a mourner reacts to grief and mourning depends upon many factors: his religious makeup and orientation and
integration of Torah attitudes and teachings; his own personal family
makeup and his particular relationship with the deceased; the status of
experiences and personal involvement leading up to the time of death; and,
of course, his own personal constitution and personality makeup.

The Rabbis have stated, "Just as no two faces are exactly alike, so, too,
the thoughts, attitudes, and emotional responses of people are not alike."[7]

Therefore it should be understood that the following are generaliza-
tions that can be made about the mourning experience, and any one or a
combination of the following emotions may be triggered at the various
stages of the grief and mourning process.

Initial Shock and Denial

The initial reaction to the news of the death of a loved one is a *disbelief* that death has actually occurred. Even when one has been around a sick and dying relative for months, when the final blow actually comes, one does not accept or fully internalize the reality of death. As has been expressed:

> Residing on the boundary line between consciousness and unconscious-
> ness is the conviction that we are indestructible; that lightning will strike
> everywhere else, but not here. This is a normal defense mechanism that
> keeps us from spending our days cringing in a bomb shelter. If we are
> confronted with a direct question, such as, "Are you going to die some-
> day?" the answer is obvious. But as soon as the questioner leaves, our
> unconscious resumes its stance of personal invincibility.[8]

This feeling applies not only to our *own* invincibility but also to that of those closest and dearest to us. There is an urgent need to recover the lost one and somehow by disbelieving it, one feels that death has not really occurred. This stage is often accompanied by shock, numbness, and confusion, and one's thoughts are frequently preoccupied with the dead person and/or the dying process. Some hallucinate and experience encounters with the deceased as though they were still alive.

It is not uncommon for the bereaved to telephone home (where the deceased lived) and listen to the phone ringing, hoping against hope that it will be answered (by the deceased). Some have reported interpreting a noise outside the door as the familiar turning of the key in the door (by the deceased), a creaking floorboard as the familiar footsteps of the lost person.[9]

It is this sense of shock and denial that often accounts for the seeming lack of mourning and grief displayed by some who have just lost a loved one. Some mourners themselves are disturbed that they don't feel more pain; some family members are distressed by the seeming lack of care about the death on the part of other relatives. Some are concerned by what they feel is irrational behavior on their part and what they may sense as a threat of impending breakdown manifesting the types of behavior described above—still sensing the "living" of the deceased.

It also accounts for the usual ability of the mourners to carry on with all the funeral arrangements, attending the funeral and burial, while seemingly presenting themselves as being "in control."

One should therefore not judge in any way the seeming indifference of the mourner. This is perhaps the Divine Wisdom from above that helps the mourners make an adaptive response to the harsh reality of death at the height of grief and aids in preparing the way for the ensuing steps of the healing process to take place.

Anger and Frustration, Guilt and Regret, Despair and Depression, Fear and Anxiety, Loneliness and Isolation

Anger and Frustration, Guilt and Regret

When the initial shock subsides and the reality of death is sinking in, a host of other thoughts and feelings arise. Initially there may be great anger and guilt: anger at *oneself* and guilt for perhaps not having done enough to prevent the death of the deceased; anger at the hospital or the particular doctor or the general medical profession for not having been able to effect a cure; anger at *God* for what the mourners see as unfair justice in bringing about the death of their loved one; and even anger at the *deceased* for having left them at this time of their lives and causing them so much suffering.

Guilt is not only felt for what could have possibly been done to prevent the death. It is also felt in self-remonstration for the way the mourner perceives his or her behavior toward the deceased when he or she was alive. They remember real or imaginary mistakes and shortcomings in the way they related to the deceased while he or she was alive. And since they can now no longer make amends, the feelings can become intense and painful. Then there is the guilt feeling that they are still alive and healthy when they perceive that perhaps it is they who should have died instead of the deceased, who may have lived more righteously than they.

During the stage of anger it is not uncommon for one to manifest an anger and irritability, hostility and apathy, toward all around. There may be a loss of warmth and closeness to others, a short-temperedness or even rudeness. One is bound up in all of the various angers described above, and this overflows to even the innocent and trying-to-be-helpful bystander. It is important to understand this so that if and when a well-meaning individual bears the brunt of this anger, he or she will not take it personally.

Despair and Depression, Fear and Anxiety, Loneliness and Isolation

Usually, after the stage of guilt and anger, we find that despair and depression begin to set in, and fear and anxiety come to the surface. There is often an intense feeling of sadness, of helplessness and hopelessness. Life has lost all meaning—there is nothing to which to look forward in the future. Everything becomes unmanageable.

The loss of the particular family member may set off a chain of practical consequences that can be overwhelmimg. Certainly if the deceased provided financial support, advice, emotional stability, affection, companionship, and an always willing and able hand—and all this is suddenly gone—there is cause for anxiety.

This situation often leads to the desire of the bereaved to withdraw from company and the broader society. Life for the deceased has ended; life for the living one has all but come to an end. One therefore brings about, by this withdrawal, the feelings of intense loneliness and isolation. These feelings are further intensified by the tendency of the bereaved to focus all of their attention on the deceased and the lost relationship, to the exclusion of all others. His or her own seeming hostility and lack of warmth toward others may be interpreted as a desire to be left alone. Company may be an intrusion of his or her privacy. Hence a cycle is introduced whereby the mourner may intensify the loneliness which he or she has created by the outwardly manifested signals sent to others.

Disorientation and Disorganization

As a result of all of the above, the mourner may become disoriented, confused, and disorganized. There is an inability to structure one's time and purpose. The mourner may display apparent purposeless activity, restlessness, and a total disorganization in relatively routine matters that need to be handled.

Physical Behaviors and Responses

During the above stages, depending on the time and the situation, many physical behaviors and responses may be manifested by the mourners.

In the more extreme cases somatic distress, such as tightness in the throat, choking, sighing and weeping, shortness of breath, panic, loss of appetite, insomnia, headaches, blurred vision, and loss of interest in personal appearance may occur.[10]

In many others, there is generally manifest a loss of energy, fatigue, an inability to concentrate, indecisiveness, and many of the other emotional feelings described in the phase above. Many of these are the natural resultants of the anger and frustration, guilt and regret, despair and depression, loneliness and isolation that have been discussed.

As has been stated previously, the type and intensity of grief reactions vary from person to person. No two people grieve or mourn in exactly the same way. Each person has his or her own unique response. It is important, however, for friends and others to be aware of what these various responses and reactions can be, and to understand that they are normal behaviors experienced and expressed at the time of the death of a loved one.

Reorganization and Reintegration

After passing through the first two stages, when the bereaved have had some time to sort through their feelings and thoughts, the slow readjustment to life without the deceased begins to take place. The emancipation from the bondage to the deceased begins to take effect, and a readjustment to the environment in which the deceased is missing begins to emerge.

To be sure there are ups and downs. The sadness, loneliness, and anger may still surface at various points, times, and places—even for quite some time after death. But at least there is some resumption of normalcy and a renewed desire to go on living despite the tragedy through which one has been. One begins a slow reorganization of the daily routine; one begins to reach out to others and to reestablish the previous relationships and friendships without the manifestations of irritability and lack of warmth; one begins to have restored faith in God and mankind.

It is hardly appropriate to tell the mourner at the height of his or her grief that time will heal the deep wounds, but in most cases time *does* heal.[11] Although memories will be awakened on special occasions such as the *Yomim Tovim*, births, *bar mitzvahs*, weddings, and *Yahrzeits*, nevertheless, the intensity of the pain will be dulled and the mourner will be able to slowly participate once again in the joyous occasions and celebrations. The sense of loss may always remain, but the *sharpness* of the pain subsides and the bereaved realizes that a way can be discovered to make a healthy readjustment to the new circumstances of life.

Often there is also a new resurgence of energy and a new desire to be creative in work and to make contributions to the welfare of others. It is not uncommon after a loss, once the healing process has taken place, for a person to tackle life with renewed purpose and zeal. It is as if the bereft one is saying to the deceased, "I shall always cherish and honor your memory and the memories of the life we shared together, but I know that you would want me to live life again despite our being torn asunder. I shall honor that silent request and do my utmost to appreciate even more the life I still have left by the grace of God."

JEWISH LAW AND CUSTOM

Having sketched a brief overview of some essentials in understanding the nature of bereavement, grief, and mourning as they relate to the general world, we can now begin to discuss the Jewish laws and customs in the particular light of reference to the *mitzvah* of *nichum aveilim*, comforting the mourners.

Although in discussing these laws, much of the rich wisdom of our traditions will be apparent as they relate to the mourners and the mourning process itself, this is not the primary focus. We will focus instead on the more practical aspects of paying the condolence call and how to conduct oneself at the *shivah* house.

In healthy mourning, the person will absorb the grief. Certainly Jewish practices help promote this and try to prevent the reverse, the grief absorbing the person, from occurring.

Our traditions assuredly address themselves to the stages enumerated above. They structure the "work" of mourning by prescribing a gradual tempo of weaning away from the trauma and the loss by effectively "working through" the acute grief and deprivation, toward a slow redirection to freedom and normal living again.

As Rabbi Samson Raphael Hirsch so aptly expresses it:

Nothing needs such vigilant precaution as the emotions of the human being. For it is just in his emotions that man swerves so frequently from one extreme to the other. Both a running wild of the emotions and a petrifying deadening of them are equally dangerous. One extreme engenders the other. The two rarely meet to mingle into a happy medium which alone would allow them their full play as designed by God, neither too much nor too little.

It is, of course, that man also eagerly goes astray when he is in the enjoyment of happy emotions. But life itself with its major and minor hardships soon sets the target and leads to the conclusion that there is far more need for a call to serenity in life than for a warning not to overlook its darker side. The feeling of grief, however, has a graver import. The surging feeling of joy, if not indulged to excess, usually produces in an honest man only a surfeit of goodliness, because, of itself it widens one's heart and, one might say, welcomes the whole universe into the loving embrace of man; and this begets love and only love.

Grief, however, because it is the outcome of some form of constraint, throws man back upon himself, fills his heart only with himself and leaves no room for anything else. Excess of the feeling of grief renders a man feeble and numb and therefore unable to master his life. But equally dangerous is the *stifling* of one's feeling of grief. For it is just by this throwing of man back upon himself that God educates him through suffering; and he who is dead to this feeling of grief is dead to the fatherly guiding hand of God.

The Torah—as in other instances, so in the emotional life of man—lays down directions and duties to guide man by its many injunctions. Our Sages, too, who were to the fore in their behests of the joyful occasions which life affords, found it necessary to draw up rules to govern our feelings of grief at the loss of that greatest blessing in our outward life—the loss by death of a fellow-man. They allowed these feelings latitude but at the same time they confined them and so they prevented these feelings, on the one hand, from being stifled, and, on the other hand, from bringing in their wake enfeeblement. They acted in accordance with injunctions implied in the Torah and also in accordance with established practice recognized by the Torah.

The provisions governing these practices are embraced in *hilchos aveilus* [the laws of mourning], and we include them in the section Edoth because they also teach us how, by symbolic observances, to commemorate what is primarily a private occurrence and the emotions which it engenders.

In the emotions engendered by death, three aspects following upon one another may be distinguished:

(1) The inevitable feeling of pain which can no more be dismissed than the physical suffering when a limb is amputated from one's own body. The ego of the human being feels that part of it has been torn away; and this hurts poignantly. This is the condition of *aninuth*, literally, one's personality is 'outraged' by a sense of loss.

(2) When the severance recedes into the past and one's ego feels only the after-effects of a loss now over—the pain is then more mental because the loss, being something past, exists still only in the mind. The pain, since it is of a mental nature, can also be mastered mentally. Its character is *aveluth,* the shrivelling of one's mortified personality.

(3) The pain has now been overcome, one's ego raises itself up again erect and independent, but it has not yet regained self-confidence, and so it neglects the outward appearance. This condition is known as *nivvul,* the inward personality which contemns one's outward appearance. The man then comes into contact with the society to which he belongs, and this is the final healing of his pains; for when an individual rejoins his associates, his feelings of sadness cease of themselves. It is the human being only as an individual that is maimed by the event of death; the community is so constructed as to expect death and it ever regenerates itself. And so it is in this feeling of 'belonging' that the last trace of suffering disappears.

Our Sages gave thought to these three aspects. They allowed each, one after the other, sufficient latitude but confined each to that latitude and so gradually led him who was grief-laden until the erstwhile self-absorbed is once again presented to life and society.[12]

To the bereaved Jew the laws of mourning represent the response of the man of faith to his God in this time of crisis. To the comforter, the laws of *nichum aveilim,* comforting the mourners, represent the guiding beacons that make the task more noble, more meaningful, and more assured of accomplishing their purpose. They do this by informing us of the infinite wisdom of the Author of death and comfort, and of the ways He has designated toward the goal of effecting this comfort. These ways address themselves to the responses and reactions of the normal mourning process, as will be shown in the coming chapters.

Because ritual observance plays a critical part in helping the bereaved, tradition discourages the "private *shivah.*"[13] Both Gorer[14] and Parkes[15] have indicated that a decline in the mourning ritual and the failure of mourners to express their distress within the first two weeks of bereavement have led to more problems later. Gorer found a direct correlation between the *shivah* and support for grief and determined that the very concentrated and overt mourning that takes place during *shivah* is of therapeutic value.[16]

5

When to Comfort

BEFORE THE FUNERAL

The *Mishnah* in *Avos* states: וְאַל תְּנַחֲמֵהוּ בְּשָׁעָה שֶׁמֵּתוֹ מֻטָּל לְפָנָיו "And do not comfort [your friend] at a time when his deceased lies before him."[1]

The actual *mitzvah* of *nichum aveilim* cannot be fulfilled before the funeral. However, it is appropriate for members of the immediate family and extremely close friends to make themselves available to the mourners to help in whichever manner they can.[2]

Numerous details have to be looked after, and the mourner who may be in a daze from the shock of the trauma may have difficulties in making all the funeral arrangements and setting up the house for the *shivah* observance.

Generally, the rabbi, the *Chevrah Kaddisha*, and the funeral home—all experienced in these matters—can be the most helpful and supportive in most of these areas. But discretion on the part of others is strongly advised.

Although it might seem strange to state, the first precaution is to verify that death has actually taken place. The following story is recounted about the *tzaddik* Rabbi Aryeh Levin, who was famous for his acts of kindness, among them his zeal for performing the *mitzvah* of *nichum aveilim*.

> When Rabbi Isaac Herzog, Israel's noted chief rabbi, was suffering from
> the illness that was to end his life, late one night a rumor spread that he

35

had passed away. It was well past midnight when the rumor reached Reb Aryeh, and by then it was being told almost as a fact. About two o'clock in the morning Reb Aryeh rang the doorbell of the Herzog home. When Mrs. Herzog opened the door, Reb Aryeh stood there speechless, waiting for her to confirm the ill-tidings. She in turn stood silent, utterly bewildered by his visit at this unearthly hour. And so they stood for several moments looking at each other dumbfounded, until at last the rabbi was able to speak and found out that the rumor of Rabbi Herzog's passing was false.[3]

From this story we learn not only of Reb Aryeh's willingness to be of comfort to the bereaved but also that it is appropriate for extremely close friends to be available to the mourners to assist them in whichever way they can.

However, it is not a time for well-meaning acquaintances to bombard the home of the mourners telling them how sorry they are about the sad news and enquiring about the details of the tragedy of the death.

Well-meaning friends can certainly contact members of the family (not the mourners themselves) and offer to take care of many of the arrangements that may be necessary for the orderliness of the funeral and the *shivah* home. Depending on what the *shul, Chevrah Kaddisha,* or funeral home provide in their services, the list may include some of the following:

1. Getting the *tallis* or *kittel* of the deceased and taking it to the *Chevrah Kaddisha* (if these will be used rather than new ones);[4]

2. Helping to call members of the *shul* and friends to inform them of the time and place of the funeral (usually each synagogue has a telephone committee arranged for such emergencies);

3. Making sure that the seven-day candle will be brought to the *shivah* home;

4. Covering the mirrors in the *shivah* home with appropriate cloths, sheets, or other drapery;[5]

5. Bringing over the low stools or other low seating on which the mourners will be sitting during the *shivah;*

6. Bringing over coat racks, etc., to accommodate the visitors at the house of mourning;

7. Making sure extra folding chairs are brought to the home if large numbers of visitors are expected;

8. Making sure that the first meal of condolence—the *seudas havraah*—has been prepared and taken to the *shivah* home;[6]

9. Making sure that other meals to be eaten during the week of *shivah* by the mourners are being sent over;

10. Arranging for at least ten male adults (a *minyan*) to be present at each of the three daily services;

11. Arranging for *siddurim, talleisim,* candles, and anything else needed for the services;

12. Arranging for a *Sefer Torah*–and appropriate box or ark in which to store the Torah–are brought to the *shivah* home for services;[7]

13. Arranging for the rabbi or other learned people who will conduct the *Mishnah* or other study texts to be learned after services;

14. Arranging for books and manuals on the laws and customs of mourning to be brought to the mourners, who may wish to read, study, or refer to them during the *shivah*;

15. Helping to arrange transportation to and from school for the children of the mourners;

16. Coordinating the special extra learning of *Mishnayos* in merit of the deceased[8] and making sure the list is hung in a visible spot in the *shivah* home;

17. Bringing charity boxes (*pushkes*) to the *shivah* home.[9]

There may be other things not listed above that can be of help to the family. A call to the nonmourning members of the family should readily ascertain these and is appropriate.

THE WAKE

As mentioned above, any actual participation in so-called comforting ceremonies or get-togethers before the funeral are out of place.

The wake, visiting the house of mourners with the deceased lying in the house, or even visiting the funeral parlor to view the deceased or to mingle with the family of mourners is totally foreign to Jewish tradition.

Generally these gatherings can degenerate into a total mockery of the deceased and the mourners. According to kabbalistic tradition, no one should view the remains of the deceased after death.[10] The only exception to this are the members of the *Chevrah Kaddisha,* who cannot help but see the body while performing the traditional purification rites of the *taharah* and the *halbashas tachrichin*–the dressing of the deceased in the traditional shrouds.

The wake is often reduced to the level of a social gathering, where the family must suffer long hours of trivial chatter in the face of their grief.

Much has been written about the detrimental consequences of viewing the deceased both from a traditional halachic perspective and from a sound psychological and psychotherapeutical point of view. *Any form of the wake is to be discouraged and avoided whenever and wherever possible under any circumstances.*[11]

AT THE FUNERAL

Similarly it is inappropriate for others (other than the rabbi or immediate family) to go over to the mourners immediately prior to the funeral, either while they are waiting in the private mourner's room at the chapel or while they are seated in the synagogue or funeral home awaiting the funeral service to begin. The deceased is lying before the mourners; it is not a time for comfort.

ATTENDING BURIAL AT THE CEMETERY

Many people attend the funeral at the synagogue or the funeral home but do not attend the burial at the cemetery. Not only is it a great *chesed shel emes* and sign of honor and respect to the deceased to be actually present at burial,[12] but it also gives one the opportunity of participating in the first traditional ceremony of comforting the mourners.

This is done immediately following the *kaddish* and the *molei rachamim* prayer after burial, when friends or those present at the cemetery form two parallel rows through which the mourners pass. As they do so they are comforted with the timeless traditional comfort formula: *HaMakom yenachem eschem besoch she'ar aveilei Tziyon veYerushalayim*—"May the Almighty comfort you among the other mourners of Zion and Jerusalem."[13]

ESCORTING THE MOURNERS TO THE HOUSE OF MOURNING

It was once customary to follow the mourners from the cemetery and escort them back to the *shivah* house.[14] Nowadays this is generally not the custom. Only close family or extremely close friends go over to the house after the funeral, usually to help with the serving of the first meal of condolence, the *seudas havraah*.[15]

Visitors who have traveled from out of town to be present at the funeral and who must return shortly (catch a plane, train, and so on) may go to the home to be *menachem aveil* (perform the *mitzvah* of offering condolences to the mourner) if no other opportunity would be possible.

THE FIRST THREE DAYS

It is widely believed that the accepted custom is not to visit the house of mourning during the first three days of *shivah*—the first day being the day of burial, no matter how late in the day burial took place; the third day being until approximately the time after the conclusion of the Shacharis (morning) services of the third morning.[16] (We are not referring here to coming to the mourner's house to attend the services and to complete the minyan. Naturally a minyan is required thrice daily even during the first three days, and when one attends the services he should recite the traditional HaMakom yenachem . . . before leaving the house.)

The above custom does have a source in Jewish writings and is based primarily on the following reasons:

1. During the first three days, grief is at its peak and the mourners may prefer to be left in solitude rather than to have to contend with the burden of communicating with visitors.[17]

2. According to kabbalistic teaching, during the first three days there is no significant decomposition or change of form of the body of the deceased. Thus a visit during this time is tantamount to attempting to comfort the mourner while his deceased is still lying before him.[18]

3. A mourner is forbidden to greet or be greeted during the three days; if greeted then, the mourner may not even return the greeting.[19] Since there may be mourners or visitors ignorant of this fact, visiting was avoided during the first three days in order to avoid the inadvertent contravening of this law.[20]

4. Others bring allusion to this law from the Torah itself, quoting the verse, "And he mourned for his son many days."[21]

It should be noted, however, that there is no halachic prohibition against a visit to the mourner during the first three days. In fact, as noted above, we actually comfort the mourner immediately after the burial, right in the cemetery. In addition, there are references in the Talmud that would infer that one may visit on the second day.[22]

Certainly if one is going to find it difficult or impossible to visit the mourners at any other time, then a visit should most definitely be made even during the first three days.[23] Similarly, relatives, extremely close friends, and neighbors may visit during the first three days.[24]

One scholar even writes that he actually knew of some rabbis who made it their practice to visit during the first three days, since they suspected that probably there were no other visitors and the mourners would be lonely.[25]

In general it should be noted that one of the best times to visit a house of mourning is at a time when it can be determined that no other visitors are there.[26]

The following story is related about Rabbi Aryeh Levin.

Rabbi Yerachmiel the Maggid, a learned scholar from Jerusalem, passed away the very night before Pesach. Since there is a halachah that in Jerusalem the body of the deceased may not remain unburied overnight, the funeral was arranged in great haste, and Rabbi Yerachmiel was brought immediately to his final resting place.

The next day, his son, Reb Bentzion, sat *shivah* only till noon, as the *halachah* requires on *erev* Pesach. The entire morning no one came to comfort him or to offer a word of solace in his bereavement. Since his father passed away so suddenly and was buried at once, hardly anyone knew of the death. And the few who did know were busy with the many details of preparing for the Passover holiday.

As Reb Bentzion later recalled, Rabbi Levin knocked on the door barely a few hours before Pesach was to begin. In a stormy rain Reb Aryeh had trudged on foot all the way from his neighborhood of Mishkenos to the Katemon section in order to pay a condolence call to the bereaved son. He was the only man who came to bring consolation on that day. Reb Bentzion said, "I can never forget that sheer kindness, nor will I ever forget the words of solace that he spoke to me then to comfort and hearten me just a few hours before Pesach began, while I was utterly alone in my grief."[27]

Returning to the question of visiting during the first three days, it has been suggested, however, that if a visit is made during that time, then the visitors should curtail their discussions with the mourners in order not to burden them by speaking during the peak of their grief.[28]

Generally, a mourner and visitors should refrain from speaking excessively, as too much talking may lead to conversation about trivial things other than the deceased or concerning the mourning. This in turn may lead to idle chatter or levity that is not in place, as it gives the impression that in this home of mourning, sorrow and mourning have been forgotten.[29] Naturally the visitors should take their cues from the mourners, for if the mourner does want to speak especially about his grief, this should not be suppressed, but rather it should be encouraged.[30]

OTHER APPROPRIATE TIMES TO VISIT

Other than the question of visiting during the first three days of *shivah*, there are no halachic restrictions on times to make the condolence call.

Some have written that it is inappropriate to visit at night, but there seems to be no real basis for this, and certainly the widely accepted practice is to visit the house of mourning even during the night.[31]

It should be noted, however, that sitting *shivah* is a *trying* and *exhausting* time, and as a matter of simple courtesy the visitor should be sensitive to the mourner's schedule. The Talmud has already stated and it is repeated in the codes, "As soon as the mourners display any displeasure, discomfort, or inconvenience with the visit, the visitors should leave."[32] *A condolence call should not be made when it is convenient for the* visitor *but rather when it is convenient and most beneficial for the* mourners.

Thus one should try to avoid visiting at times that are usually set for mealtimes. The mourners, too, have to eat! In addition, visits late at night can be very taxing on the mourners who, already exhausted, may wish to retire a little earlier in order to prepare for the long and arduous day ahead. One should not use this as an excuse for not visiting, but discretion is urged at all times.

Perhaps this is the place to mention a word about visiting other than at times of services. While it certainly is a great *mitzvah* to ensure that there is a *minyan* available at the services, in many cases there is an overabundance of people at this time. It is also difficult to really sit down with the mourners and exchange words of solace other than the traditional phrase of *HaMakom yenachem.* . . . If one does come at this time, then it would be more appropriate to come a few minutes before the services (more applicable to *Minchah* and *Maariv* rather than *Shacharis* services), or stay a few minutes after services are over, rather than to come when services begin and leave immediately afterward.

MULTIPLE VISITS

Similarly, many write that it is certainly a *mitzvah* to visit a mourner more than one time. While in our times we are lucky if we get one visit in, the point is, if we can, we shouldn't think that a second visit is out of place.[33] Only among some Sephardic Jews is there a custom that one does not visit a *shivah* home twice—either once or at least three times, but not twice. As Rabbi Dobrinsky writes:

> Among the Syrians, there is a unique tradition wherein a visitor may pay only one condolence call during the *Shibah*. If he is to come twice, according to the tradition of the Jews of Aleppo (but not Damascenes), he would have to pay a third visit. This may be because the second visit symbolizes that death could return again to this family. However, the third visit would indicate that this was not the reason for the second visit, but that the second visit, like the third, was simply to further express empathy for the mourner in his time of sorrow. Thus, if someone makes a second visit and cannot come back for a third visit, he should merely walk out of the house and reenter for a few moments, so that this coming back will constitute the third visit, and thereby remove any ill-boding notions about the second visit.[34]

One who does visit several times, either to *daven* or to comfort, should say the phrase of comfort *each* time.[35]

THE CUSTOM OF COMFORTING IN *SHUL* ON FRIDAY EVENING

Among many of the Ashkenazic communities and synagogues, the custom on Friday evenings is the following. After the conclusion of the singing of the *Lechoh Dodi* before beginning the recitation of *Mizmor Shir LeYom HaShabbos*, the mourners are called into the sanctuary. The rabbi or the *shammes* (synagogue sexton) calls out, *"Nichum aveilim"* or "Come forth to comfort the mourners,"[36] and the congregation then recites the traditional phrase of comfort, *HaMakom yenachem eschem besoch she'ar aveilei Tziyon veYerushalayim.*[37]

This custom probably originated from the source found in the *Pirkei d'Rabbi Eliezer.*[38] In Prague the custom was actually to form two parallel rows through which the mourners passed, as was done in the cemetery immediately after the burial.[39] It would seem that the reason for this custom is to afford to those members of the *shul* who did not actually make a condolence call to the house, the opportunity of extending their condolences at this time and to fulfill the *mitzvah* of *nichum aveilim.*[40]

It is not recited on a Friday evening that coincides with a *Yom Tov*[41] (if seven days have already elapsed since burial, or if *Yom Tov* begins Friday night[42]), nor when *Shabbos* immediately follows either Purim or Shushan Purim,[43] or Simchas Torah.[44] It should also not be recited if the mourners were delayed for some reason and came to the synagogue after the recitation of *Mizmor Shir LeYom HaShabbos* had been started, for there is no public mourning on *Shabbos.*[45]

If the mourner was already in the synagogue to lead the *Minchah* service, some say that he should *not* exit before *Kabbalas Shabbos* to return later before *Mizmor Shir.*[46]

This *minhag* also applies to a mourner who was sitting *shivah* for a *shemuah kerovah* (i.e., the news of the death reached him after seven days and before the end of the thirtieth day.)[47]

ON *SHABBOS, YOM TOV,* AND OTHER SPECIAL DAYS

Reference is made in the Talmud[48] and the *Shulchan Aruch*[49] permitting condolence calls on *Shabbos* and *Yom Tov.* Nevertheless, it is the accepted practice among all Ashkenazic Jewry *not* to pay any condolence call on these days.[50] Among Sephardic Jewry the custom remains to permit condolence calls on these days.[51] However, the traditional comforting phrase is changed and the words *Shabbat hi milenachem unechamah kerovah lavo* are substituted for the words pronounced during a weekday visit.[52] Since the custom among most Sephardic Jewry is to say, even during the week, *Min Hashamayim tenuchamu,*[53] some have the custom on *Shabbos* of saying *Shabbat tenachemchem.*[54]

Among some Sephardic Jews the custom is for others in the synagogue to come and sit beside the mourners to display that they share in the mourner's sorrow.[55] The custom among the Judeo-Spanish Jews is as follows:

> Toward the end of the service, the *shamash* (sexton) makes a public announcement, *Visitar gemilut hasadim kehal kodosh,* at which point (before *Pitum haketoret*) the entire congregation goes to join the mourner in his section, so as to "visit with him" and thereby demonstrate through their commiseration that they have empathy for him. Following the service, most members of the congregation (especially family and friends) will accompany the mourner to his home, where they will again have a special *limud*, this time not by reading the *Mishnayot*, but by reciting the *Alfa Beta*. This is followed by the *Kaddish deRabbanan,* and the *Kaddish* is recited by the mourners.[56]

ROSH CHODESH, CHOL HAMOED, CHANUKAH AND PURIM

On *Rosh Chodesh*, *Chol HaMoed*, Chanukah and Purim,[57] it is customary for all to offer condolences to the mourners.[58]

TISHAH B'AV

On Tishah B'Av one may come to the home to offer condolences after midday.[59]

AFTER *SHIVAH*

If one did not have the opportunity of visiting the mourners during the *shivah*, what should he or what may he say if he meets the mourners after the *shivah*?

If he meets one mourning for relatives other than a father or a mother within thirty days, or one who is mourning the loss of a mother or father *within twelve months*, then he may comfort them by using the traditional phrase of comfort—*HaMakom yenachem eschem. . . .*[60]

If he meets them *after* this time, he should not use the traditional phrase nor should he mention the name of the deceased. He may, however, indirectly offer words of comfort and say, "*Tisnachem*"—"May you find solace."[61]

The Talmud, in explaining why after this time one does not use the usual phrase of comfort (nor mentions the name of the deceased) offers the following comparison:

"Rabbi Meir said: If one meets a mourner after twelve months [on the loss of a father or mother, or after thirty days on the loss of other relatives] and tenders him [the regular] words of comfort, to what can this be compared? To the case of a man whose leg was broken and then was healed. A physician met him and said, "Come to me and let me break it again and reset and heal it to show you how good my remedies are."[62]

The obvious lesson of the above is that once the wound has healed, why reopen the sore and bring back the pain? One therefore should not reopen the pain of the mourning by mentioning the deceased by name or by extending the full mourning comfort. However, out of courtesy and repect for both the deceased and the mourner, one may allude to the event and acknowledge that he is thinking of them.

If one meets a man who had lost his wife and is now remarried, he should not offer any words of comfort nor mention the passing of the former wife in front of the present wife. When not in the presence of the new wife, he may, if appropriate, allude to the passing indirectly and wish the husband long life and only happy occasions in the future.[63]

6

The Meal of Condolence

NOTE: In many instances the mourners may be required to complete some of the prayer services that they missed while they were in their state of *aninus* (after death and before burial). This is not treated in this volume. A rabbi should be consulted for the particulars of which prayers should be recited before partaking of the meal, if applicable. A volume pertaining to these laws, and general laws relating to the mourner during *shivah,* is in preparation.[1]

Also, it is the custom among most Sephardic Jews to perform the *keriah,* the rending of the garments, upon returning to the *shivah* house after the burial, before partaking of the meal of condolence.[2] These laws have been treated extensively by the author in his Hebrew work, *Zichron Meir al Aveilus,* chapter 7.

As mentioned above in chapter 5, the mourners are obligated upon returning from the cemetery to partake of the traditional *seudas havraah,* the first meal of condolence. Usually only nonmourning relatives and extremely close friends or neighbors are present, and their purpose in being there is to help with the serving of this meal. The mourners are not allowed to prepare this meal themselves, neither should the meal consist of food that belongs to the mourners, but rather must be food bought or brought over by others and prepared by them.[3]

ORIGIN

The origin for this law is based on a verse in the Bible (Ezekiel 24:17). We find numerous references to the custom in other places in the Bible and the Talmud, and some of the traditional foods eaten can even be traced back to the times of Adam and Eve, when they mourned the death of their son Abel.[4] We also find reference to this in the famous story of Jacob and Esau, when the birthright was sold for the pottage of lentils, which the Talmud tells us was the meal of condolence being prepared for Isaac on the day of the death of his father, Abraham.[5]

The *Midrash* relates how women went to unbelievable ends in order to provide this meal to their mourning neighbors.[6]

There is even discussion as to whether this law is even biblically or only rabbinically binding.[7]

REASONS

Many of the laws and customs concerning mourning are deduced in the Talmud from what the Almighty commanded to the prophet Ezekiel when He informed him of the impending death of his wife. There Ezekiel was instructed *not* to perform most of the mourning rites, and from the converse of those instructions, the Talmud infers what the normal laws of mourning should be.

Among the instructions the Almighty said to Ezekiel was one telling him, "And do not eat the bread of other people."[8] From here we deduce that in regular mourning situations the mourners must first partake of other people's food.[9]

Abarbanel in his commentary to Ezekiel there, states simply that the reason for this custom is to relieve the grieving mourners of the burden and bother of preparing their own meal.

One of the most interesting explanations for the law of the condolence meal focuses on the psychological and emotional state of the mourner. This is but one instance of how clearly we see how *halachah*, custom, and tradition address the practical nature of the stages of the grief process as mentioned above in chapter 4.

The tendency of the mourner upon returning from the cemetery and during the peak of grief would be to totally neglect the physical neccessity of eating. "How can I be concerned with eating when we have just left the cemetery and the deceased is lying alone in the cold grave?" At this stage a mourner may even be harboring desires to die and join the deceased and does not wish to attend to the physical life-sustaining exercise of eating. Therefore, to safeguard the mourner's health and to ensure that he would eat, others were obliged to come to the home, prepare the meal, and ensure that the mourners would partake of the food.[10]

Another explanation for this custom bears directly on the *mitzvah* of *nichum aveilim*, showing the mourners that they are not alone and forgotten after the burial is over.[11] Some explain that in order to ensure that visitors would come to comfort, they were required to bring the meal. At the same time, they would probably offer words of comfort.[12]

Until now we have been more in the spectator role. Now we assume the role of comforters, as active participants providing a tangible service for the mourners. To show such physical concern for them as to provide them with the sustenance of life, their first meal, after the trying time of the funeral and the burial is itself a great comfort and relief to the mourner. In addition, we show the mourners that they have strong ties and links to the community at large. They are not alone or isolated but part of the greater family of the *Klal Yisrael*. What can be more comforting knowledge when feelings of isolation and loneliness engulf the mourners? As Rabbi Samson Raphael Hirsch so aptly puts it:

> It has already been mentioned several times how the assuaging of one's anguish at a death can be fully achieved first by uplifting oneself nearer to God and secondly by a sense of belonging to the community.
>
> Through the latter, orphans will again find their parents, parents their children, brothers and sisters their brothers and sisters, the widow her husband, and the husband the woman who will manage his home and be a mother to his children. For the community in the aggregate must become everything to the individual within it, receiving the orphaned and taking the part of the widowed. Those who are bereaved of children and to whom it seems that they have lost the *raison d'être* of their lives will find it again in the bond of the community, in the Holy Brotherhood of Israel for which we strive. He who is an integral part of it, lives with it—he never dies. And so, as soon as the insuperable state of sorrow in *aninuth* has passed and the sadness has become more spiritual and thus can spiritually be overcome more easily, the *avel* should be made to feel his link with the community; and thereby healing will gradually come to him.[13]

Another reason offered for the meal of condolence is just the opposite of the above, but also takes into consideration the nature of the mourner. It was feared that if the mourners were to partake of their own food, then in an attempt to drown out their grief, they may do just the reverse and *overindulge* in food and drink to the point of intoxication. This seeming preoccupation with eating and drinking would itself be a slighting of the deceased and the mourning ritual. This risk of overindulgence was greatly minimized by the realization that others were preparing and serving the meal, and the mourners were not to partake of their own food.[14]

There is yet another explanation offered by the Rabbi of Dvinsk, Reb Meir Simchah, the author of the classic *Meshech Chochmah*. Jewish philosophy postulates the concept of *nahama dikesufa*, the bread of shame. The entire reason why the soul descends from its heavenly abode, where it is basking in the radiance of the Divine Presence, is because the soul would be ashamed to exist eternally by receiving, so to speak, a free handout purely from the munificent hand of God. It would rather earn, in its own merit, the eternal spiritual rewards of the delights of the other world. It comes down, therefore, to this world, where by winning the struggle of allowing the soul to champion over the physical desires of the body, it earns its "bread," the reward of entering for eternity the World to Come.

When a mourner is confronted with the reality of death, which has now been finalized with the burial, he or she may question God's actions and wonder what the purpose of creating a person is if one is to be taken away and die. Therefore, immediately upon his or her return from the cemetery, we offer "free bread," bread that he or she has not earned but rather is provided by others at no charge. This is to serve as a reminder of the purpose of having brought life to the deceased, who having now earned his or her share in the World to Come, can enjoy eternal rest in peace. At the same time it reminds the mourner of his or her own purpose in life, to continue with the task of making the most of his or her remaining days by observing the Torah and *mitzvos* by which future rewards will be earned in the Afterlife.[15]

Another explanation offered is that at this point, rather than minimize the mourning, we should intensify it, to drive home the lesson that burial is not the end but rather the beginning of a new stage of the mourning process. When one is dependent on others for his food, rather than being independent of them, the food is bitter and increases his discomfort.[16]

There are yet other reasons offered using kabbalistic notions.[17]

GENERAL LAWS

A Mourner Fasting

There is a difference of opinion among the codifiers as to whether a mourner may choose to fast on the first day of the burial. Some say he may, and in fact it is even praiseworthy to do so.[18] Others maintain that he *must* partake of the meal of condolence and may *not* fast.[19] Although it would seem that the prevailing opinion is the first, nevertheless in actual practice it is uncommon for mourners to fast; in almost all situations they do partake of the meal of condolence.

Only the First Meal from Others

There is another interesting difference of opinion as to whether the obligation of the mourner to eat only the food of others applies only to the *very first* meal after burial[20] or even extends to any subsequent meals of the first day.[21] Again the preponderance of opinion follows the first notion and only forbids the mourner to partake of his or her own food for the very first meal.

Foods Not Bound by This Restriction

The verse in Ezekiel from which the obligation of this meal is derived only mentions bread. Therefore, there are opinions among the Rabbis that maintain that the mourner's obligation is to eat only the *bread* of others. Others include cake in this prohibition.[22] He or she may, however, partake of other foodstuff such as cooked vegetables, salads, fruit, and certainly beverages—soft drinks or tea and coffee, that belong to him or her.[23]

Others forbid any kind of food, but do permit any kind of drink.[24] Yet others maintain that the mourner may not partake of anything belonging to him or her, even beverages.[25]

Although the custom is to follow the stringent view of the latter and to partake only of that which has been brought and served by others,[26] nevertheless, in any situation where this may be difficult to follow, one may certainly rely on the more lenient views.[27] Thus, if upon arriving from the cemetery, the meal of condolence has not yet been brought to the house of mourning and the mourners desire greatly to partake of food and drink, they may partake of their own light refreshments.

WHO IS OBLIGATED TO PROVIDE THE *SEUDAS HAVRAAH?*

Neighbors

Tradition places the foremost obligation to provide this meal on the most immediate Jewish neighbors of the mourners.[28] In fact, the Jerusalem Talmud puts a curse on neighbors who, by not providing this meal, cause the mourners to eat of their own food.[29] (Perhaps in those times everyone knew and was friendly with their neighbors. I'm not sure if this is the case today. And even if it is, unfortunately, not every Jewish neighbor observes the laws of *Kashrus.*)

Friends, Nonmourning Relatives

Therefore, nonmourning relatives—preferably those who do not reside normally in the mourners' house and are not supported by the mourners[30]—or close friends usually help to provide the meal of condolence.

Chevrah Kaddisha

There were communities in the past, and perhaps there are still some today, where traditionally the members of the *Chevrah Kaddisha* provided for the *seudas havraah*.[31]

Men Serving the Meal to Women

The *Shulchan Aruch* states that men should not serve this meal to women.[32] This, however, was only to protect the laws of modesty and the noncontravening of the laws of *yichud* (forbidden seclusion). In any situation, however, when the female mourner is in the company of males, such as her husband, brother, or son, then this restriction would not apply.[33]

Women Serving Men

There is an opinion that only men should serve male mourners.[34] However, in any situation where the laws of modesty and propriety will be maintained, most opinions would permit women to serve male mourners.[35]

A Husband Providing the Meal for His Wife

Since a husband is duty bound to provide for his wife, in essence the food that a husband would provide to his wife would actually be hers. Since a mourner may not partake of his or her own food, a husband may not, therefore, provide the meal of condolence for his wife.[36] He may serve it to her, but the food must belong to others.

A Wife Providing the Meal for Her Husband

In the same manner, and even more so, a wife may not provide the meal of condolence for her husband, for the food is actually his.[37] She may, of course, serve the food of others to her husband.

A Son Providing the Meal for His Father

Many rule that a son supported by his father may not provide his father with the meal of condolence.[38]

TO WHOM DOES ONE SERVE THE *SEUDAS HAVRAAH*?

The Seven Relatives

The *seudas havraah* must be served to anyone mourning the loss of one of the seven relatives for whom one is obligated to mourn. They are a husband or wife, a father, a mother, a son, a daughter, a brother, or a sister.[39]

A Minor

Since there is no obligation for a minor (boy under thirteen; girl under twelve) to mourn, there is no obligation to serve them the *seudas havraah*, and they have no obligation to eat one.[40]

One Mourning the Death of a Child

There is an opinion that states that one is only obligated to eat from the *seudas havraah* if he or she is mourning a child who was at least one year old.[41] This opinion is rather difficult to understand, for it is clearly stated in the Talmud and repeated in the *Shulchan Aruch* that one is obligated to mourn for any infant who lived for at least thirty days.[42]

If a child was born and lived for more than thirty days but was kept alive in an incubator, a rabbi should be consulted.[43] It would make a difference according to some *Poskim* whether the child was born prematurely or was carried to the full nine-month term.[44]

Suicides and Excommunicants

Most opinions write that one mourning the death of a suicide should not be provided with the *seudas havraah*.[45] However, there are many factors that determine whether one is halachically considered a suicide or not.[46] There is also a question of the honor of the mourners.[47] Thus if the mourners themselves desire to be provided with the meal, their request should most certainly be honored.[48]

Similarly, if one is mourning the death of one who was halachically excommunicated, the same law would apply.[49] However, one who is a *menudah* (who has been excommunicated) should not be served the *seudas havraah*.[50]

When Another Death Occurs during *Shivah*

If another death in the family occurs during *shivah*, even though a *seudas havraah* was eaten on the day of the first burial, another one must be served on the day of the second burial.[51]

When Two Burials Take Place Simultaneously

If two relatives die and are buried simultaneously, there is an obligation to eat only one *seudas havraah*.[52]

When One Ate His Own Meal

If a mourner ate his own meal either unwittingly, being unaware of the obligation to eat from others, or for any other reason, there is no longer an obligation for others to bring him the *seudas havraah*.[53] However, if people were unaware that he had already eaten, and they brought him the *seudas havraah*, it is still customary for the mourner to partake of that meal.[54]

Shemuah Kerovah, Shemuah Rechokah

One is obligated to eat the meal of condolence if news of the death reached him any time within thirty days of the burial.[55] After this time there is no longer any obligation to serve or to eat from this meal.[56]

Bride or Bridegroom

A bride or bridegroom whose relative died after the time of the *chuppah* but *before* the marriage was consummated customarily observes shivah for the seven days, then observes the week of *Sheva Brachos*.[57] Thus there would be an obligation to serve him or her the *seudas havraah*.[58] In circumstances where he or she first observes the *sheva brachos* and then the *shivah*, he or she should not be visited or offered condolences during the days of *sheva brachos*, even though the rest of the family is sitting *shivah*.[59]

One Who Was Not Brought the *Seudas Havraah*

A mourner who was not served the *seudas havraah* may technically fulfill his obligation by halachically transferring ownership of his food to another and then by partaking of that food.[60] Another way of doing it would be for each mourner to provide the other mourner with the meal, even if they are mourning the same deceased. However, no one may stipulate that he or she was giving the meal in order to receive one in return.[61]

If a mourner is all alone somewhere and there is absolutely no one around to serve him or her the *seudas havraah* or no one to whom he or she may transfer the food as above, most authorities agree that he or she does not have to fast till nightfall in order to obviate the obligation. The mourner may partake of his or her own food.[62]

There are those, however, who maintain that he or she should try his or her best to fast till nightfall.[63] If this is difficult the mourner should restrict him- or herself to light refreshments as much as possible.[64]

On *Rosh Chodesh*, *Chol HaMoed*, Chanukah, and Purim one does not have to be stringent in this matter if one was not sent the meal of condolence.[65]

SPECIAL TIMES WHEN OR WHEN NOT TO SERVE THE *SEUDAS HAVRAAH*

When Burial Took Place during the Day and the Family Returned Close to Night

When burial took place during the daytime but there was no time to serve the meal upon the return from the cemetery before nightfall, there is no longer any obligation to serve or eat from the *seudas havraah*.[66] Some say that in this case, too, the first meal at *night* should be the *seudas havraah*.[67]

Burial at Night

However, if burial took place at night, then there is an obligation to eat the *seudas havraah* upon returning from the burial at night. If there was no time for this at night, then the first meal in the *morning* should be the *seudas havraah*.[68]

One Who Fasts

There is no obligation to serve the *seudas havraah* to a mourner who fasted the first day of the burial.[69]

Erev Shabbos

On Fridays, most opinions maintain, the *seudas havraah* should not be served after nine hours of the day.[70] However, if the mourner is going to eat after this time anyway, then he or she should eat first from the *seudas havraah*.[71]

Some maintain that if there was no time to serve the *seudas havraah* before *Shabbos*, then it should be served on *Motzoei Shabbos*.[72] This is not the prevalent custom.[73]

Erev Yom Tov

The above law applies also to *erev Yom Tov*.[74] However, on *erev* Pesach the *seudas havraah* is only served if the mourners returned from the cemetery before the time that the prohibition to eat *chametz* commences.[75]

On *erev* Yom Kippur if mourners returned for the *seudah hamafsekes* (meal before the fast), some say that this should be a *seudas havraah*.[76]

Shabbos and Yom Tov

There is no *seudas havraah* on *Shabbos* or *Yom Tov*, even on the second day of *Yom Tov*.[77] Some say that when one is buried on *Yom Tov*, then there is an obligation to serve and to eat the *seudas havraah* at night after the conclusion of *Yom Tov*.[78] Others maintain that once there is no obligation on the day of burial, the obligation is over and the meal need not be served at any makeup time.[79]

Chol HaMoed

The *seudas havraah* is served on *Chol HaMoed* to a mourner if the burial took place on *Chol HaMoed*.[80] However, the traditional mourning foods[81] are not served, just cake and coffee (or tea),[82] and the mourners sit at the regular table to eat.[83]

Some authorities maintain that the special *minhag* of the city of Jerusalem is to serve the *seudas havraah* only when one is mourning the death of a father or mother, but not one of the other five relatives.[84] In this case, if other mourners are present some maintain that they should also be served the *seudas havraah*.[85] On *Chol HaMoed* Succos the meal should be eaten in the *succah*.[86]

Rosh Chodesh, Chanukah, and Purim

The *seudas havraah* is served on *Rosh Chodesh*, Chanukah, and Purim,[87] but it is customary to serve only cake and coffee or tea, as on *Chol HaMoed*, and not the traditional mourning foods.[88]

On a Fast Day

A mourner who fasts on a public fast day is not obligated to break his fast on a *seudas havraah*, since the day of burial has actually passed.[89] Even if for some reason one is unable to fast on a public fast day, there is nevertheless no obligation to serve or be served the *seudas havraah*.[90]

On the Day of a Bris

If the mourner is the father of a baby who will be circumcized on the day of the burial, and the *bris* takes place before the mourners eat, some say that the *seudas havraah* should consist only of cake and coffee or tea, as above.[91] Others maintain that the regular *seudas havraah* should be served first and then the *bris* should take place, followed by the *seudas habris* (the *bris* feast).[92]

WHAT IS TRADITIONALLY SERVED AT THE *SEUDAS HAVRAAH*?

Bread

The most important part of the meal is bread, as the verse in Ezekiel specifies. It is customary among many to use a bagel, which is round and therefore symbolizes mourning.[93] Some authorities maintain that bread or bagel *must* be served, and if not, one did not fulfill his required obligation.[94] Others maintain that it is not an absolute prerequisite for fulfillment of the obligation.[95] The bread or bagel should not be dipped in salt as the usual custom requires.[96]

Lentils and Eggs

Traditionally, lentils[97] and eggs[98] (cold,[99] and hard-boiled[100]) are served. The main reason for this custom is the fact that these foods have no "mouths" (clefts or openings) and they are round.[101] This alludes to the mourner who has no mouth (does not wish to speak, or may not speak too much)[102] and to the fact that death will roll around to everyone; it is inescapable.[103]

Some say that the egg also symbolizes unfinished life (as the egg did not hatch to life) and alludes to the unfinished life of the deceased.[104] Others maintain that the egg alludes to the future life of resurrection. Just as life may issue and be hatched from the egg, so, too, the life of the deceased is not ended by seeming physical death, but a new life now issues for eternity.[105]

Another possible explanation for the egg is what the Chasam Sofer has written in connection with the custom of eating eggs at the *seder* table. The egg is one of the only foods by which the longer it cooks, the harder it becomes. This signifies a message to *Klal Yisrael* that despite the travails of the many exiles and persecutions, they will nevertheless remain steeled against all adversity and will eventually triumph over their adversaries.

Similarly, we hint to the mourners that although they are now facing adversity and grief, God will strengthen them so that they will be able to bear the tragedy. And as they brace themselves for the difficult days ahead, they should know that ultimately they will be favored with God's comfort and they will triumph over their grief.[106]

It is also customary to peel the eggs before handing them to the mourners. Some say this is merely a courtesy to the mourner to spare him or her

the trouble.[107] Others say this is to avoid the appearance of being raven-
ous (overanxious to eat) on the part of the mourner.[108]

Meat and Wine

The *Shulchan Aruch* states, "Where it is customary to serve meat and wine,
this should be done, but first one should serve eggs or a lentil stew as a
reminder of mourning, and afterward they may eat whatever they desire."[109]
Some write that meat and wine *must* be served at this meal.[110]

    The Talmud relates how at first ten special cups of wine were drunk
at the *seudas havraah*, but after some mourners became intoxicated they
abolished this.[111] The Talmud states in another place, "Rabbi Chanin said:
Wine was created only for the purpose of comforting mourners . . . as it
says (Proverbs 31:6), 'Give strong wine to the mourner and wine to the
bitter of spirit.'"[112] Today when wine is served, it should be served in moderation.[113]

    If burial took place after *Shabbos*, when the mourner returns home,
he may recite the *havdalah* over a cup of his own wine even before partaking of the meal of condolence.[114]

    Some write that meat is not appropriate for this meal,[115] but custom-
arily there is no such restriction, and it may be served.[116] There are, however, some Sephardic communities that do not eat meat during the *entire
shivah*.[117]

Fish, Cheese, or Olives

Some have the custom of serving either fish,[118] cheese,[119] or olives[120] at
this meal.

Beverages

It is also customary to serve at the meal some form of beverage (besides
wine), such as water, juice, coffee, or tea.[121] The custom is not to use a cup
from which the mourner has drunk unless it has been washed out. On
Shabbos, however, one need not be particular.[122]

OTHER CUSTOMS

Not Eating with the Mourners

Among many Sephardic Jews it is customary for nonmourners to join with
the mourners.[123] This is not the custom among Ashkenazic or chasidic
Jewry.[124] In any event the meal should not become a social gathering, nor

should any air of partying or noise of idle chatter be present. It certainly does not belong in a house of mourning and is not an honor to the deceased.[125]

Handing the Bread Directly to the Mourner

Unlike at any other meal, where one should *not* hand the bread directly into the hand of the recipient, at this meal it should be given into the mourner's hand.[126] This custom is alluded to in the Book of Lamentations (1:17).[127] Some write that this tradition of handing the bread directly to the mourner should be carried out with all the other foods that are part of the *seudas havraah*.[128] The mourner does not cut his or her own bread, except on *Shabbos*.[129]

Sitting on the Floor or on Low Stools

In keeping with the general laws of the *shivah* period, a mourner should not sit on any chair or stool that is above approximately eleven inches.[130] This restriction applies also to eating any of the meals, including the *seudas havraah*.[131]

Eat Your Bread in Joy

One author mentions that it was customary in his region to say to the mourners as they were about to eat the *seudas havraah,* אֱכֹל לַחְמְכֶם בְּשִׂמְחָה— *echol lachmechem besimchah*—"Eat your bread in joy." The beginning letters of the three Hebrew words spell the Hebrew word אָבֵל, *aveil*—a mourner.[132] He brings no source for this, neither does he explain this seemingly inappropriate remark for this occasion.

It occurred to me that what we are telling the mourner is the following: "I know you are extremely anguished at this moment of despair and mourning, and it is probably useless for me at this time to comfort you by saying time will heal your broken heart and shattered spirit. But know that the time *will* come when you will once again eat your bread in joy. As the *Midrash* says, 'There is a time to weep and a time to laugh; a time to mourn and a time to dance.' *A time to cry* refers to the period of mourning; *a time to laugh* refers to the period *after* mourning. *A time to mourn—during* mourning; *a time to dance—after* the mourning period is over."[133]

The Mourners Should Not Eat Together

Some write that mourners should not eat together in order not to have to join in a *mezuman* for *bensch*ing (grace after meals).[134] Others maintain that if they so desire, they may initially sit together in a circumstance that would require them afterward to join to a *mezuman* of three, but not to one of ten.[135]

Special *Bensching*

Some, especially Sephardic Jewry, are still accustomed to reciting the special blessings at *bensching* that are mentioned in the *Shulchan Aruch*.[136] Others say it is not customary anymore for us to recite these special blessings.[137] (See Appendix I.)

BRINGING FOOD TO THE MOURNER'S HOUSE DURING *SHIVAH*

The obligation for the *seudas havraah* is for the first meal only (or, according to the other opinions mentioned above,[138] for meals only on the first day of burial). However, it is customary for nonmourning family and friends to prepare meals for the mourners all during *shivah*.[139]

This has nothing to do with the obligation of the *seudas havraah*, but is simply a kindness shown to the mourners during this difficult time. The mourners have other things on their mind, need to attend to the many visitors, and do not have the patience to figure out menus and to be occupied with them.

Some have offered another beautiful reason for doing this, although it would apply more to past days than to the present. A mourner may not work during the *shivah*. A poor man who relied on daily work to provide the money to buy food for his family would be hard-pressed to do so during the week of *shivah*, in which he could not work. Thus others began to provide poor families with their meals during *shivah*. However, this became somewhat embarrassing, for it identified who was poor and needy and who was not. To spare the poor this shame it became the custom to provide rich and poor alike with their meals during the *shivah* period.[140]

However, it is only the essential meals that should be provided. It is not appropriate to bring gifts of candies and chocolates, baskets of fruits, bottles of liquor, and so on, to the house of mourning. In fact, this may contravene the law of not sending any presents to the mourners during their entire mourning period.[141]

There is, however, no obligation on the part of the mourners to insist that these presents be taken back.[142] This may offend the well-meaning but uninformed visitor, and it may also cause the contravention of the custom of not taking anything out of the house of mourning during the *shivah* period.[143]

NOT TO EAT IN THE HOUSE OF THE MOURNER

It also bears mentioning that it generally is not appropriate for visitors to eat in the house of mourning, nor to drink *LeChaim* (except on the seventh day, when the mourners rise from *shivah* when it is customary to do so).[144] Besides the oversocial and partying overtones, which are out of taste in a house of mourning,[145] it is unfair to the mourners to have to be concerned with providing their visitors with food and drink.

The exception to this may be among Sephardic Jewry, where there is a particular custom to have people recite many blessings over the food, they provide special food for the scholars after special learning sessions, and they invite poor people into the house in order to feed them. All these are done with the singular purpose in mind of doing these *mitzvos* for the benefit and merit of the deceased.[146]

In addition, some serve a light breakfast refreshment to the men who participate in the morning *minyan* service, who otherwise would perhaps have to rush off to work without eating.

There is also the situation where visitors may have traveled long distances to come to offer condolences and may not have had a chance to eat on the way. However, discretion must be urged. Whenever and wherever possible, the mourners should not have to be burdened with ensuring that these matters are taken care of. And in no situation should others sit and eat with the mourners, who may then be drawn into the social atmosphere of such company.

7

Visitation Obligations

WHO IS OBLIGATED TO VISIT THE HOUSE OF MOURNING?

Adult Jews

Every male and female who has reached the age of being obligated to perform *mitzvos* (male, thirteen years old; female, twelve years old) is required to fulfill the *mitzvah* of *nichum aveilim*. There are no limitations in time, place, or circumstance.[1] Parents should educate their children to perform this *mitzvah* and should have them accompany them when they go to comfort mourners.[2]

When Others Are Present

When there are others visiting specific mourners, one's obligation to visit those mourners is somewhat diminished.[3] However, whenever it can be ascertained that one's visit will increase or enhance the comfort of those mourners, then one should not rely upon the visits of others but should rather make a personal condolence visit.[4]

One Studying Torah

One who learns Torah all day may in certain circumstances be released from his duty and obligation to perform the *mitzvah* of *nichum aveilim*, if he can only visit during the hours he usually devotes to Torah study.[5] Naturally he should endeavor to fulfill the mitzvah during times that would not interfere with his set hours of Torah study.[6]

The Talmud relates numerous cases where the great Tanna'im and Ammora'im went to perform this great mitzvah.[7]

It is especially a mitzvah to visit one who would normally have no visitors,[8] or mourners who are sitting shivah for one who died without leaving any children.[9]

Rabbis Visiting Congregants and Others Who Are Expected to Visit

Although the mitzvah of nichum aveilim is incumbent upon all, it is especially a mitzvah for those who are normally expected to pay the condolence call as part of their rabbinic or organizational duties. Mourners may feel hurt or slighted if the rabbi, president, school principal, and so on, do not pay them a condolence call.

Judging Favorably Those Who Do Not Attend

On the other hand, the mourners must be careful to judge such individuals favorably if by some chance a visit was not made. I have heard of a case where congregants became enemies of the rabbi for not having paid them a condolence call. The rabbi happened to be out of town taking care of his own dying father and was unaware of the death. Had the family judged the rabbi meritoriously, much self-imposed aggravation, animosity, and ill feelings would have been spared both the rabbi's family and the bereaved family.

Of course this comment holds true for any person who is expected to visit and for any mourner who is expecting the visit. It has personally happened to me several times that I was not informed of the death of certain individuals and had no idea that the family was sitting shivah. In some cases it was only many months later that I became aware of the death.

This principle is taught in the Torah when it states, "You shall judge your fellowman with righteousness."[10] It is reaffirmed in the Ethics of the Fathers: "Judge all men favorably."[11] Abiding by this principle also brings great additional merit to the deceased and the mourners, for our sages taught, "He who judges others favorably will himself be judged for merit."[12] The sages there recount the following story:

A man from Upper Galilee was hired by a man from the south to work for him for three years. On the day before Yom Kippur he approached his employer and requested his payment so that he could return home and support his wife and family. His employer told him that he had no money.

"Then give me produce," he asked.

"I have none," he replied.

"Give me land."

"I have none."

"Give me cattle."

"I have none."

"Give me linens."

"I have none."

The distraught employee slung his sack over his shoulder and went home with a sorrowful heart.

After the festival the employer took the complete salary in his hand, together with three laden mules—one carrying food, another, drink, and the third, various delicacies—and traveled to the home of the employee. After they had eaten and drunk, the man was given his entire wages. The employer then asked him, "Tell me, what did you think when I told you I had no money?"

He replied, "I thought that perhaps an opportunity had just arisen for you to obtain some bargain merchandise in which you had just invested all of your money."

"And when I said I have no cattle?"

"I thought that you had hired them out to others."

"And when I said I had no land?"

"I thought that perhaps you had leased out all your land to others."

"And when I said I had no produce?"

"I thought perhaps you had not yet tithed your produce (and it was therefore forbidden to be eaten)."

"And when I said I had no linens?"

"I thought you had perhaps dedicated all of your possessions to Heaven."

The employer then said to him, "I swear to you that it was so. I vowed away all my property because of my son Hyrcanus who would not study Torah, but when I went to my companions in the south, they absolved me of all my vows. And as for you, just as you judged me favorably, may the Almighty always judge you meritoriously."[13]

Rabbi Aryeh Levin always strove to judge all Jews favorably. Even in extreme cases where he seemed to have no choice, he would retort, "But do we know everything about that man?" Or he would prefer to keep silent and change the conversation. He once explained how he reached this level of behavior:

"One day I attended the funeral of Reb Eliezer Rivlin, one of Jerusalem's pure-minded Jews. That esteemed man had a dear friend, Rabbi Shmuel Kook, a brother of the first chief rabbi. The two had been very close, shared a splendid friendship, and worked in the same field for thirty years.

"All at once I saw this true friend of his leave the funeral procession, which was just about to leave for the cemetery. He was not accompanying his dear friend on his last journey, to his final resting place, as he certainly should have done. Instead, he entered a flower shop nearby to buy a pot for planting!

"Nu, I thought to myself: Is this how a man should act toward a true friend who passed away—a friend who treated him so well while he was alive? Could he not give him this last kindness and pay him this last honor? Could he not find some *other* time to buy the flowerpot? Did he have to buy it right now during the funeral?

"Well, you know, the Torah commands us: 'You shall not hate your brother in your heart; you shall surely rebuke your friend.' So I went over to him and scolded him to his face: Teach me, so that I also will know. Were you not more like a brother than a friend for so many years to this man who has just departed this life? Why, then, did you leave the funeral procession to go buy a flowerpot?

"He explained the following: 'For years I have been visiting and attending to a Jew stricken with leprosy. Yesterday he died, and the Gentile doctors ordered that all his clothes and belongings must be burned. Among his possessions were a pair of *tefillin* and I couldn't bear the thought that these holy *tefillin* would be burned. I spoke earnestly and pleadingly with one doctor, and he agreed to allow me to bring a flowerpot today before noon, and place the *tefillin* in this earthenware container. I could then bury it in the ground with the *tefillin*, in accordance with our religious laws.

"'So you see, I was compelled to hurry off to buy the flowerpot in order to make the deadline and save the holy *tefillin* from being burned.'

"Since then," said Reb Aryeh, "I firmly resolved to judge every person favorably."[14]

A Great Scholar or an Important Person

The obligation to fulfill the *mitzvah* of *nichum aveilim* rests upon even the most eminent scholar or sage of Israel and upon any other prominent person. It is also incumbent upon them to visit even the most *unimportant* or humble member of the Jewish people. Such great men should neither be concerned with their pride or honor, nor should they consider it an affront to their dignified position when they visit mourners who are of humbler status.[15]

Many of the commentators prove this from the Almighty Himself, Who visited the patriarchs Isaac and Jacob during their bereavement.[16] The *Midrash*, in fact, says, "And if the evil inclination would come to mistakenly advise me not to go to comfort mourners, saying that I am a great person [and it is not fitting to my honor to visit others who are inferior to me], I would not listen to him, but I would go to comfort them. Why? For I would say that I am no better than my Creator, and He in His own Honorable Self goes to comfort [the people of] Israel."[17]

Stories abound about the great sages who made condolence calls. The following is related about the Chazon Ish: The only child of a friend of Rabbi Yitzchok Greenberg, *menahel ruchani* (spiritual leader) of Lomze Yeshivah, contracted polio and died. The father of the child was deeply depressed, but because people were afraid of the communicability of polio, they did not come to console him. This added to the father's depression. The bereaved father asked Rabbi Greenberg to request the Chazon Ish to pray for him. When the message was related to the Chazon Ish, he asked Rabbi Greenberg if he felt that his personal visit to the father would prove beneficial. "I'm certain it would," replied Rabbi Greenberg. Immediately, the Chazon Ish ordered a taxi and refused Rabbi Greenberg's offer to pay for the fare. The Chazon Ish soon arrived at the *shivah* house and for twenty minutes spoke comforting words to the mourner, who was greatly consoled by the visit of this great man."[18]

WHOM ONE VISITS

Men Visiting Women or Women Visiting Men

The Torah demands that at all times we conduct ourselves in a manner of *tznius* (sexual propriety and modesty). This also applies to mourning occasions.[19]

Therefore, when there are many members of a family sitting *shivah*, if it is at all possible, it is appropriate to have separate rooms for male visitors to visit with male mourners and for female visitors to visit female mourners, in order to restrict inappropriate comingling of the sexes.[20]

However, there is no prohibition for a man to visit a female mourner or for a woman to visit a male mourner, provided that the laws of *yichud* (forbidden seclusion of the sexes) and immodesty are not contravened.[21]

Where there are only women mourners sitting *shivah*, and there is a *minyan* in the house for the services, then many maintain that men should attend the services and offer brief condolences following the service.[22] If there are no services being conducted at the *shivah* home, then it is preferable for a man to accompany his wife or other men when visiting, and to offer condolences with her or them.[23]

Visiting an Enemy

The Torah states, "And thou shall love thy neighbor as thyself" (Leviticus 19:18). There is, therefore, a prohibition against hating one's fellow man. However, circumstances may arise that create animosity, and enemies are made. When unfortunately this does occur, some authorities prohibit one antagonist from visiting the other in the house of mourning. The mourner may infer that his enemy is glad to see him in his bereaved state, and this could increase his aggravation and add to his distress and antagonism.[24]

However, all circumstances are to be measured by the degree of the animosity and by the nature of the parties involved. In many instances, such a visit may breach the resentment and actually restore peace, harmony, and true friendship between the antagonists.[25] In any event, it may be proper for the person contemplating the visit to notify the mourner of his intent and to ensure that there is no objection to the visit.[26]

Visiting a Wicked Person

Whoever is included in the term *my nation*, unto him one is obligated to do kindness.[27] Therefore, a *mumar letei'avon* (a Torah transgressor due to temptation) is still included in the fold of Israel, provided that he believes in the thirteen cardinal principles of faith. It is a *mitzvah* to have mercy on him and to extend acts of kindness to him in his time of need.[28]

However, a *mumar lehachis* (a brazen Torah transgressor out of malicious spite), even of only one *mitzvah*, is classified as an *apikores* (a disbeliever). Similarly, one who publicly desecrates the Sabbath excludes himself from the fold of Israel. The same applies to a *malshin* (an informer). All are excluded from the brotherhood of Israel, and one should not extend kindness to them.[29] The above applies only when the guilty person has not repented. If he has, then nothing stands in the way of repentance. It is also true only if his guilt has been established beyond any shadow of a doubt. Mere suspicion or unconfirmed rumor does not exclude one from brotherhood, and one is obligated to act kindly to him, including visiting him during his bereavement.[30]

Today, we need careful reflection before we categorize *any* person as one of the above Torah transgressors. We could and perhaps should judge them meritoriously and include them in the category of *tinok shenishbah*, a person who sins out of ignorance or due to his upbringing. These are not excluded from the brotherhood of Israel, and it would be a *mitzvah* to act kindly toward them.[31]

One should also not forget that in times of bereavement one is closer to repentance, and by visiting him at this time, one may find the mourner more receptive to embracing Torah and *mitzvos*. Thus, it may even be a greater *mitzvah* to visit mourners who fall within this category.[32]

Visiting One Who Does Not Observe *Shivah*

Rabbi Lamm writes, "Condolence calls may be paid mourners who have returned to business during *shivah* (if it was religiously permissible to do so) the same as to other mourners. If the mourner returned to work in violation of the tradition, he *need* not be visited. He has denied himself the solace of religious consolation" (emphasis mine).[33] Others maintain that one who brazenly disregards the tradition of *shivah should* not be visited.[34] Perhaps even in this respect we can judge the mourner as a *tinok shenishbah*, one who is unfamiliar with the proper observance of the *shivah* laws and customs, and therefore has not forfeited his right to receive consolation.

As I write this, I am reminded of the following story:

An aged scholar expired, and his sons, who were industrial magnates, visited the *shammes* (sexton) of the synagogue. They requested him to recite *kaddish* for their father for the eleven-month period and promised a substantial remuneration for this service. The *shammes* agreed to do so. The next day the sons made another visit to him and asked if he would sit *shivah* on their behalf, as their commercial duties prevented them from observing *shivah* themselves. Again, a large remuneration was promised and the *shammes* agreed.

The following day the sons came to see the rabbi to ask a *sheilah* (a halachic question): "Are *they* obligated to make a condolence call to the *shammes* who was sitting *shivah* for *their* father?"

As one rabbi comments on the above, "The moral of this episode is self-explanatory. We are witnessing the degradation of mourning in America!"[35]

Visiting Mourners Who Are Sitting *Shivah* for a Wicked Person, an Excommunicant, or a Suicide

It is difficult today to know who to classify as a *rosho* (wicked person), as was mentioned above. It is also difficult to know who is classified as a suicide according to halachic parameters.[36] Another important factor is the honor of the living mourners and the shame that they would bear were visitors not forthcoming to their home.[37]

Therefore, in almost all cases it is permissible and a *mitzvah* to visit mourners who are sitting *shivah* for any of the above.[38]

Rich Man, Poor Man, Scholar, Layman

Where it is known that a rich mourner has many visitors, it is more of a *mitzvah* to visit a poor mourner, even if the former is a scholar. However, in a case where a scholar and a poor man are both mourners and equally require consolation, the honor due to the Torah scholar dictates that his visit receive priority. If the poor man, however, is a notably pious individual, and the scholar is not, the pious man has priority for the consolation visit.[39]

Visiting a Bride and Groom

According to custom, in certain circumstances where a bride or groom becomes a mourner, if the marriage has not yet been consummated, the bride and groom first observe *shivah* and afterward the week of *sheva brachos*.[40] Naturally, during the week of *shivah* they should be extended a condolence visit.

However, if the marriage has been consummated before the death, then in most cases, the week of *sheva brachos* is observed first, and only after its conclusion does the bride or groom sit *shivah*.

In this case, during the week of *sheva brachos*, they should not be visited as mourners and offered condolences, despite the fact that the rest of the family is sitting *shivah*.[41]

A bride and groom may visit a mourner during their week of *sheva brachos*, but they should not do so on the day of their wedding after the *chuppah*.[42]

One Mourner Comforting Another

Although a mourner should not leave his home to pay a condolence call to another mourner, nevertheless it is appropriate to call or write[43] another mourner to offer condolences. Even mourners who are sitting *shivah* together should extend the traditional phrase of comfort to each other.[44]

Converts

It is permissible to pay a condolence call to a *ger toshav* (an incomplete convert) as one would visit any other Israelite.[45] A *ger tzedek*, a bona fide convert, holds the status of a full Jew and one is obligated to visit him.[46]

Visiting a Non-Jew

It is appropriate to visit non-Jews who are mourners, especially when the visit will lead to increased peace and harmony and when one's abstention from the consolation visit may cause additional hatred and animosity between Jews and non-Jews.[47]

A House Where There Are No Mourners

It is customary to visit a house of a deceased person even if there are no mourners in existence in any location.[48] According to the Talmud the soul of the deceased hovers in the home during the first seven days and the soul receives comfort when it is visited during *shivah*.[49] Therefore, if at all possible, a *minyan* should congregate for services in the home during *shivah*.[50] When it is difficult to arrange this, at least a *minyan* should go to the home for the *first* service (*Shacharis*, *Minchah*, or *Maariv*) after the burial.[51]

Private *Shivah*

Although mourners should be educated that it is appropriate and proper to open their homes for visitors during *shivah*,[52] nevertheless, when mourners do not wish to have visitors and announce or inform the public that they wish to observe a "private *shivah*," their request should be honored and visitors should not call on them.[53]

8

Visiting the House of Mourning

BEFORE ENTERING

One should *not* be deterred from making a condolence call because of the fear of not knowing what to say.[1] Nevertheless, if it is at all possible, one should prepare appropriate thoughts and words of comfort before one enters the *shivah* house.[2]

Often, the visitor may recall personal incidents that transpired between him or her and the deceased or had personally witnessed or heard many of the good deeds of the deceased. Being able to relate these to the mourners will bring them pride and comfort. If one gives the matter some forethought, it may be possible to think of extremely appropriate words to say to alleviate the suffering of the mourners.

Remember, however, that one's mere presence is a comfort to the mourners for it shows honor to them and to the deceased and shows that the visitor cares. One should not be concerned, therefore, if no particular thoughts come to mind before entering the *shivah* home.[3]

Rabbi Hirsch stresses the role of the comforter as displaying society's concern for the mourner.[4] Rabbi Lamm expresses it beautifully in the following words:

> The fundamental purpose of the condolence call during shiva is to relieve the mourner of the intolerable burden of intense loneliness. At no other time is a human being more in need of such comradeship. *Avelut* means

71

withdrawal, the personal and physical retreat from social commerce and the concern for others. It is the loss that he alone has suffered. All the traditions of mourning express this troubled loneliness in diverse ways, covering the spectrum of social life–from the excessive growth of hair in indifference to social custom, to the avoidance of greetings, the minimum social courtesy.

Recognizing this state of mind, the visitor comes to the house of mourning, silently, to join the bereaved in his loneliness, sorrowfully to sit alongside him, to think his thoughts and to linger on his loss. The warmth of such human presence is inestimable. Practiced as the tradition prescribes it, true consolation is the distillation of empathy. The sum effect of the visitation of many friends and relatives, some long forgotten, others members of a community who may rarely have paid the mourner any attention at all, is the softening of loneliness, the relief of the heavy burden of internalized despair, and the affirmation that the world-at-large is not a hateful and angry place, but a warm and friendly one. It is a beckoning with open arms for the mourner to return to society. Comforting the mourners, says Maimonides, is *gemillat chasadim*, a genuine kindness to both the dead and the living."[5]

DOORS OF THE HOUSE ARE GENERALLY OPEN

Traditionally, the doors of a *shivah* home are open (not locked), and it is not necessary to ring the bell or knock on the door before entering.

Visitors are expected, and since there may be only mourners at home, it is inappropriate to have them come to the door to greet or welcome visitors to their house of mourning. It is forbidden for one to greet a mourner and similarly forbidden for the mourner to greet a visitor.[6]

PRIVATE *SHIVAH*

Although it is generally not customary to close the house of mourning to visitors, nevertheless, in a case where no visitors are wanted and the mourners wish to have a "private *shivah*," prior notice will be given or mentioned in newspaper obituaries, or word of mouth will get around quickly enough. If it didn't, the doors will be locked or a notice will be pinned to the door. In that case, it is inappropriate to impose an unwanted visit contrary to the wishes of the mourners.[7]

In this respect it may be appropriate to quote here a few words that may change the minds of the mourners.

At first right it seems false to impose custom on so intense and private an emotion as grief; yet the very loneliness of the crisis and the intensity of ambivalence, cries out for a supportive structure. Both the attenuation of leave-taking and the gradations of customary mourning set a time for the conflicts of grief to work themselves out and sanction their expression, defining the relationship between the bereaved and the rest of society.

Thus mourning customs can help to articulate grief, expressing its impulses in symbolic acts, containing them within a recognized period of social withdrawal, and setting a term for their resolution. These rites and gestures of remembrance continue a relationship with the dead into a world he or she no longer inhabits. They attenuate the loss and help to incorporate the meaning of the relationship in the continuing stream of life.[8]

Those contemplating a private *shivah* should give thought to the supportive structure they are abandoning at this critical time.[9]

SIGN-IN BOOKS

In traditional homes, visitors will generally not find a sign-in book for autographing to verify one's attendance at the *shivah* house.

There is actually nothing halachically objectionable to signing such a book placed in the *shivah* home.[10] However, mourners should be cognizant of the fact that since this is not done in most traditional homes, many people may visit and be unaware that such a book exists. Therefore, the book should not be taken as an accurate record of the visitors. In addition, many people visit the home for services when it may be inconvenient or not expedient to stand in line to sign in the book.

While no one should shirk his duty and obligation to visit a *shivah* home, many people often have legitimate reasons for being unable to do so. They may be ill, out of town, did not hear of the death (as has happened to this author on numerous occasions), and so on.

Not having signed the book can either mistakenly or correctly highlight one's absence from making the *shivah* call and can cause hard feelings between the mourners and the nonvisitor. Perhaps this is reason enough to justify the practice in most traditional homes that do not call for a sign-in book.

The mourners should be careful to judge favorably those who did not visit them while they were sitting *shivah*.[11]

NO GREETINGS

As mentioned briefly above, a visitor is not allowed to extend greetings to a mourner,[12] nor is a mourner allowed to greet a visitor.[13] It is also not

appropriate for one visitor to greet another visitor in a house of mourning.[14]

Some authorities write that this prohibition of *she'eilas shalom* (greeting) is only when the usual traditional word of greeting, "*Shalom*," is used
for the greeting, but not if a simple "Hello" or "Good morning" is used.[15]
Shalom means peace, and there can be no true peace in a house of mourning. It is, however, best to refrain from any kind of greeting.[16]

The mourner, too, is not allowed to greet a visitor. He or she should
also not respond to a greeting offered during the first three days by a visitor
who was unaware of the law that the mourner should not be greeted. After
the first three days the mourner may respond reluctantly in an undertone.[17]

Greetings are out of place in a house of mourning. Peace is not present
there. There is no good morning or good afternoon or good evening or
good night in a *shivah* home. There is no place for a cheery "Hello! How
are you?" These normal social niceties do not belong in a home where death
has struck. And, in deference to the feelings of the mourners, it is not cour-
teous for one visitor to greet another in the *shivah* home, while its inhab-
itants are in mourning.[18]

Even on *Shabbos* it is not apropriate to say *Shalom* to a mourner, but
one may say "Good *Shabbos*" to him.[19]

If one feels uncomfortable entering the *shivah* home without some form
of greeting, then a simple nod of the head in the direction of the mourners,
which indicates the desire to greet, if this were permitted, may be done.[20]

If a mourner wishes to acknowledge the presence and departure of a
group of visitors, he or she is permitted to say, "Go to your homes in peace."
This exception is permitted in order to give honor to the public and may
be said even during the first three days.[21]

OFFERING ONE'S HAND TO THE MOURNERS

Where the custom is to do so, there is no objection for a visitor to offer his
or her hand to the mourner when entering or leaving, especially during
the time when he or she is offering the mourner a blessing, words of comfort, and wishing him or her "long life," and so on. This is not taken (and
in no way should be meant) as a gesture of greeting, but rather as a gesture of sympathy and comfort.[22] It is, however, not appropriate to do this
where this is not the custom, and certainly not where it may lead to the
improper practice of men shaking the hands of women or vice versa.[23]

Kissing should also be discouraged in most circumstances. Besides
the obvious halachic objections contravened by many, it is unfair to place
the mourners in a position of having to accept these social graces when
they may be in no mood to do so.

MAZEL TOV WISHES

Notwithstanding the above, one may wish a mourner *mazel tov* wishes on the occasion of a *simchah* and express all sorts of blessings such as "I wish you long life," "May you have no further sorrow, only *simchas*," "May you live to take all of your grandchildren to the *chuppah*," and so on.[24] Similarly, a mourner may extend good wishes and a *mazel tov* to a visitor and may even phone a sick person or a woman who has given birth to wish them a *refuah sheleimah* (speedy recovery).[25]

BRINGING PRESENTS OR FLOWERS

It is against *halachah* to bring or send presents to a mourner during the entire mourning period.[26] Certainly, flowers have no place in the house of mourning. The only exception to this is the appropriate food brought in by those who are preparing the basic meals for the mourners during the *shivah*.[27]

As previously stated, should a visitor unknowing of these traditions bring a gift of food or anything else, there is no obligation on the part of the mourner to reject it or send it back.[28]

RELIGIOUS ARTICLES

The other exception to the above is when the mourners are in need of religious articles such as a pair of *tefillin*, a *siddur*, a book on the laws of mourning, and so on.[29]

BRINGING CHARITY

In addition, it is entirely appropriate to bring checks or cash that will be placed in the various charity boxes in the home.[30] It is also appropriate to send condolence cards, letters, and so on, especially when accompanied with a notification that charity has been pledged in memory of the deceased.[31] All of these *mitzvos* increase the merits of the deceased and are not only appropriate but also the proper thing to do.[32]

A MOURNER SHOULD NOT RISE

A mourner is not obligated to rise before any visitor, even if the visitor is a great rabbi or scholar.[33] Although some permit him to do so if he desires,[34] others forbid him to do so.[35] However, all agree that he is permitted to make a slight bowing motion as if to indicate that were he permitted to rise he would definitely do so in honor of his esteemed visitor.[36]

DO NOT SAY "SIT"

If a mourner, unknowing of the previous law, did in fact rise to greet a visitor, the visitor should not say to him or her, "Sit where you are," for inadvertently he is telling him or her to sit and remain in his or her state of mourning, an inappropriate statement.[37] He may, however, say, "Don't trouble yourself to stand up."[38]

Because of the tendency to automatically say this, some state that a mourner may not rise even if he or she wishes to do so, in order not to cause this inadvertent slip of the tongue on the part of the visitor.[39]

A VISITOR SHOULD NOT INITIATE CONVERSATION

Visitors are not permitted to initiate conversation with the mourners but rather must wait for the mourners to begin speaking to them.[40] The Talmud actually deduces this law from the verses in Job (3:1 and 4:1) where it tells us that the classic mourner Job spoke first and only then did Eliphaz answer him.[41]

Whenever possible, it is appropriate for the mourners to begin conversation with the words *Boruch Dayan HaEmes*.[42]

A mourner may not desire to engage in conversation. He or she may justifiably be wrapped up in his or her own thoughts of grief. To intrude on these thoughts, to forcibly draw him or her out of his or her silence, is neither fair nor appropriate.

Often, rather than the distracting trivial chatter that is bantered around the mourner, silence would be preferable. The same holds true for the many well-meaning but often hollow and even sometimes annoying remarks: "Well, he lived to a ripe old age," "He was suffering so much this was far better for him," "He could have lingered on in so much pain," and so on. The different combinations of hundreds of these phrases, all meant to be words of comfort, may strike the wrong chords! It is far better to take one's cue from the mourners and to try to adjust and address one's remarks to them. If, for instance, a mourner himself says, "Well at least my mother lived to a ripe old age," it is certainly not appropriate to interject a contradictory remark such as "It doesn't matter how old one was, a mother is a mother and it's always painful when she dies."

King Solomon in Ecclesiastes 3:7 informs us, "There is a time to be silent and a time to speak." The Talmud notes, "Reward comes to the one who remains silent in the house of mourning."[43] Some commentaries say this refers to the mourner himself,[44] while others say this refers to the visitors.[45] Both are correct. For generally when either begins to overtalk, the conversation leads to idle chatter, frivolity, or the like, so contrary to the mood that should be present in a home of mourning. Again the cue is from the mourner. If he or she is not talking about the *shivah*, one must use a great deal of discretion in bringing the conversation around to the deceased. However, it is not appropriate to admonish the mourner directly and cause hurt feelings.

The purpose of the visit is to offer comfort, and it is not always easy to find the right words. Silence is often golden. The meeting of the eyes where the mourner reads the genuinely expressed heartfelt sympathy of the visitor, and the very presence of the visitor who took the time and made the effort to visit, may be more comforting than any verbal communication that can transpire between the mourners and the visitors.[46] As Rabbi Lamm writes:

> The strategy of true compassion is presence and silence, the eloquence of human closeness. Sad, muttered words are clumsy openers of the heart compared with the whisper of soft eyes. The comradeship demonstrated by the expression on the face speaks volumes that the ancient bards could not match with mere words, no matter how beautiful. It fulfills at once the mourner's desperate need for both companionship and privacy. It was, therefore, an old custom, unfortunately lost to our generations, for visitors to sit silently on the earth with, and like, the mourner. How magnificent an expression of compassion.[47]

WHEN ONE MAY SPEAK FIRST

In circumstances where it is obvious that the mourner is in the mood for talking but is either unaware of the law that he or she must open the conversation, or perhaps feels that in deference to the greatness of his or her visitor, the visitor should speak first, then it is permissible for the visitor to initiate the conversation.[48] (If possible, the visitor should inform the mourner of this custom and request the mourner to speak first.)[49]

This is important to know, for there are many mourners who are unaware of this tradition. I was informed by a rabbinic friend that he once visited a house of mourning where the mourner did not know this law, and in deference to the rabbi he was waiting for him to say something. The rabbi, on the other hand, thought it important to adhere strictly to the law of not initiating conversation and thus did not say anything. After the *shivah* a mutual friend told the rabbi that the mourner had been quite hurt that the rabbi had not found anything at all to say to him at the *shivah* visit.

It must also be noted that if a visitor enters the *shivah* house and finds the mourner already engaged in conversation, then he does not have to wait for the mourner to initiate conversation directly with him, but may join in the conversation even though he will be speaking to the mourner before the mourner speaks to him.[50] Some say that once the mourner has begun to speak on any day during the *shivah*, then one may initiate conversation with him on any subsequent day.[51]

Obviously, the entire restriction of not being able to initiate conversation only applies to one who is coming to comfort the mourner. If one merely enters the mourner's home to ask something of the other members of the family or friends, no such restriction applies.[52]

In any event, even when it is obvious that the mourners do not wish to speak and the visitors have been sitting silently with them, upon leaving, they are permitted to say the traditional mourning phrase, "*HaMakom yenachem eschem* . . . ("May God comfort you . . .").[53]

CHARITY—MERIT FOR THE SOUL

It is a great merit for the deceased when charity is donated in his or her memory.[54] Therefore, it is appropriate to have charity boxes or plates in a conspicuous part of the house of *shivah* and for visitors to donate charity. This would also be an appropriate time (when giving the charity) to offer the short prayer mentioned on page 141.

Others have the practice of donating to a charitable organization that sends out a card of condolence to the mourners informing them that a charitable donation has been made (by the contributor) in memory of the deceased. If the deceased had a favorite charity, it is not inappropriate for the mourners to mention this in an obituary notice and to ask those who wish to memorialize the deceased, by donating charity in his/her merit, to donate to that specific cause.

TORAH STUDY

Similarly, it is a great merit for the deceased when portions of the *Mishnah* and Talmud are studied and completed specifically in merit of the deceased.[55] (We are not referring here to the specific studying actually done in the *shivah* house. This is not the discussion here.) It is customary, therefore, in many houses of mourning to post a list of all the mishnaic and talmudic tractates and for the mourners and visitors who are able to study them to select a tractate and to fill in his name on the line opposite that tractate.[56] Ideally, the form should have a place for a phone number of each volunteer learner, so that the mourners or the one who is coordinating the memorial study will be able to contact the volunteer to remind him of his commitment and of the anticipated date of completing the learning cycle. Some have cards printed, leaving space for the tractate to be selected and informing the volunteer of the date of completion (usually the day of the *shloshim*—the thirtieth day). A copy of the forms can be found in Appendix II.

NOT TAKING ANYTHING OUT OF THE *SHIVAH* HOUSE

There is a widely known custom that a visitor should not take anything out of the house of mourning.[57] Obviously, this refers to belongings of the *shivah* house. One, of course, may certainly bring in a coat, hat, pocketbook, and so on, and retrieve them on the way out.

Some authorities maintain that this custom was really meant only for taking articles out of the room in the house where the death actually took place.[58] Others extend this to mean any room of the house as long as death occurred in the house.[59] If, for example, as is prevalent today, death occurred in the hospital or elsewhere, then they maintain that there is no reason to be concerned with the above *minhag*. Some even maintain that the whole custom arose mistakenly.[60] Therefore, others[61] have writtten that in regard to this custom, we may apply the talmudic dictum of "When one is not particular, they are not particular with him."[62] In essence this means that if one is not worried about the consequences of *harm* related to a certain custom, then he may not have to practice that particular custom.

The general practice seems to maintain this custom as much as possible and does not needlessly disregard it. One who wishes to be scrupulous in complying with it should not even borrow a book from the mourner's house.[63] Some Sephardic Jews (especially because of this custom) do not eat anything in the *shivah* house.[64]

For a completely different reason, if one's possessions were in the house of the mourner prior to his or her becoming a mourner, one may retrieve them only if really necessary and provided that the mourner does not benefit financially from their removal.[65]

COMFORTING OVER THE TELEPHONE

Although the *mitzvah* of *nichum aveilim* is fulfilled more completely by an actual visit to the house of mourning,[66] nevertheless, when this is difficult or almost impossible, that is, when one lives in another country or city, then there is *most definitely* a *mitzvah* to phone the mourners during *shivah* to extend condolences.[67]

A mourner may come to the phone to receive the condolence call. Some maintain that in keeping with the injunction of not greeting, the mourner should not say "hello" when he or she comes to the phone.[68] However, others rule that this is no worse than "good morning" and so on, which does not actually breach the law of extending greetings.[69] Therefore, when it would be difficult to initiate the conversation in another manner, it is permitted.[70] As stated above a mourner may call to wish someone a *refuah sheleimah,* or to call for his or her own needs for the *shivah,* such as getting together a *minyan,* and so on, but he may not call anyone—even his or her own family—to enquire about their welfare.[71]

WRITING SYMPATHY LETTERS AND CARDS

Similarly, if it is difficult to reach the mourner by phone, then it is certainly appropriate and a *mitzvah* to write a condolence letter.[72]

If the letter will reach the mourners before the end of *shivah,* it may even be preferable to write rather than to phone. For one thing, the mourner is not disturbed while in the company of other visitors. For another, it takes a lot more effort to write than to phone. And thirdly, whereas the words over the phone may be forgotten, the printed words of a letter can be read and reread, and one usually puts in a lot more thought into what one writes than into what one says.

I do not mean to infer that one should only write a condolence letter if the wording is eloquent and beautiful. It does not have to be a long letter filled with deep philosophical or theological references. A few personal, tender expressions of genuine support and sympathy will be treasured by the recipient. If one finds it difficult to write, merely sending a printed condolence card of sympathy is far better than nothing at all. At least it lets the mourners know that you were thinking of them in their time of sorrow. If at all possible, a few personal words of feeling should be added in the sender's own handwriting. This transform the impersonal card into a really personal note. If this is the method used, then it is particularly appropriate to use cards that are sent out by organizations informing the mourner that charity has been donated in memory of the deceased. This accomplishes a twofold *mitzvah.*[73]

While each person would want to make his or her addition to the sympathy card a personalized expression, the following examples may be of help:

"To these words we add our love and concern. We are physically sepa-
rated by hundreds of miles, but our hearts and spirits are right there
with you."

"You are constantly in our prayers and thoughts, and we just want
you to know that we send all our love and heartfelt sympathy in
these sad days."

"We cannot find the words to adequately express our sympathy and
concern, but please know that we feel your loss deeply, and send
you our love and heartfelt condolences."

Naturally, the traditional phrase of comfort should be added in all
cases.

It is not always better to write than call. Obviously, there are times
when the personal phone call will be more meaningful to the mourner,
depending on the relationship between mourner and caller. A letter should
not only be written if it is to reach the house during shivah. A letter can be
written any time (preferably during the period of mourning, which for
mourners of relatives other than for a mother and father is thirty days) [74]
Perhaps a telegram should be sent at first to reach the home during shivah,
and a phone call or letter should follow.

Although, as stated above, the card may be written during the entire
course of the mourning period, nevertheless it is wise to make every effort
to write as soon as possible. The strong emotional impulse you feel when
you first hear the sad news should be utilized immediately. Delaying makes
the task more difficult, and we offer ourselves at that time a host of excuses: "I really don't know what to write. What shall I say?"; "My letter
probably won't make that much difference. They probably have received
so many already"; "They probably have far more important things to concentrate on than my letter." These rationalizations are a natural way of trying
to avoid a task that is unpleasant. But, in truth, they are misleading deni-
als of what can turn out to be the fulfillment of a very important mitzvah.

These are just guidelines. Each person will know what is the right thing
to do in his or her situation.

As I was finishing the last draft of this book, I came across two binders,
one containing some of the letters and cards we received after my son
passed away; the other, the letters and cards our family received after my
father, z"l, passed away. I cannot remember all of the sentiments that were
expressed verbally and who exactly came to express them. However, these
letters are a timeless record of those who wrote and the beautiful sentiments they expressed.

I have excerpted phrases and sentences from them for further mod-
els of what one can write:

We have just heard the tragic news and I felt I wanted to let you know how deeply sorry we are and how much we feel for you all. It is so terribly hard for me to write, as everything I think of seems so inadequate. We just pray that time will be a great healer and you will only have *simchas* in future for many years.

. . . Even though there are no words in my mouth to console you on your great loss. . . . Nevertheless I want to share from the distance, but from very close as far as the feelings of my heart, in your deep pain. We know that the hidden things belong to God; *HaShem* gave and *HaShem* took, may His Name be blessed for ever. Our prayers and blessings are that you should merit from now on to inform us only good news in good health and with much *nachas* from the rest of the family.

What can we possibly say to comfort you on the loss of your precious Ephraim, *a'h*? It was just two short years ago that we rejoiced with you from afar at his birth, and now we share your grief, again from a distance, at his untimely passing.

You've had many tribulations in the past, and we've seen you face them with courage and faith. Now God will have to bless you with exceptional strength and fortitude, added to your unfaltering belief, so that you will be able to carry on.

We think of you constantly and just thought we'd tell you so. How can we really tell you, though, what is in our hearts? We wish we could be with you to bring you some words of comfort, to help in some way.

I just sit here thinking. I want to write, but what does and can one write? Friends belong together in times of *simchah* and they belong together at times of sorrow. As I couldn't come in to be with you, I want to share in your pain from far. . . .

Now it may be hard to accept this as a *nechamah* [comfort], which is only natural. But the *Ribbono Shel Olom* has given us the gift of "forgetting." And though today we say, "We'll never forget"; "How can I ever forget"; "I'll always remember as clearly as I do today"—but *HaShem* put "forgetting" in the world to *make* us forget, because a person couldn't possibly go on living with a sorrow forever, if it were so vividly in front of him. And though for a time it will get harder before it gets better, when it, God willing, does become bearable to think about, and when the pain can be born without tears, maybe it will be a comfort to you to think that you had the merit of being *mezakeh es horabim* [bringing merit to the public]. It will be a *zechus* [merit] for you that others did *teshuvah* because of you; that others searched their deeds because of Ephraim, *a'h*."

We appreciate that the written word is incomparable with a personal conversation and visit, but trust that, nevertheless, this letter will be of some comfort to you at this sad time. May the Almighty give you and the family the strength to bear your tragic loss and to face the future and all its tribulations.

It is difficult to find the right words to express my very deep sorrow on hearing of the passing of your very dear husband and father. I shall always remember him for his kind and gentle *middos,* and he shall be deeply missed by us all.

We know that words are quite inadequate to comfort you at a time like this. May you, however, find a certain amount of comfort in the knowledge that Myer, *z'l,* had a full life span and was loved and respected by everyone who knew him. He had real Jewish *nachas* and devotion from all of the children who are carrying on their lives in the true Jewish tradition.

Living so far away from you all and seeing each other so rarely doesn't make it any less sad for us, as the bonds of family are always with us. We only wish we had been nearer to be able to help and comfort you all.

We were very saddened to learn of the loss of your beloved father, *alav hashalom.* He was a man of distinguished character and will long be remembered by all who had the privilege of knowing him. May the good deeds of the wonderful life he led help you and your family in this very difficult period of mourning.

To you we send our fondest love at this difficult time and earnestly pray that the Almighty Himself will comfort you and grant you a long and healthy life.

It was with deep regret that we just heard that Myer has passed away after an extended illness. I realize that my lines will be too late to reach you during the shiva. But as a friend and admirer of many years I feel I must express some words of comfort.

I belong to the category of people who, when judging others, and their achievements in life, have due regard for their background. Some *talmidei chachamim* [Torah scholars], when weighed on the scale against their ancestors, turn out to be only lightweight. Whereas others, not so knowledgeable measured by the same yardstick, are veritable giants. Myer certainly belonged in the latter category. His constant endeavor to improve his knowledge, his simplicity, his truthfulness so devoid of any deviousness have always struck me as belonging to someone who had never shed the innocence that marks our childhood.

It is these qualities I have always admired in him, and it is because of these qualities that it was always a privilege to be counted among his friends. That such men leave behind children who each are a credit to our tradition is not due to good luck but to the example they have set throughout their lives, not only in public, but—most important—at home, in the privacy of their four walls.

Looking back on having shared a life with such a person is indeed something to be grateful for and must be your most comforting thought at this time.

May you and all yours be comforted among the mourners of Zion and Jerusalem.

In sympathy and continued friendship. . . .

I also wish to record some fragments of letters of consolation from the great *rosh hayeshivah* Rabbi Hutner, *ztz'l.*[75]

A son is the foot of his father.[76] Why just a *foot*? Why is he not considered as the *hand* of his father? People are considered in this world as "going." But the dead and the angels are considered to be only "standing." As it says in the verse . . . (Zechariah 3:7). When a man dies he is freed from doing *mitzvos*, and without *mitzvos* there is no "going any higher." There is just "standing in one level." The foot is the limb by which man "goes." That's what is meant by the son being the "foot" of the father. For even if the father himself is in a position of only "standing," nevertheless, if he leaves behind a good son, then his son turns his father into a stance of "going." . . .

What shall I say, what shall I speak?—I have no words of consolation in face of this great breach. Only the Master of Comfort, from Whom nothing is impossible, has in His treasure house the healing ingredients for the brokenhearted and the crushed of spirit. . . . My hope is that *HaShem* will open up this treasure house of comfort, and rain droplets of comfort into the wounds of the heart. *HaMakom yenachem.* . . .

To comfort you?—I don't know how. I only know of one statement, to which tens and tens of thousands of *Knesses Yisrael,* hosts of *HaShem,* broken souls, have cleaved to with their lips, and have nurtured from it strength and life, in the time of their strongest afflictions:

Yisgadal veYiskadash Shmei Rabbah—Magnified and Sanctified shall be His Great Name.

I am walking around here and there with a throat full of obstruction. My powerful desire is to bring forth words from my mouth, but each word is choked within my throat, for in truth every expression of consolation is cut off from my mouth. It is true that my hand falls short from being able to comfort you. But it is impossible for me not to be in contact with you at this stormy time. When one is in close proximity, it is possible to find a form of contact besides the expressions of the lips. The choked throat becomes visible through the look in one's eyes. The squeezing of the hand unites the hearts. But when one is at a distance, the eye cannot look, and the hand cannot squeeze. All we have left are the words, the letters, and the sentences. And when those words become choked, against their will they burst out with the cry: *HaMakom yenachem oscho.*

With pain, silence, and empathy. . . .[77]

RESPONDING AND REPLYING TO VISITATIONS, LETTERS, AND CARDS

Although one may thank the visitors for coming, it is not in any way an obligation of the mourners to respond or to reply in writing to any visitations or correspondence. People must understand that the bereaved would be overwhelmed if they had to respond or reply to the many calls and letters received.

However, it is appropriate to place, and not uncommon to find, in a local *shul* bulletin or Jewish newspaper a notice of thanks to all who came to share in the family's grief during *shivah*. Similarly, one may choose to print a simple card to send to those who wrote or called, depending on the closeness of the family to the caller or writer and whether they feel the need to acknowledge their thoughtfulness.

I have reproduced the card we sent out after the passing of our son (we wrote the cards close to Rosh HaShanah—hence the *kesivah vachasimah tovah*).

בס"ד

We thank you for the kind sentiments

you expressed in the recent loss

of our beloved Ephraim ע"ה

Your caring and sharing in our sorrow

have been a source of strength and comfort to us

during these difficult days.

May we share from now on

only in each other's Simchas.

כתיבה וחתימה טובה

Aaron and Chanie

9

What to Say and What Not to Say to the Mourners

INTRODUCTION

Before reading this chapter, please refer once again to certain sections in chapter 8.[1]

NO IDLE CHATTER OR FRIVOLITY

We have already discussed the inappropriateness of making trivial, frivolous, or jesting remarks in a house of mourning.[2] Many people make the mistake of thinking that making small talk and light conversation, which will distract the mourner and take his or her mind away from the death, is the appropriate thing to do. Some try to adopt a false tone of cheerfulness and even resort to telling jokes to change the somber mood.

In fact, trying to *divert* the mourner from the reality of death is like trying to camouflage the death. Usually the mourners can see right through this, and when the visitors leave, reality hits home even harder. It is hard to face the actual death, but that is what the mourners *must* do in order for the healing process of the grief cycle to take place. Therefore, attempts to distract and divert this process are not helpful to the mourners; on the contrary, they impede the healing process.

Many rabbis have unfortunately been told by mourners about the anguish caused by the invasion of "cheerful" visitors. "My heart was breaking and they were telling jokes. For a while I wasn't sure whether they had come to a house of *shivah* or to a cocktail party" is the way one widow expressed herself.[3]

One writer has also pointed out that this very problem may be the reason why some people choose to have a "private *shivah*," which is not in consonance with tradition. He writes as follows:

> "Proper Shiva" Not "Private Shiva."—In the modern Jewish community, it is not uncommon that families request a "Private Shiva" in the week following death. The very term, however, "Private Shiva," is a religious contradiction. Shiva, as understood throughout centuries of Jewish life, has always been a communal activity. It is the time for family, friends and community to gather together to mourn, console the bereaved, and to remember the life of the deceased. The announcement "Private Shiva" serves to discourage and limit communal participation in the Shiva, thereby cutting mourners off from a source of support and consolation.
>
> However, it is not difficult to understand why a family might choose to request a "Private Shiva." Often what takes place in a Shiva house is reminiscent of a party—loud talking, laughter and frivolity, and all the guests enjoying food and drink. Hence, families choose to avoid such a scene and grieve in quiet and among intimate family members.
>
> This dilemma can be resolved by understanding the difference between a "Private Shiva" and a "Proper Shiva." It is usually the latter which people want—a Shiva that is observed with integrity and with respect to the mourners and for the deceased. A "Proper Shiva" is a communal Shiva in which the needs of the mourners are taken into consideration. A "Proper Shiva" takes place in a respectful atmosphere where time and energy are given to the act of mourning and remembering the deceased. Such a properly observed Shiva can lead to reconciliation among family members, reinforcement of the family bond, and a genuine emotional healing in the face of death.[4]

One great rabbi writing on this subject states:

> Therefore, all must be extremely careful to ensure that in the house of mourning, no insignificant words are spoken, that is, words containing no wisdom, no *mussar*, words leading to self-betterment, no comfort, no *derech eretz,* plain courtesy. These words are neither helpful nor advantageous to the soul of the deceased, but rather increase the pain, sorrow, and bitterness [of both the soul and the mourners]. But Israel is a holy nation, and they can devise many things to do [in addition to what I have said above]. Each one should seek out the appropriate methods to honor his [deceased] parents or relatives, to ensure that he

affords them the proper peace of mind in both this world and the World to Come.[5]

TALK ABOUT THE DECEASED

As mentioned above, many feel it is appropriate to distract the mourner from the death. They think that speaking about the death and the deceased may only cause a new flow of tears and lead to more anguish.

In reality, the opposite is true, not only from a traditional point of view,[6] but even from a psychological and emotional perspective. The more the mourner talks about the deceased, the better off he or she will be. Many unconsciously try to *suppress* their feelings of grief. The more these feelings are brought to the fore, the more the mourner expresses his or her grief and cries, the easier and more therapeutically sound will the healing process of grieving be accomplished.[7]

Talking about the deceased, relating incidents and experiences that one shared with him or her in ordinary circumstances or on some special occasion, can add treasuries of memories to the mourner. It also re-creates a living picture of the deceased that replaces the picture of him or her in death.

Speaking of the merits of the deceased, his or her goodness, fine character, a particularly outstanding trait or quality that he or she possessed—all of this brings merit to the deceased and alleviates the anguish of the mourner.

If one did not know the deceased that well, there's nothing wrong in saying, "I unfortunately never had the pleasure of knowing your father. I heard he was a fine man. Tell me a little about him." In one instance when this happened with a woman who had lost her brother, she talked about her brother with a visitor for over an hour. Afterward she said, "I feel relieved now for the first time since he died."[8]

Generally, however, the mourner needs good *listeners*. He or she may wish to unburden his or her grief. He or she may wish to relieve some guilt feelings. *Talk little and listen much.* One writer expresses it this way: "The measuring stick for the success of a visit to a house of mourning is 'if your friend [the mourner] has said a hundred words to your one, you've helped a lot.'"[9] Try to draw him out so that he speaks about the deceased. But don't *force* it out of him. *Don't push, and don't intrude.* One should certainly not bombard the mourners with questions relating to details of the illness and death of the deceased unless, of course, the mourners themselves wish to talk about them. In this respect one mourner wrote the following: "Do not put additional strain on the *aveil* by asking him to constantly relive the deceased's sickness and the last painful days of his life. Ask, instead, questions about his accomplishments, pleasures, and satisfactions. Having to recount details about his illness and death are extremely painful for those mourning him. Speaking, however, about his past while he was still well can be very rewarding."

WHEN THE MOURNER IS ANGRY WITH GOD

Perhaps one of the most difficult parts of conversation is how one should react to seemingly blasphemous remarks on the part of the mourners who, in their grief, express their anger against God.[10]

While this problem may be more pronounced among mourners who have very little religious background and are weak in religious faith and conviction, this feeling does not necessarily escape even the one most observant in Torah and *mitzvos* and one strong in his faith of God.

The Talmud says, "A man is not held responsible for what he says in the time of his distress."[11] Even the most devout can sometimes let slip from their mouths, in their time of grief, seemingly unholy words. Our mother Rachel said to Jacob, "Give me children, and if not I would rather die." Jacob angrily replied, "Am I in place of God Who has held back from you the fruit of your womb?"[12] Nachmanides comments that Jacob was punished for this. "Is this the way one answers the broken-hearted?"[13]

Thus, one has to first know that these reactions, words, and thoughts are not uncommon at a time like this. The visitors themselves should know this, and they may make the mourners aware of this. Expressing unholy words in the height of grief does not call into question one's commitment to Torah and to God.

Therefore, one must be careful and use great discretion when responding to such words. To chastise the mourner and say, "How can you talk like that? You are blaspheming God!" will not serve any purpose and only add to the burden of grief. To tell him not to be angry in his time of anger or to try to stifle and repress the anger will also accomplish little.[14]

Certainly, however, whenever possible, one must gently help the mourner be *matzdik es hadin*, accept the decree of Heaven. According to many, this is the *main* purpose of the *mitzvah* of *nichum aveilim*.[15]

Certainly one should be extremely careful not to interject any complaint against God or His justice and thus stir the mourner to doubts of religious faith.

In this respect we have learned in the glosses of the *Shulchan Aruch*, "One [a mourner] should not say, 'I have not been punished enough for my wicked deeds,' or anything similar, for one may not tempt fate. [And] a visitor should not say to the mourner, 'What can you do? You can't change anything now.'—for this is like blasphemy . . . but rather one should accept upon himself the Heavenly decree of the Almighty with love."[16]

After the death of Aaron's two sons, Nadav and Avihu, the Torah tells us: *"Vayidom Aharon"*—"and Aaron remained silent" (Leviticus 10:3). The *Midrash* tells us that this means that Aaron accepted the decree of God without complaint, and he was justly rewarded for it.[17]

The story is told that when Reb Lipman of Radomsk, the son-in-law of the Tiferes Shlomo, the *rebbe* of Radomsk, came to the Kotzker *rebbe*, the *rebbe* asked him to tell him a Torah thought he had heard from his father-in-law. Reb Lipman replied, "Our sages highly praise Aaron the High Priest for remaining silent when hearing about the death of his two sons. But even greater is that which is written about King David, 'So that my soul might sing to you *velo yidom*, and *not* be silent, *HaShem* my God, forever will I thank you' (Psalms 30:13). Even when King David was in the greatest distress—not only did he not complain; not only did he accept the decree and remain silent; he even continued to sing the praises of God."[18]

The rewards that can accrue to a person for fully accepting the decree of Heaven without murmuring against divine justice is epitomized by the following incredible story: It is told that the Vilna Gaon (Rabbi Elijah of Vilna) had a daughter who passed away very shortly before going to the *chuppah* on her wedding day. The mother of the Gaon appeared to him in a dream and said: "If you would know the Heavenly reward you received for the manner in which you accepted this decree, you would have danced at her funeral more than you would have danced at her wedding."[19]

It is told of Rabbi Aryeh Levin that he was especially careful to fulfill the *mitzvah* of *nichum aveilim*. He explained why this was so important to him: "When a misfortune or tragedy befalls a person, apart from his anguish and suffering, his faith also becomes affected to some extent. When a person goes to comfort a mourner, not only does he renew his spirit and courage by sharing in his sorrow; he also returns the mourner's faith to its original strength."[20]

I can perhaps agree with Harold Kushner, who says we shouldn't tell the mourners they deserve the tragedy that has just occurred because of their sins.[21]

I can agree with him that one shouldn't say suffering is a wonderful happening because it uplifts and ennobles him [the mourner] spiritually.[22]

I can agree that one shouldn't say to the mourners, "Maybe God is trying to teach you a lesson or use the death of your loved one to teach others a lesson."[23]

I can agree that one shouldn't say, "Don't worry, you'll be all right. God never sends us a burden that we cannot bear."[24]

I can agree that one shouldn't say to a parent who has just lost a young child, "This is a time for rejoicing because your son has been taken out of this world of sin and pain with his innocent soul unstained by sin."[25]

My agreeing, however, does not mean that I negate the truth of some or all of the above. It only means that I concur that these sentiments are not the appropriate ones to express to the mourner.

Rabbi Kushner states:

> Sometimes, because our souls yearn for justice, because we so desperately want to believe that God will be fair to us, we fasten our hopes on the idea that life in this world is not the only reality. Somewhere beyond this life is another world where "the last shall be first" and those whose lives were cut short here on earth will be reunited with those they loved, and will spend eternity with them.
>
> Neither I nor any other living person can know anything about the reality of that hope. . . . Belief in a world to come where the innocent are compensated for their suffering can help people endure the unfairness of life in this world without losing faith. But it can also be an excuse for not being troubled by injustice around us, and not using our God-given intelligence to try to do something about it. The dictate of practical wisdom for people in our situation might be to remain mindful of the possibility that our lives continue in some form after death, perhaps in a form our earthly imaginations cannot conceive of. But at the same time, since we cannot know for sure, we would be well advised to take this world as seriously as we can, in case it turns out to be the only one we will ever have, and to look for meaning and justice here.[26]

This is precisely the point of departure from traditional thought that the above author takes. Consequently it leads him to explain that when bad things happen to good people, these bad things do not come from God at all. *They are beyond His control.* "They happen at random, and randomness is another name for chaos, in those corners of the universe where God's creative light has not yet penetrated."[27]

I agree with the author that the subject is a difficult and troublesome one. I confess that I am totally inadequate to debate and explain the problem of evil in the universe. I agree that it is heartbreaking to see the many tragedies that befall this world. I feel with true empathy the pain he suffered by the loss of his beloved son. I, too, lost a son and went through the agonies of the tragedy.

The *Mishnah* states, "Rabbi Yannai says: 'It is not within our ability [to understand or explain] the tranquillity of the wicked or the afflictions of the righteous.'"[28]

The great *tzaddik*, the Chofetz Chaim, once said: "With *emunah*, with faith, there are no questions; without faith, there are no answers." Faith in the fact that there is another world is mentioned all over the Talmud. Interestingly, on the verse where Mosheh Rabbeinu asks God to show him His ways (Exodus 33:18), the Talmud explains that Mosheh asked: "Why are there righteous people who suffer, and righteous who only have good; why are there wicked people who suffer, and wicked who have only good?"[29] My *rebbe*, Rabbi Dovid Kronglass, *ztz'l*, pointed out the following: If you look carefully at the text you will notice that Mosheh was not at all troubled by the question, "How come there are righteous who suffer, and wicked who prosper?" The answer to that question was obvious to him. There is *this* world, where even the wicked receive recompense for their good deeds; retribution they will receive later. There is the World to Come where the righteous will fully enjoy eternal reward and bliss; in this world they must receive retribution for any evil that they may have done. What Mosheh wanted to know was the difference between the righteous— some of whom suffer and some of whom prosper—and between the wicked—some of whom suffer and some of whom prosper.

It is true that the notion of the eternal reward and bliss of the World to Come is foreign to us. The prophet Isaiah says, "No eye has seen it [O God] but Yours."[30] Maimonides tells us that to describe the World to Come is like trying to describe to a man, blind from birth, what color is, or to a man, deaf from birth, what sound is. It is impossible. But my *rebbe*, Rabbi Mordechai Gifter, *shlita*, once said the following:

> It is true that we cannot fully grasp the meaning of spiritual bliss in the World to Come as long as we are encased within our earthly bodies. But even here on this earth we have examples that clearly demonstrate to us the greater power of the *spiritual* or *intangible* over the *physical* and *tangible*. For example: We have all seen a crane swinging a few-ton iron ball and smashing it into a building that is being demolished. It may take several hours of doing this to finish the building. A hurricane can do the same thing within seconds. The former consists of a very real and tangible physical power—the massive iron ball; the latter is intangible, mere air, no actual physical substance to it. A second example. There are very real and tangible physical pleasures that man enjoys on this earth—eating, sleeping, listening to beautiful music, smelling fragrances, beholding beautiful sights—pleasures that are enjoyed by all the five senses of man. There are, similarly, physical examples of pain— hunger, tiredness, abrasive sound, bad odors, and sights which are painful to behold.
>
> On the other hand, there are intangible pleasures or displeasures that are far more powerful than any of the above. To obtain these intangible pleasures, a man would forego any kind of physical pleasure. To be spared these intangible displeasures, a man would subject himself to almost any kind of physical pain. For example: take the intangible pleasure called *nachas* [delight and pleasure from one's children or grandchildren], or honor, fame, and pride. A man would give up will-

ingly all the money in the world to obtain these. Conversely, what physical pain would a man not be willing to endure in order to be spared
shame and humiliation? Can you touch, taste, smell, see, or hear *nachas,*
honor, fame, pride, shame, or humiliation? Yet, we see that the latter is
far more powerful. And if this is the case even within this world, the
physical world, where spiritual pleasures are greater than physical ones,
how much more so can we begin to understand the pleasures of the
spirit in a totally spiritual world.

The *Mishnah* says in *Avos:* "One hour of repentance and good deeds
in this world is more valuable than all of the World to Come. And one
hour of *koras ruach* [intangible pleasure] of the World to Come is more
valuable than *all of this entire world.*"[31] At first glance we might think that
the first part of the *Mishnah* contradicts the second. Is this world more
valuable or is the World to Come?

There are millions of levels in the World to Come. One hour of repentance and good deeds in *this* world is far more valuable than the *previous* level one had attained in the World to Come. For in this hour he has
elevated his portion in the World to Come and exchanged it for a far greater
level. This world is extremely valuable to us for it is the world wherein we
labor to attain our status in the afterworld. Once a person dies he can no
longer work to attain a higher level (except for the good deeds of others
that accrue to him through his own deeds and influence). *However, the
ultimate pleasure of the World to Come is far greater than any of this world.*

Rabbi Dessler explains this in the following incredible manner:[32] Firstly,
what is meant in the *mishnah* above by the words *koras ruach* [intangible
pleasure]? Picture a poor man walking in the street and passing by a ban-
quet hall where a wedding feast is taking place. It is a hot summer night,
the air-conditioning has broken down, and therefore the windows are wide
open. They are serving the main course of the feast—roast duck. The poor
man once tasted roast duck many years ago, and now, as the aroma of that
sizzling delicacy is wafting through the open window, he pauses to inhale
the pleasant smell. "Ah! How wonderful, I remember that time when I actually enjoyed eating this delicacy." This time, he didn't actually *taste* the
duck, he didn't even feast his eyes on it. He merely had a *whiff* of the tantalizing aroma—and what pleasure it afforded him. That's what *koras ruach* is.
We're not even talking about the *actual* pleasure of *Olom HaBoh,* the World
to Come, we're merely talking about a "whiff" of it. And that is more valuable and more pleasurable than *all of the pleasures of this world.*

Now let's examine the last few words—*all of the pleasures of this world.*
Close your eyes for a moment and think of your most exquisite pleasure.
You can have this for a day—undisturbed. A week, a month, a year—a life
time. That's only *one* of your pleasures. Combine the hundreds of pleasures and compress a lifetime of those pleasures into one hour. Can you

possibly imagine the intensity of pleasure. But that's only *your* pleasures. It says in the *mishnah—all of the pleasures in the entire world.* For that, you have to combine *all of the pleasures since creation, of every single individual that ever lived*—and that you must compress into an hour of pleasure. The sheer delight and ecstasy of that hour is not humanly conceivable. Says the *mishnah*: *The pleasure of just one whiff of the World to Come is far greater than that one hour we have just described—greater than all of the pleasures of this world combined.*

If we had this faith and belief in the above *mishnah*, we would have no questions. For there is another *mishnah* in *Avos* which teaches us, "According to the pain, so shall the reward be."[33] This means that corresponding to the sorrow and pain that one endures in this world, if he accepts it righteously and follows God's commands and Torah, then he will be rewarded accordingly in *Olom HaBoh*, the World to Come.[34]

It is another axiom of the Jewish faith that there will be a *techiyas hameisim*, a resurrection of the dead. The Talmud is full of references to it.[35] The Talmud points out where we see this from the Torah.[36] Thrice daily we say in the *Shemoneh Esrei* prayer found in the *siddur*: "You are eternally Mighty, my Lord, the Resurrector of the dead are You; abundantly able to save. He [God] sustains the living with kindness, resurrects the dead with abundant mercy, supports the fallen, heals the sick, frees the imprisoned, and maintains His faith to those who sleep in the dust. Who is like You, O Master of mighty deeds, and who is comparable to You, O King Who causes death and restores to life and makes salvation sprout! And You are faithful to resurrect the dead. Blessed are You, *HaShem*, Who resurrects the dead."

It is one of the thirteen cardinal principles of faith that separates the believing Jew from the nonbeliever. "I believe with complete faith that there will be a resurrection of the dead, whenever the Creator—blessed is His Name and exalted is His mention forever and for eternity—so desires it."[37]

The Talmud states and Maimonides so rules: "All Israel has a portion in the World to Come, as it is said. . . . The following have no portion in the world to come: (a) He who denies the resurrection of the dead. . . ."[38]

In one of the talmudic references alluded to above, it tells of the scoffer who said to Gebiha ben Pesisa, "Woe to you the wicked who maintain that the dead will be resurrected. If even the living die, shall the dead live?" He replied, "Woe to you the wicked who maintain that the dead will not be resurrected. If what *never* existed comes to life, surely that which *has lived* [and died] can be brought to life again."[39]

As Rabbi Lamm expresses it:

The second major device in the spiritual arsenal of the Jewish tradition is the concept of the world beyond the grave as the locus where the scales of justice are finally balanced. This is not conceived by the tradition as a cop-out, to rationalize and make up for the apparent injustice of this world, where the wicked prosper and the saintly suffer. . . . To the contrary, it is a corollary of our belief in a just God—that there is where God fulfills His spiritual justice; of a merciful God—that the God who healed us in this world will be merciful in the world to come. . . . Thus, in the special *Kaddish* recital at burial, for the phrase in the standard Kaddish: *"B'almah Di Vra Chirutei*—the world which He created according to His will," a special phrase is substituted: "the world in which He will create anew and in which He will revive the dead who lie in the dust, and whom he will raise up to eternal life."[40]

The beautiful parable of Rabbi Tuchachinsky[41] makes it easier to grasp the reality of another world. And again, although it may be difficult to mention to the mourners many of these theological truths, and discretion certainly has to be used, nevertheless the *visitor* must be convinced of these truths and may then perhaps find the appropriate time, place, and words to offer them to the mourners.

In order to combat the other false notion mentioned by Rabbi Kushner that God is powerless to prevent death, we have just quoted from our daily *siddur*, which explicitly states the contrary. It may also be appropriate to quote from the traditional prayer of the burial service, which also addresses this point.

The Rock! His work is perfect, for all His ways are justice; a God of faithfulness without iniquity, He is righteous and upright. The Rock! He is perfect in every work. Who can say to Him, "What have You done?" He rules below and above, brings death and brings to life, brings down to the grave and raises up [from it]. The Rock! He is perfect in every deed. Who can say to Him, "What do You do?" O He Who says and fulfills, do undeserved kindness to us, and in merit of him [Isaac] who was bound [on the altar] like a lamb, hearken and grant [our requests].

O righteous One in all His ways, O Rock Who is perfect, slow to anger and abundant of mercy, please take pity and please spare parents and children, for to You, O Master, are forgiveness and mercy. Righteous are You, *HaShem,* to bring death and to bring back to life, for in Your hand is the safekeeping of all spirits. Far be it from You to erase our memory. May Your eyes please watch over us in mercy, for to You, O Master, are mercy and forgiveness.

Whether a man be a year old, or live a thousand years, what does it benefit him? He shall be as though he never was. Blessed is the Judge of truth, Who brings death and brings back to life. Blessed is He for His judgment is true, He scans everything with His eye, and recompenses man according to his account and sentence. All must give His Name acknowledgment.

We know, *HaShem*, that Your judgment is righteous; You are righteous when You speak, and pure when You judge, and one should not murmur in his heart about the attributes of Your judgment. You are righteous, *HaShem,* and Your judgment is upright. O true Judge, Judge of righteousness and truth, Blessed is the Judge of truth, for all His judgments are righteous and true.

The soul of every living creature is in Your hand; righteousness fills Your right hand and Your power. Have mercy on the remnant of the sheep of your flock and say to the Angel [of Death], "Hold back your hand!" Great in counsel and abundant in deed, [O You] Whose eyes are open upon all the ways of the children of Man, to give man according to his ways and the fruits of his deeds. To declare that *HaShem* is just, my Rock, in Whom there is no wrong.

God has given and God has taken, may the Name of God be blessed. He, the Merciful One, will forgive iniquity and will not destroy, frequently withdrawing His anger, not arousing His entire wrath.

Again, Rabbi Lamm expresses it this way:

A corollary to the feeling of injustice is the mourner's sense of the powerlessness of God. If he must affirm, because of his traditional belief, the absolute justice of God, then he has to begin to doubt the omnipotence of God. Since God cannot be unjust, perhaps He simply cannot help it. Perhaps, in fact, the stubborn Angel of Death catches up with all, and makes no distinction whether they are good or bad, deserving or not. Perhaps He is simply not selective. In that case, death is Almighty. But then the Almighty would not be all-mighty! I believe that the *Halakha* understood this very well. The rabbis of the Talmud advise us that when people visit a house of mourning during the *Shiva*, it is not proper for the visitor, indeed it borders on sacrilege, to speak of the inevitability of death (something which we mention unthinkingly and which falls so glibly from our lips). It borders on sacrilege, the rabbis felt, because it is as though one were saying that, in fact, the death may not be just, and God would have altered the decree if only He could have changed it. Evidently, death is inevitable.

That the rabbis took this questioning of God's omnipotence into serious account is evidenced by their inclusion of it in the fifteen-time recital of "justice" and "judgment" in the *Tzidduk Ha'din* [the burial service quoted above] at the burial. There is a phrase which is insinuated into that paragraph which, on the surface, does not appear to belong: "Have mercy on the remnants of your flock . . . and say to the Angel of Death: 'Stay your hand!'" We are saying, in the very prayer that affirms the justice of God, that God can indeed say to death: "Stay your hand," that God has the power to do so, but that He chose not to say it. It was God's choice, and God's choice is just.[42]

This idea of accepting the decree of Heaven is included in the command not to weep or mourn excessively. The Talmud relates also to this point:

> When Rabbi Avahu lost a young child, Rabbi Yonah and Rabbi Yosi came to comfort him. Because of their great reverence for Rabbi Avahu, they were unable to express their condolences. Thereupon Rabbi Avahu himself said:
>
> "After the execution of a person condemned by an earthly court, where deception and bribery may have existed, the man's relatives are required to come to greet the judges and witnesses pleasantly to demonstrate that they have no grievance in their heart against them, because they have judged truthfully. How much more so must we humbly accept the decree of the Heavenly Tribunal where no human defects or shortcomings exist."[43]

Rabbi Yisrael Salanter explains the verse "The Rock (God), perfect is His working, for all His ways are justice, a God of trust without iniquity, righteous and upright is He" (Deuteronomy 32:4) in the following manner.

When a man is imprisoned for a crime and remains in prison for a long time, his wife and family suffer, too. In truth they had not committed any crime and do not deserve any punishment or pain that actually is brought upon them. The justice of the sentence is therefore not perfect. Actually judges of flesh and blood cannot help that. They must punish the criminal, and if by doing this, they also punish the family or other people who are directly or indirectly affected by the imprisonment, that can't be avoided.

But God's working is perfect. Before He punishes anyone, He scrutinizes the lives of anyone who will be affected by that individual's punishment. If in some measure anyone affected does not deserve to bear the pain, inconvenience, or suffering that is caused by punishing the offender, then that punishment will be suspended or lessened to an extent where no one will suffer unjust consequences. Only the Almighty has the power to render punishment or justice in such a perfect manner.[44]

I once attended the *bar mitzvah* of the son of a dear friend of ours who had lost her husband (the father of the *bar mitzvah* boy) a couple of years earlier. At this emotion-filled *simchah* I offered the following thought to one of the relatives. The Torah says: Do not harm any widow or orphan. If you do and he cries to Me I shall surely hear his cry. And My anger will be kindled. And I shall kill you with the sword and your wives shall become widows and your children orphans (Exodus 22:21–23).

Seemingly strange is it not? Here God demands from us that we be especially careful not to harm, aggravatge, or cause any pain to a widow or orphan. It is so severe a crime that if we do we forfeit our own lives. But who made the widow or orphan? You, *HaShem*, You Yourself caused them the very same pain from which You are so stringently warning others to abstain!

But in light of what we said before it's not strange at all. The Almighty has His *cheshbonos*, His considerations and reasonings. His decrees are perfect. "What I have to do for the good of the ultimate divine scheme, which is ultimately for the good of all, I have to do," says *HaShem*. "If I decree widowhood or orphanhood, that's My judgment. But now that I so decreed, don't *you* dare cause the slightest bit of extra aggravation that was not included in my decree. On the contrary. Be compassionate and kind to them!" So precise is the depth of divine justice!

Much that has been said above not only applies to anger with God, but to any of the many angers expressed against oneself, the doctors, the hospital, and so on.[45]

Again, be a willing listener. Don't be judgmental or argumentative. It is not a time to try to convince the mourner of anything, not a time to engage in any battle, theological or otherwise. It is a time for personal reflection and contemplation, and the visitor can add much-needed solace by his or her very presence and willingness to listen to the mourner vent his or her grief.

WHATEVER GOD DOES IS FOR THE GOOD

The Talmud says, "Whatever God does is for the good."[46] That is why we are obligated to bless God when something seemingly bad happens to us, just as we are obligated to bless Him when good happens to us.[47] The Talmud even says that one should receive and make a blessing over the bad with *gladness*.[48] While one has to really be on a high spiritual level to do this, it nevertheless drives home again the lesson that we should try to accept that all that God does is good. The Talmud states, "This world is unlike the World to Come. In this world, for *good* tidings, one says, 'Blessed be He who is good and doeth good'; on *evil* tidings he says, 'Blessed be the True Judge.' In the World to Come on *all* tidings, one will say, 'Blessed is He Who is good and doeth good.'"[49]

The following stories exemplify the above level of acceptance.

When the daughter of Rabbi Zundel of Salant died, he pronounced the blessing of *Dayan HaEmes* (the judge who is true) without any visible sign of grief. The head of the burial society related that he had the same concentration and peace of mind as someone pronouncing a blessing of gratitude to the Almighty.[50]

Shortly after Rabbi Avraham Grodzensky became the *mashgiach* (the spiritual supervisor) of the Slobodka Yeshivah, his wife died leaving him with eight young orphans, the two youngest only one and two years old. Rav Avraham did not recite the blessing of *Dayan HaEmes* immediately after hearing about this tragedy. He constantly taught that we should not fulfill commandments out of mere habit, but should have a conscious awareness of what we are doing and saying. He waited two days, until he felt he could recite it properly in the manner that the Talmud (*Brachos* 60b) states, that it should be with joy. When he did recite the blessing, he internally felt complete acceptance of the Almighty's judgment.[51]

The Chofetz Chaim lost a beloved and brilliant son, who died at the age of twenty-three. During *shivah* he said the following:

"During the Spanish Inquisition in 1492 the blood-thirsty murderers slaughtered two beloved children in front of the eyes of their saintly mother. That woman of valor lifted her eyes Heavenward and with a brave heart uttered the following: 'Master of the Universe, I have always loved You. But I must confess that as long as I had my beloved children, my heart was split into two parts as I made room also for the love of my dear children. Now that my children are no longer, my heart turns once again to loving you completely. Now I shall be able to truly fulfill the *mitzvah* of: "And you shall love the Lord your God with *all* your heart and with *all* your soul."'"

When the Chofetz Chaim finished the story he proclaimed heartily: "Master of the Universe, the love that I had for my son till now, I now pass over to You."[52]

When Rabbi Chaim of Sanz returned from the funeral of his seven-year-old son, Aryeh Leibishel, it was very early in the morning, even before the morning *Shacharis* services. Before they began to *daven* he said the following:

"A man was walking peacefully down the street and suddenly felt a hard smack on his back. He whirled around angrily to see who hit him, but it was his very dear friend who was slapping him on the back as a gesture of love and friendship. There is no doubt that even if originally he was going to get upset at the person who hit him, now he would even be happy when he realized that his beloved friend was openly displaying his warm friendship.

"I, too," added Reb Chaim, "received today a powerful blow. But when I realized from Whom I received it, I said to myself: 'It was the Creator, may He be blessed, who hit me. The One Who I love so much. If so, I will certainly accept it with love.'"

When he finished these words, he began his holy service, the *Shacharis* prayers, and proclaimed loudly: "Give thanks to *HaShem*, call His name, make known among the nations His works; sing to Him, make music to Him."[53]

As one writes: "*We* do not always understand what is good for us and what is bad, but *He* knows all."[54] We may not understand this in our finite state of existence and with our limited minds, but the Infinite One understands this.

The great Rabbi Mendel of Kotzk once remarked: "What? You question that the ways of God are mysterious and hidden? Of course they are. I would never be able to crown upon myself a God Whose ways were understood by every human being."[55]

Rabbi Moses Chaim Luzzatto writes the following:

This means that even suffering and hardship which appear in one's eyes to be evil are, in reality, true goodness. For example, the surgeon amputates a muscle or a limb which has been injured in order to preserve the health of the rest of the body, and to save the person from death. Though this seems cruel, it is in reality a true act of mercy, and meant for the good of the person upon whom it is performed. The patient does not love the surgeon any the less because of what he has done to him; on the contrary, he loves him all the more. In like manner, when a person realizes that whatever the Holy One, blessed is He, does to him, whether it affects his body or his possessions, even though he does not see nor does he understand how this can be for his good, it is definitely intended for his benefit, then neither suffering nor hardship would lessen his love for God in any way. On the contrary, his love would even become more intense and fervent. But the true men of understanding do not even need this reasoning, for they have no selfish thoughts whatsoever. All their prayers are only to increase the glory of God and to bring Him satisfaction. The more they are faced with obstacles and the more they need strength to overcome them, the more they will strengthen their hearts and rejoice in being able to display their strong faith. Just like an army general noted for his valor who will always pick the most difficult battle in order to demonstrate his might when he is victorious. This commonly applies to each person who loves another who will always rejoice at the opportunity to demonstrate how far his love for that person extends.[56]

Rabbi Meisels tells of the incident that happened to him when he was caught wearing his *tallis kattan* in the concentration camp:

I was caught. One day, when I left the bath-house, the guard Penicks (a German Communist serving a life sentence), who was there to see that no one took more than one set of clothing, noticed the difference in my appearance. He ordered me to come over to him so that he could see the reason. He felt my clothing and discovered the *tallis kattan*. Enraged, he demanded to know what this was and why I was wearing it. In order that he should not think that I had stolen it, I replied that this was *ein Gottes-kleid*—a religious garment—which I had brought with me from home. Immediately, he began to rain murderous blows upon my head and body and shouted that I should come to his private quarters, where he would teach me something about God.

When I heard this terrible order, my hair stood on end, for everyone knew the meaning of this order—certain death through a cruel and merciless beating from his powerful hands. I could do nothing, and was compelled to follow him to his room. He began his beating again, angrily shouting, "You pig! You speak of a *Gottes-Kleid* when you see with your own eyes how every day your people and your family are being destroyed in every cruel and violent type of death. In these circumstances you are still able to mention the name of God and to believe in Him, and that He governs the world. How can you say or think that there is a God who rules the world? Why does he not prevent the Nazis from removing you from the world with tortures and torments the likes of which no human beings have ever endured before? . . ." So he continued in this vein while I lay upon the ground like a stone. I was silent, overcome by despair and pain. The blood ran from wounds on every part of my body. He ordered me to get up and give him some satisfactory explanation for my continued belief—otherwise I would not leave his room alive.

I knew that this cruel beast would kill me if I did not find some rational explanation which would quiet his murderous wrath. So I said, "I will give you a parable. Unto what is this like? To a famous professor of surgery who is noted for his success in performing a certain difficult operation on critically ill patients. He is called in to perform such an operation on a great nobleman. In order to carry it out successfully, he begins to cut very deeply into the patient's body, and makes a number of incisions which he believes necessary. A shoemaker watching the operation, who does not understand anything about the disease or its cure, will wonder and say to himself, 'To what purpose is the professor torturing this patient? Not enough that he is gravely ill, but he has to add terrible torture and pain by cutting the healthy parts of his body to pieces. When I repair shoes, I do not cut the hide where it is strong and good.' But would you think the professor would stop what he was doing because of the ignorant shoemaker's opinion? Even though no one else understands what he is doing, he himself does. He will, therefore, not stop until he completes doing what he knows must be done.

"So it is with the conduct of the Creator. The truth is that we do not understand His actions at all. We do not grasp why He makes these 'incisions' in the best and most lovely part of the people of Israel. But we must realize that we are flesh and blood, with limited understanding. The fact that we do not understand Him does not diminish Him in our eyes."

I explained this parable at length and concluded with a word from the Rebbe of Yarislov, who said that the reason he lived to such a ripe old age was that he never asked questions about what the *Ribbono shel Olam* did—but accepted everything lovingly. He was afraid that if he did

ask such questions the Almighty would say to him, "If you don't understand, just come up to Heaven and I'll explain it to you." Since he wasn't
quite ready yet to go up to Heaven, he never asked questions. "So," I
advised Penicks, "don't ask too many questions or they may invite you
to come up to Heaven for the answers."

Praised be the All-Merciful, my words found favor in the eyes of
the wicked kapo. With a little smile he said, "You are a clever Jew; you
can leave in peace."[57]

I have always said that I do not judge anyone who survived the Holocaust who lost his or her faith. The *Mishnah* says, "Do not judge your friend
until you have been in his place."[58] Yet it bothers me when those who never
experienced the Holocaust use it as a reason or rationalization to deny God
and religion. There were literally untold tens of thousands who as holy
martyrs went to their deaths with *Ani Maamin* and *Shema Yisrael* on their
lips. There are unbelievable accounts of the sacrifice and lengths that believing Jews went to in order to perform the *mitzvos* under impossible circumstances.[59]

One survivor of Auschwitz said the following:

It never occurred to me to question God's doings or lack of doings while
I was an inmate of Auschwitz, although of course I understand others
did. . . . I was no less or no more religious because of what the Nazis
did to us; and I believe my faith in God was not undermined in the least.
It never occurred to me to associate the calamity we were experiencing
with God, to blame Him or to believe in Him less or cease believing in
Him at all because He didn't come to our aid. God doesn't owe us that,
or anything. We owe our lives to Him. If someone believes God is responsible for the death of six million because He didn't somehow do
something to save them, he's got his thinking reversed. We owe God
our lives for the few or many years we live, and we have the duty to
worship Him and do as He commands us. That's what we're here on
earth for, to be in God's service, to do God's bidding.[60]

In my younger years at *yeshivah* I remember being told the following
parable:

There were two simple brothers who were reared in the city and had
never stepped out of the confines of the city to visit the countryside.
They were also quite naive and unschooled in agricultural matters.

One day they decided to visit the country and came across a
beautiful, lush, and smooth piece of land. While they were admiring
this expensive piece of real estate, along came a man (a farmer) and
began to plough the field, turning it into a mass of shallow rough
ditches.

"Hey, do you see what sort of crazy people they have here in the country?" said one brother to the other. "They purposely ruin a beautiful and expensive piece of land for absolutely no reason."

"Let's be patient and wait a while and see what's going to happen," replied the other brother. "Perhaps there is a reason why he did that."

The next day they returned to the field just in time to see the farmer empty some sacks of good wholesome grain into the narrow ditches (furrows) that he had dug the day before.

"I don't believe my eyes," said the skeptical brother. "Did you see what he just did? He took good food and wasted it; he threw it on the ground and covered it with earth. I'm going back to the city where the people are normal. If we stay around here any longer we may become influenced by their *meshugene* country behavior."

So he went home. But the other brother, a little more trusting of the country folk, decided to stick around to follow up the curious ways of the farmer. Perhaps after all, there was a method to the madness. The remaining brother visited the field every day and as time went by he noticed straight rows of green stalks sprouting up from all of the furrows.

"So that's what it's all about," he said to himself. "The grain that the farmer threw into the ground produced these beautiful plants. That's amazing!"

He quickly phoned his skeptical brother, who had returned to the city, and told him that he must come back to the country immediately.

"You won't believe what happened," he said. "The farmer was not so crazy after all. Come back and you'll see why he ruined the land and the grain!"

Well, what do you think happened on the day the brother from the city joined his brother in the country? Just on the day that he arrived and as he was showing his brother the field with the beautiful plants that had grown out of the "ditches" and were now in full bloom, along came the farmer with his reaper and chopped down all the plants (shoots of grain). What was before a beautiful field with orderly rows of lovely plants had turned into a disorderly mess, a scene of wilfull destruction and wanton waste.

The two brothers stared at the field in horrified shock. "Is this what you called me back for?" asked the skeptic of his brother. "Did you want to subject me to viewing more madness? You are a fool for being so trusting. Come back with me now, before you turn crazy, too."

But the trusting brother decided to wait. He watched patiently as the farmer bound the fallen stalks into bundles. He watched as he threshed the bundles, separating the straw from the kernels and the kernels from the chaff. He watched as the kernels were piled high, loaded into a wagon, and taken to the mill. For a moment, after the grinding, he was disappointed to see that the kernels had been turned into a white powdery dust. "Again you have destroyed," he thought to himself. But he was beginning to see that obviously there was some pattern of activity that was going on. So he decided to be patient and follow the pattern to the very end, so he obtained permission from the farmer to accompany him and watch everything that ensued.

The farmer put the powder (flour) in sacks, took them home, and mixed the flour with water. The brother was puzzled with the "whitish mud," but knew that something exciting was about to happen that would unravel the entire mystery. Sure enough, the farmer fashioned the "mud" into a square-shaped loaf, put the loaf in the oven, and waited. Finally he opened the oven and a tantalizing aroma wafted through the air. The brother couldn't believe his eyes. There in the farmer's hand was a freshly baked crisp brown bread, better than any bread the brother had ever seen on his kitchen table in the civilized and normal city where he lived. As they savored together the delicious bread, the farmer turned to the trusting brother. "Now," he said, "now you understand!"

We are like naive city boys who descend on this earth, God's country, for a few years and are confronted with what seem to us to be some very strange and incomprehensible sights. But the Almighty has a divine plan for the world that can span six thousand years. We only see disjointed fragments of that plan. We cannot follow the process from beginning to end. But we must be patient and trusting, having faith that everything— even that which seems tragic, painful, and destructive—is part of an ultimate Divine plan that will create an end goal of beauty, happiness, fulfillment, and eternal reward.[61]

On March 1, 1990, corresponding to *Adar* 4, 5750, I accompanied the great *Maggid*, Rabbi Sholom Schwadron, to the airport. I asked him two things: first, to tell me a story about *nichum aveilim*; second, to explain how one answers someone who has questions on the justice of the Almighty when tragedy happens? He told me the following:

The Ramban (the great talmudic scholar and kabbalist, Nachmanides) went to visit a young student who was very ill. When he came into the room he told the student that since he [the student] was a *tzaddik*, a righteous person, he was going to be elevated in Heaven and transported from one *heichal* (sphere) to another. When he was to enter a particular *heichal* the Ramban instructed his student to say: "I would like to ask a question." The student asked what question he was to ask, and the Ramban answered that he should ask, "Why did I have to die so young?"

The student died and came soon after to the Ramban [in either a dream or through another medium]. The Ramban asked, "So did they take you from this *heichal* to that one, as I had indicated?" "Yes," replied the student. "And did you come to that particular *heichal* that I spoke about?" "Yes," replied the student. "And did you ask the question that I asked you to ask?" "No," replied the student. "And why not?" queried the Ramban. "Because I did not want to embarrass my *rebbe* [meaning the Ramban himself]," answered the student. And he explained: "You see, *Rebbe*, on the door of that *heichal* the following words are inscribed: דִּמִּינוּ אֱלֹקִים חַסְדֶּךָ בְּקֶרֶב הֵיכָלֶךָ—*Dimeenu Elokim chasdecha bekerev heichalecha*—'We have hoped, O God, for your kindness, in the midst of your *heichal* [sanctuary].' (Psalms 48:10). The word for God, *Elokim*, is used always when referring to the *stern* and *strict* justice of God [*midas hadin*]. According to this simple translation of the verse, would it not have been more appropriate to use the word *HaShem*, God's attribute of *kindness*? The answer is that we can interpret the verse in another way altogether, putting the comma after the word *Elokim* and translating the first word, *dimeenu*, not as *hope*, but rather as from the word *nidmeh*, what appears to us. In this way the verse is saying the following: What appears to us (what we think is) *Elokim*, God's stern justice, we now clearly see, when entering this *heichal*, is rather in reality, Your kindness, O God."[62]

Parenthetically, I heard a similar story about the *chasid* who always went to his *rebbe* to pray for him whenever misfortune or problems came his way. The *rebbe* would pray and the *tzorus*, the troubles, would go away. Then one day the *rebbe* died, and the *chasid* could no longer go to him. One day in the midst of a troubling situation the *chasid* decided to go to the *rebbe*'s grave to importune him to intercede for him before the Heavenly throne. But nothing happened and the trouble persisted. One night the *rebbe* appeared to the *chasid* in a dream and said to him, "Do not think that I did not hear your supplications and that I did not want to help you. You should know that when I was on earth I prayed for you because I thought your troubles were not to your benefit. Now that I am in Heaven and have an understanding of the divine plan, I realize that all of one's troubles are for a divine purpose and are for the good of the sufferer."[63]

The same idea is vividly portrayed in the following true story:

A certain man was beset with many different kinds of pain and suffering. Sickness afflicted both him and his family, he had a very meager livelihood, and other difficulties and problems were his lot in life. One day he informed his wife that he was going to travel to the *tzaddik* and kabbalist, Rabbi Sholom Shrabi, *ztz'l*, to seek advice in understanding what *HaShem* wanted from him and how he could perhaps improve his situation.

When he arrived at the rabbi's home, he was requested to please wait until the rabbi would be able to meet with him. He seated himself on an armchair and, being exhausted from the trip, soon fell into a deep sleep. And he had the following dream.

He found himself reaching Heaven on a path that was absolutely desolate; not a soul was visible on the horizon. Total silence blanketed that place. Slowly, he began to press forward on the path before him. Suddenly, he was aware of a large carriage beside him, filled with angels, dazzling white as snow. The carriage zoomed by and was soon out of sight. There was silence once again, and the man continued on his way. Soon after, another carriage passed by, then many others. All were filled with dazzling white angels, some big and strong, some small and puny. When the band of carriages carrying white angels ended, a giant band of carriages carrying frightening black angels began to whirl past him.

The sights he had just beheld aroused his curiosity. He hurried his steps and soon found himself at an enormously expansive plain, where all the carriages were stationed. The angels had alighted and were approaching a giant scale in the center of the plain. The white angels began to enter one pan of the huge scale; the black angels, the other pan. The man didn't understand what was going on until they explained to him that he was witnessing the Heavenly court in the midst of judging a man's deeds.

The Mishnah says, "When a man does a mitzvah he acquires [creates] a defending angel; when he sins he acquires [creates] a prosecuting angel."[64] They explained to him that all the angels were created from the deeds of the man being judged. The strong, robust, and heavy white angels were created from mitzvos that were performed perfectly. The small, light, and puny ones—from mitzvos created imperfectly. The strong and robust black angels were created from sins that were done intentionally and with a strong desire; the small and puny black angels were created from unintentional sins and sins that were performed accidentally or under duress.

After this explanation his glance fell on the sides of the chariots stationed there. He observed that, painted on the sides of the chariots, were identifying mitzvos or sins. On the chariots from which the white angels had alighted were painted different signs: Torah Study, Prayer, Honor and Respect of Parents, Acts of Kindness, Shabbos Observance, Kashrus Observance, and so on. On the chariots from which the black angels had alighted were: Bittul Torah (wasted time that could have been used for Torah study), Lashon Hora (evil gossip), Shabbos Desecration, Theft, Jealousy, and so on.

The balance of the scale kept swaying up and down as different angels entered the two giant pans. The man became curious to know who was being judged. When they told him that it was he, himself, he became terrified. Most of the angels had climbed onto the scale, and the balance was tipping in favor of the black ones. He realized that if this was the final balance, then he would be judged a wicked man and his end would be very bitter.

The scale was still. A voice rang out, "Are there any more angels to come?" "No," came the response. "Perhaps there were pains and suffering," the voice rang out, "and if so, we can add that to the merits of the man being judged." Immediately there was a great stir as a gigantic chariot filled with angels created from the man's sufferings pulled into the plain. For each angel of suffering, they took off the balance many black angels of sin, for suffering eradicates sin.[65]

For the moment, the scales of balance began to swing again. Each angel of suffering canceled out many angels of sin. The pans were almost equally balanced. They had brought forward the last angel of suffering, but still the scale tipped very slightly to the black side. The man was petrified. Soon the judgment would be announced, and the balance was not in his favor. In his distress he screamed out, "Bring upon me a few more sufferings."

From the noise of the scream, the man awoke from his dream. Rabbi Shrabi and his family, alarmed by the scream, ran to his side and asked what happened. Only now he realized that it had all been a dream. He arose from the armchair and made his way to the door. "But you traveled all the way here to speak to the rabbi," called out the *rebbetzin* (the rabbi's wife). "There is no longer any need," the man replied. "I received the appropriate answer from Heaven."[66]

To answer my second question, Rabbi Schwadron told me the following:

I was once on a bus traveling from Haifa to Jerusalem and a man seated next to me, who obviously understood I was a rabbi of some sort, started to ask me questions on the *Chumash*, the Bible. I could see at once that he didn't know too much about the *Chumash*, but I just listened as he threw out his questions to me, and I did not respond. After he was finished, I said to him, "May I ask you what your occupation is?" He told me that he was an architect [engineer] and that he was on his way to supervise the construction of a building in Jerusalem. I asked him if he had any architectural plans with him and he immediately produced them and proceeded to explain to me what the plans were all about. "This is where the entrance of the building is; this is where the front stairs leading to the building are; this is where the side entrance will be," and so on. I listened attentively, and after he finished, I said, "I have a few questions." I then proceeded to tell him that it would seem to me that the steps should be a little more to the front, and the side entrance should be a little more to the right, and the second floor should be a little closer to the first, and so on. He looked at me with some astonishment and said, "Rabbi, you strike me as quite an intelligent man, but I can't understand how you can question me on these plans. Are you an architect or engineer? Have you ever studied either of the two?"

I then replied, "Let your ears hear what your own mouth says. Have you ever really studied the *Chumash*? Are you a Torah scholar? If you are an intelligent man you should realize that in order to ask any questions, you really must first know your subject matter and what you are talking about."

I had a peaceful journey the rest of the way. No more questions on the *Chumash*.

And so he said to me, "Do we really have any conception of how the Almighty runs His world? We have absolutely no notion of so many of the miracles of the universe and so many of God's dealings with all that goes on. How dare we ask questions, or even think we shall begin to understand the depths of His ways. The more one comes closer to God, the more he studies about Him, the more one will come to see and understand that God's ways are infinite and above any human comprehension.[67] 'It is a decree from Me; do not murmur against it.'"[68]

NOT TO MOURN EXCESSIVELY

In reference to mourning, the Torah states, "You are children of the Lord your God; you should not mutilate yourself nor tear out your hair [in grief]."[69]

On this, Ibn Ezra comments, "Once you realize you are children of the Almighty, and He loves you even more than a mortal father loves his children, you will not grieve excessively over whatever He does to you. Whatever He does is ultimately for your good. At times you might not understand His ways, just as a young child does not always understand why his father does certain things. Nevertheless the child trusts his father. You, too, should trust the Almighty."

Harold Kushner, when discussing the Book of Job, concludes that the "anonymous author"

> takes the position which neither Job nor his friends take. He believes in God's goodness and in Job's goodness, and is prepared to give up his belief in proposition (A): that God is all powerful. Bad things do happen to good people in this world, but it is not God who wills it. God would like people to get what they deserve in life, but He cannot always arrange it. Forced to choose between a good God who is not totally powerful, or a powerful God who is not totally good, the author of the Book of Job chooses to believe in God's goodness.[70]

In other words, according to Harold Kushner, God was saying to Job, "You think it's so easy to control evil. Evil is a force even bigger than I, and I can't control it. I feel bad for you, but I can't do anything to help you." Kushner would rather deal with bad luck than a seemingly bad God. He's ready to accept a God who is not all-powerful rather than a God who is powerful but can bring evil. It must be stated that this is not traditional Judaism's point of view.

How are we to learn the authentic traditional view? The answer lies clearly in the first six verses of the last chapter of the Book of Job. There it states clearly that God came to Job and brought about a reconciliation and total acceptance on Job's part, and a clear statement that Job himself acknowledges that God can do anything and everything.

"Then Job answered the Lord and said, 'I know that Thou canst do everything, and that no design can be withheld from Thee. Who is he that hideth counsel without knowledge? Therefore have I spoken that I have not understood, things too wonderful for me which I did not know. Please hearken to me and I shall speak, I will enquire of You and You shall make it known to me. *I have heard of Thee by the hearing of the ear, but now my eye sees Thee.* Wherefore I abhor myself and repent in dust and ashes.'"[71]

Nachmanides, the famous biblical commentator, explains that the answer lies in the second to last verse quoted above [italicized]. Job was saying, "Until now my relationship with You, O God, was that of a purely intellectual experience. And when I had questions, then I questioned our entire relationship and Your ways of justice. Logically the pieces did not fit together. But now that You have brought me close to You and showed me the marvels of all creation and talked to me and established this close-knit emotional bond that never existed before, I now perceive You on a close emotional level." This relationship took away all the questions. For to paraphrase Ibn Ezra quoted above, when you have an implicitly trusting relationship, be it with a father or a spouse, nothing can breach that trust, and no one can convince you that they mean harm to you in any way. Job became so close to God that his questions ceased to be questions. He had an implicit faith and trust that God can do him no harm or evil.[72] May we be blessed to receive the midrashic blessing, "Just as I returned and comforted Job, so I shall come to comfort you."[73]

The Talmud actually states, "Whoever indulges in excessive grief over his dead will weep for another. . . . Our Rabbis taught, 'Weep not for the dead, neither bemoan him' [Jeremiah 22:10], that is, weep not in excess, nor bemoan him beyond measure . . . after that the Holy One, blessed is He, says, 'You are not more compassionate toward him [the departed one] than I.'"[74]

There are clear laws and bounds for mourning; excessive sadness and grief call into question the just ways of the Almighty. One writer expresses the difference between mourning and sadness in the following manner: "What is the difference between mourning and sadness? Mourning takes hold of one's heart, but not one's mind, while sadness takes hold of the mind. Mourning leads to thinking, while sadness stops one's thoughts. Mourning stems from the light in one's soul, while sadness comes from the darkness of the soul. Mourning arouses one to life, while sadness brings to the opposite. The Torah obligates mourning when it is appropriate, while it forbids sadness and commands we serve the Almighty with joy."[75]

THE DECEASED HAS NOT LEFT US

We firmly believe that the deceased has moved to another abode. He has not left us entirely, but has returned home from his earthly abode to his heavenly one.

On the verse quoted above, which speaks about the prohibition of excessive grieving, *Or HaChaim* comments:

> A basic Torah concept is that when a person dies, he does not disappear into oblivion. Rather, the situation is analogous to a father who sent his son on a business venture to another city. After allowing his son a certain amount of time to make some profit, the father sent a message for his son to return home. When the son returns to his father, the son's existence has not ended. He has merely moved from one location to another. Moreover, when he returns to his father, he is back home and that is the best place for him to be. Similarly, when a person dies, his soul returns to his Heavenly Father.[76]

As the Talmud says, "Cry for the mourners, not for the deceased, for it [the deceased] is at rest, but we are in sorrow."[77]

The following incident is related about Rabbi Aryeh Levin.

> A former mayor of Rishon l'Tziyon who knew Reb Aryeh well had lost his family in the Nazi Holocaust. Once, while in Reb Aryeh's house, he revealed the burden that weighed down his heart. "The truth is that my faith in the Almighty was shaken by that tragedy. What sin did my little child ever commit, that this should happen to him?"
>
> Reb Aryeh rose from his seat at once, took the man's hand in both of his, and began caressing it. "There is a *tzaddik*," he said, "a righteous devout person; and there is a *hasid*, a man of kindly piety. But a *kadosh*, a hallowed person, is only one who was put to death for his religion and his faith. Then I have to stand in your presence, because you offered up not one sacrifice to sanctify God's name, not one kadosh—but two."
>
> "You know," he added, "when a child is born and comes into the world, all are rapturous with joy—and the child itself cries and wails. When someone dies and his life-spirit leaves the world, all mourn and grieve—but that living spirit itself exults and rejoices. It has gone from a world of darkness to a world of light. . . ." In this vein Reb Aryeh continued talking and explaining, till he sensed that his words were reaching and calming the bereaved father, to bring him some inner tranquillity. From that time on there was a strong bond of friendship between the two.[78]

A similar thought is expressed in the following *midrash*:

Rabbi Pinchas said, . . . When a child is born all are happy; when a man dies all are sad. But it should not be that way. For when a person is born one should not yet rejoice for one does not know what his actions will be, righteous or wicked, good or bad. But when he dies, there should be gladness over the fact that he passed away from this world with a good name and departed this world in peace.

This can be compared to two ships that crossed on the high seas. One was just leaving the port; the other was returning. All were happy to send off the one that was departing; the one that was returning did not stir too much rejoicing. There was a wise man there who exclaimed, "It should be just the opposite. There should be no rejoicing over the ship that just left the port for no one yet knows how it will fare. How many rough seas will it encounter? How many accidents may occur to it? But over the one that is entering all should rejoice, because we see it has returned in peace."

So it should be with the human being. When a man dies we can be glad and full of praise that he departed this world with a good name and in peace. This is what King Solomon meant when he said, "And the day of his death [is better] than the day of his birth."[79]

TWO FAMOUS BEREAVEMENT LETTERS

I would like to record here two famous letters (freely translated, one from the original Hebrew, the other from its original Hebrew and semi-Yiddish. The italics are mine for emphasis). The first was written by a father while he was alive, to be handed to his family after his death. The second is by the great *Gaon* Rabbi Yehonoson Eibeschutz to his sister-in-law in the year 1743. Many of the sentiments written above and throughout this chapter are expressed in these letters.

To my dear and beloved sons and daughters.

I write this letter to you with the hope that you will only be reading it in many years to come. My purpose is to console you over the fact that I am no longer alive. No person knows when his time will be up, but the day will come (may *HaShem* bless us all with long life) when I shall dwell in my eternal abode—but you will be orphans.

My beloved, I have seen many orphans, most of whom find themselves in darkness without counsel or hope. Young orphans are jealous, thinking, "Everyone has parents, but me." Even older ones are shaken and feel that their world is crumbling. I saw only few who were able to brace themselves and bear their loss bravely and to even elevate themselves after their tragedy. When I reflected on this I said to myself: "Before one can comfort mourners it is essential to teach them how to deal with and bear their loss. I hope I succeed in my endeavor to teach you this. May you understand these words so that they illuminate your lives.

The key to the mystery of life is faith in Eternal Living God, the Creator of the universe. It is God's power that sustains the entire world–each and every blade of grass, and surely so each human being. The force of this life spirit is the essence of everything, and the most important part of a person is his spirit and soul.

My beloved children, I trust that I have merited to raise you to have faith in God. Now, strengthen your faith and realize that in this is also hidden the key to the secret of the mystery of death. *If the death of the body meant the end of man himself, there would be no other comfort for mourners other than the ability to forget. But this is not so. The body passes away, but the person continues to live.*

Our great teacher (Rabbi Yeruchem Levovitz) wrote in a letter of consolation: "Death should be understood only as if one has moved from one city to another. This is the real truth. Your father, may his memory be blessed, has not died. He is alive. He has merely moved away. *To the one who understands things more deeply, on the contrary, the deceased is now even closer to the living than when they were alive. For now there are no separations.*"

How great a thought! Only our great and holy master could reveal to us such a wonderful thing. *This is a fact. Faith does not know of death. The truth is that the deceased is alive. He is aware of and feels everything, and he is close to his relatives at all times.*

However, one still needs to find comfort from the pain of the physical separation. Children are accustomed to seeing their parents, hearing their advice, receiving their help. Even after they move away from home they rely on them and draw strength from knowing that they are close by. Who can fill this void?

But know, my beloved ones, that if you really loved me when I was with you, and if your love was not just superficial, you can always picture your father in front of your eyes. You will know what he would have said and how he would have advised you. Take, for example, what our sages say about *Yosef HaTzaddik* who withstood temptation because of the vision of his father that appeared before his eyes.

Thanks to this, each of you who will carry the vision of your father in your heart, will be able to draw strength and encouragement. *The main thing to keep in mind is that the essence of a person is the spiritual, and his spirit continues to live and exist.*

Another point I wish to tell you–a feeling I had when I was orphaned from my parents. All people feel an urge to come closer to *mitzvos* and good deeds at a time of mourning. Even those who are nonobservant come to say *kaddish*, they don a *tallis* and *tefillin*, and pray. What is the source of this inner force?

There is a deep reason for this. Our sages teach us that there are three partners to every human being: his father, his mother, and the Holy

One, blessed be He. Now a child is used to seeing only his father and mother. The third partner is invisible. However, when the physical partners leave him and go the next world, there is an inner feeling in the person that is rooted in the deep faith that lives within the heart of every Jew that pushes him to cast his reliance henceforth upon the third partner.

One whose faith is strong understands and feels this simply and conclusively: "My father and mother (may) have left me—but *HaShem* will gather me to Him."

The truth is that the physical parent was merely a messenger from his true Father in Heaven. Now that the physical father's mission is over, the son binds himself with a strong bond to his Heavenly Father, and, "It is better to trust in God than it is to trust in man."

This is what I felt when I mourned the death of my parents, and this I hand over to you, my beloved children. Know that this is the most important fundamental for all people of all ages, especially for orphans: to strengthen greatly one's faith, to sense *HaShem*'s real providence, to realize how *HaShem* guides and leads you daily and provides you with all of your physical and spiritual needs and supports your steps. You will not lack anything if only you will keep your faith strong.

And only one who lives with this faith can be consoled. Behold a person's environment—his family, his teachers, his friends—all of them help him to properly maintain and elevate his life. A person's goal in life is to always rise higher, not to go lower, God forbid. Now, when a relative passes away, may *HaShem* spare us, one of the supports to his spiritual stature has been removed. A person is comforted when he merits once again to feel the support of others who raise his spirits and strengthen him, helping him to continue with life. This is what the Torah teaches us about *Yitzchak Avinu*, who was comforted over the death of his mother Sarah, when he took Rivkah "who took the place of his mother." He found comfort through her over the loss of his former home and situation. . . .

Now my beloved ones, do this and be comforted. *Come closer to each other, help each other, encourage each other, and banish all abandonment of hope and despair from your hearts.* Your friends should be wholesome in faith, lovers of Torah, and of those who study Torah. Always be willing to learn and to improve. . . . Know with absolute certainty that *HaShem* will surely comfort you and will help you continue in your ways to be strong in faith and in Torah; to build loyal homes with the aim of fulfilling *HaShem*'s *mitzvos*. Your actions shall then serve to benefit me as our sages say: "When one leaves behind a good child, it is considered as if the father has not passed away."

This is my advice and request and my parting words to you, my beloved ones. Have faith, and your faith will be fulfilled and then a light will shine on your paths forever.

With love,
Your father[80]

The second letter is as follows:

Peace to my sister-in-law, may she live and be well, and to her children. May the Almighty comfort you, and spread His wings over you, to be as a Father and Patron to you; to heal your broken hearts.

I am really unable to write because of the terrible pain and sorrow. It is truly difficult for me to comfort especially you and your dear children and specifically my beloved and honored Michal, he should live and be well. My eyes flow with tears, my heart is a vacuum inside of me. Heaven is my witness that I did not have as much pain and feeling of sorrow on the demise of my own brother *z'l*, as upon my departed brother-in-law, *z'l*. Heaven is my witness that on the *Yahrzeit* of Mosheh Rabbeinu when I spoke words of reproof to my congregation in *shul*, I mentioned him, and made a private mourning, appropriate in every way befitting his honor. But I have yet been unable to comfort you as befits the dictates of *halachah*, for I have been made silent due to my extreme anguish.

I request from you that you give honor to God and not to overly distress yourselves. You, my dear sister-in-law, are anyway not a strong woman. And now you will need to give more attention to your children than before. You must strengthen yourselves and accept all decrees from God with love. He wounds and He heals. You have lost a human father. In his place you have received God, blessed is He, as a Father, for He is called "the Father of orphans and the Judge of widows" (Psalms 68:6).

We see clearly in the world that most of the young people who are successful in Torah, wisdom, and business are orphans. For the Holy One, blessed is He, pays special attention and gives special supervision to them for He has mercy on an orphan.

But O how blind are people, and how wisdom is concealed from them. For what reason should we cry on the acts of God? Do we know what is good and what is bad? Are we as wise as God? Are we as merciful as He? Bestowers of good as He? Merciful on orphans as He? Lovers of kindness and mercy as He? Ones who see the future as He? Charitable as He? For He is the source of wisdom, mercy, and truth itself.

It is most definite, that if He in His wisdom would see that there was yet to come from him [your father] a thousandth of a thousandth of good that was needed to come for him or another, he would have, without a doubt, remained alive. For when God is confronted with meting out tribulation and there is an opposing reason for goodness, He pushes off tribulation and chooses the good. Therefore He is called "Good"— "the Good One, Who does good to evil people and to good people" (High Holiday *Machzor*). And King David says in Psalms (145:9), "God is good to all, and His mercies are upon all of His works"—without exception!

Especially to His nation Israel, and even more so to a person who conducted himself in the performance of *mitzvos* and actions, with perfection and uprightness, God is more particular on each second that he should yet be able to live. He, blessed is His Name, counts all of the

seconds until the exact time comes for the righteous man to be born;
much more so to determine the exact time that he should die. It is clear
that He in His infinite wisdom has decided that this is the ultimate good.
And "Difficult in the eyes of God is the death of His pious ones" (Psalms
116:15). So why should we be in distress? Do we not want to acknowledge the goodness of God? Does He not have pain and mercy on the
widow and particularly on the young orphaned children, who are likened after the death of their father to stray sheep, in no less measure
than the family who is steeped in pain?

Does not God feel pain when man is in pain, and especially the
pain of widows and orphans who did not taste sin? God feels pain even
for one who worships idols, who curses God, who is stoned and hung
by the courts—God says, "My Head is too heavy for Me, My Arm is too
heavy for Me" (Mishnah, Sanhedrin 6:6). And much more so for anguish
such as this. As it says, "In all their distress, there is distress to Him"
(Isaiah 63:9). And God is not like a human being who does not always
have the ability to change or remove his pain. He can change anything!

Therefore it should be easy to understand that had He not found
that this was for the ultimate kindness and goodness, He would not have
brought this trouble. He found that this leads only to good, despite the
fact that it comes, undoubtedly, with great suffering.

Take, for example, a child who is brought to his teacher to receive
a punishment; or a sick person who, on doctor's orders, needs painful
treatment. Certainly one would let the child scream from pain, and all
should feel his pain. Nevertheless, everyone knows that this is for the
good of the child or the sick person. Mercy, in such a situation [with-
holding treatment], is actually cruelty. And so it is with the King of Kings,
the Holy One, blessed is He. He knows that He cannot, so to speak,
withhold His actions because of the great pain and worries that ensue,
since this is for the benefit of the pure soul of the deceased, and for the
benefit of the orphans, even though we cannot understand this. For how
do we know what is good? There are many sick mothers who recover,
but who are subjected after this to unbearable suffering through their
children. They would have been much happier had they died. But God
found this time that it was better for them to endure the suffering as
atonement for their sins. Had He seen the opposite to be better, He would
have brought death.

Why would a blind man shout at his guide that he is not leading
him in proper paths? He is blind; his guide can see and is an intelligent
person. In contrast to God we are all blind. But God sees. He discerns
and sees till the end of all generations. For what reason should we cry
and shout upon the death of a person? To whom is God obligated to
award how many years he shall live? Just as when a man lives eighty
years, one should not be so distressed at his death [for he has lived a
full life], similarly, one should not be distressed when someone dies at
age thirty. It is all the same—a man, even were he to live a thousand years,
it is as if he never was.

Would we be distressed over a dream? Some sleep and have an enjoyable, lengthy dream. If we would wake such a man, he would certainly be upset that he was woken in the middle of such a pleasant dream. But after all, that is not real distress for dreams are mere unreal vanities of the world. So is the world itself like a dream. Some awake in the middle of the dream, some sleep all through the dream—some, most of it. It's all the same. A dream is a dream.

Why should we distress ourselves over the death of a person while we are in exile? A time when we see only sorrow and pain for our nation Israel who has been cast off from its mother, the holy *Shechinah*. A time when we stray like sheep who have been shunted from one place to another. Our lives are mere spasms, as one who is being lead to death. We are dead on the inside, for all we have in this world are fears, troubles, and alarms.

And even when we actually die, there will be a time of redemption when we exit our graves. This is called *techiyas hameisim*, the resurrection of the dead, a time when we shall be redeemed from the grave and attain life in the true world, which is totally true and fair. That place is a world of joy, where trouble and groaning flee. There, there is no weakness or tiredness, for all bask in the radiance of the Face of the everliving King.

There have been in the past many individuals of other nations who took their own lives, thinking that they would leave this dark world and reach a world that was all light. God has forbidden us to do this as it is written, "And you should be exceedingly careful to guard your lives" (Deuteronomy 4:15) He knows when is the time for life or for death. Therefore we live or we die—all by the will of God.

Therefore my dear sister and children. Guard your health. This is even more important than the *kaddish* that you will say for your father, z'l. For this is a greater *mitzvah*—to watch your health and to accept all from God with love. This will be greatly pleasing to God.

A king sends his servants to other countries on a mission. As long as he sees that there is still something to accomplish there, he would be a fool if he would summon them back. But once he sees that there is no more need to remain there, they are called back home immediately. We are all here in this world to fulfill our holy mission for the Almighty. That is why we were created. If God sees that one can still accomplish more in his mission, He certainly won't recall him from this world to the World to Come. Why therefore should we bemoan his death? Don't we all know that the World to Come is much better than this world? Therefore there is not any reason to mourn the death of a person, only the minimum, as little as possible. The exchange of a transitory world for an Eternal World is a good exchange!

Should we weep over the fact that the dead leave behind widows and orphans? Does man have the ability to save anyone? Can he even help himself, much less a wife and child? Bad is the salvation of men. What are we? What is our salvation? For nought is the salvation of man.

Now if God saves—that is salvation! He lives and exists for ever and ever. He does not need the help of man. He is quite capable Himself of helping widows and orphans, and He truly does this. There is no urgent need of support from the father of the family.

And if crying comes because we have longings for the dead, this is really the animal nature and instinct that is within us. But this is not the way of Israel, a nation saved by *HaShem*. For how long are the years of a man in this world? And afterward we all come together in the Land of Life.

A king sends the children of his officers to be trained in a different land. Children of great stature do not remain long in the foreign place. However, bad children are held for a long time. So it is with God. The one He loves, He recalls to him quickly. Therefore we say, "You are children to the Lord your God; do not cut yourselves" (Deuteronomy 14:1). We should not fret over the death of a person, for really the son has just returned to his Father, so what reason is there to be so distressed? We are obligated to accept all of God's decrees with love.

Behold eleven years ago when he was dangerously ill, were it not for the abundance of God's mercy, he would have died and already been forgotten. And so, my sister, is God not now the same Merciful One as he was at that time? "I am God; I have not changed" (Malachi 3:6). He, blessed is His Name, is not subject to change. It is therefore easy to posit that now He has found no greater kindness than this.

I ask of you, my sister, be serene. God will grant you joys from your beloved orphans. Your broken heart will return to its strength. Dear sister, be consoled by the breach of Zion and Jerusalem, which we are obligated to remember and mourn, as a woman who cries over the husband of her youth.

We, Israel, are all orphans and widows. Jeremiah the Prophet laments, "We have become orphans and have no father; our mothers are widows" (Lamentations 5:3). In addition, we wander in exile without a leader, a High Priest, the Sanhedrin (Court), Prophets, *Urim VeTumim,* altar, and many other prized possessions of which we have been deprived.

In truth, my dear sister, whoever can be called a Jew, were he to take to heart the destruction of Zion and Jerusalem, it would be an amazing thing were he not to take his own life. For we have been plunged from such heights to such lowliness and exile, which has lasted for so many years. But to do this on our own is forbidden. More, we are consoled by the fact that God will certainly save us and comfort Zion when the end and time of redemption come. Just as a fruit that ripens on the tree lasts longer than a fruit that is plucked off the tree before it ripens, and just as we hope and expect without a doubt that this salvation will come, God helps much more so to heal all broken hearts. He will comfort all orphans and widows. Just remember that the mercies of God never end. They are without limit and unceasing. Because of our many sins there have been this year many troubles, which are half a consolation, one greater than the other. Without doubt God will have mercy on you for he pities the orphan, and he will not allow your feet to falter. Do not fret in this world, which is in reality only vanity of vanities.

Darius was a great king and an only son. When he was very young he was about to die. He commanded his wife and his mother not to cry over his death until someone came and reported to them an evil deed that the king had committed. Only were this to happen could they cry without respite, over the short number of years that he lived.

After his death, they kept the command of the king and withheld themselves from crying. And they waited for someone to come and report to them an evil deed that the king had done. But since no man ever came, they were never able to cry. This was recognized by all the wise men to be great wisdom. For it taught everyone that there is no reason to cry over the actual death of a person; the only reason to cry is over his evil deeds. If a man dies and no evil deed can be found that he did, there is absolutely no reason to cry.

Therefore dear sister and children; I wish to end with this. Be happy that he died with a good name, and without any blemish. The Talmud (Bava Basra 10b) says: "And who is a son of the World to Come? He to whom are applied the words, 'And before his elders shall be honor' (Isaiah 33:16)." If all wise people say good about him afterward, this is called, "He died with a good name." So why should we cry and shout? For who knows? Perhaps if he would have lived longer, he may have spoiled that reputation. Just as good wine must be drunk before it turns sour and spoils. Therefore one uses good wine with which to comfort mourners, for to this is compared the righteous; only bad wine must remain for a very long time until one can reuse it.

Therefore, my dear sister, let us live with hope to God for "Those who have faith in God shall be blessed with renewed strength; they shall soar as eagles" (Isaiah 40:31).

> From me, your brother-in-law,
> Yehonoson, son of the departed *rav*, Noson Nota, *z'l'hh*
> Residing in the city of Metz and suburbs[81]

WHEN THERE ARE GUILT FEELINGS

As has been discussed in chapter 4, there are often mourners who are laden with guilt feelings. However, all comes from the hand of God, "even the erring of the doctor."[82]

In such cases, however, where guilt is manifest, the visitor would be wise to try to gently steer the mourner away from the counterproductive thoughts of guilt to practical ways of how to honor the deceased. Since the mourner can no longer make amends for what he or she feels guilty about from the past, then at least if he or she feels something can be done in the future, this will greatly help to alleviate the guilt.[83]

Donating to worthy charities, setting up scholarship funds, and doing small daily activities of kindness in addition to the all-important improvement of one's religious observances—when done to honor and to bring merit to the deceased—can help negate the guilt feelings.

In addition, anything that the visitors can do to get the mourner to show respect for the deceased will help alleviate the guilt feelings, for instance, teaching the mourner the proper laws of *shivah* and mourning so that he can perform his or her religious duties at this time in the proper manner or getting the mourner to speak positively about the deceased and to relate his or her virtues and meritorious deeds. One writer has said, "Just as there must be witnesses at the reading of the will, so there must be 'witnesses' at the recounting of the spiritual legacy of the deceased. *Thinking* about the deceased's virtues only increases guilt feelings; *speaking* about the deceased's virtues can relieve these feelings."[84]

It is told that a distinguished scholar who meticulously looked after his elder father felt tremendous guilt when his father passed away. He feared he had not done as much as he could for his father and hence felt he was somewhat to blame for his father's death. This *rosh hayeshivah* felt so much suffering there was an actual danger to his health. Later at a rabbinical meeting at Vilna, the scholar met the Chofetz Chaim, who was aware of the man's guilt feelings. The Chofetz Chaim spoke to him at length about the value of sincere repentance, stressing repeatedly that repentance not only atones for one's transgressions, but transforms one into a new person. He is no longer the person he was the day before and hence need not feel guilty for the past. The scholar gained peace of mind and said, "I am a new person and have no reason to feel suffering about the past."[85]

When a certain man in Jerusalem became ill from heart disease, his daughter, an only child, left her own home and came to take care of him. When he saw that she was taking too much trouble over him, spending far more energy than she could afford, he pleaded with her to go back to her own home, where she was needed. He insisted that he could look after himself. The daughter refused to listen. Finally he said, "If you want to respect your father, you must do as I say. Go back now to your home." Since it now became a matter of the Torah requirement to obey a parent, she yielded and went home.

A few days later the man died of a heart attack. His grief-stricken daughter was not to be comforted. She blamed herself for abandoning her father when he was so ill. Convinced that she was guilty of his death, she became emotionally ill herself. Then Reb Aryeh Levin came to talk to her: "Listen to me," he said gently. "Even if you remained by his bedside, he would not have lived any longer. A man's lifetime is fixed and set by a Higher Power. And then, if you had remained and he died, you would have been twice as stricken with grief—because you did not fulfill your obligation to honor and respect him. After all, he clearly told you to go back home. You would have been sure that by refusing to leave, you caused him anguish and that hastened your father's death while he suffered with his heart."

Reb Aryeh continued in this same vein, on and on, until the truth of his words struck home and she was comforted.[86]

Another piece of advice to remember when one hears expressions of guilt feelings is not to argue but rather to try and reassure. A husband may say he should have been more considerate of his wife. A wife may say that she should have made fewer demands of her husband. A parent may say that he should have spent more time with his child.

These may not be justified feelings but they are natural. Anyone who loses a loved one feels that they "could have done" or "should have done" more. These feelings must work themselves out of the emotions of the bereaved mourners. Don't contradict or argue with the mourner. Just gently try to reassure that in all probability the mourner was a good husband, wife, or parent. If one knows of specific instances where strong family ties were displayed and were known to have existed, gentle allusion to these are appropriate.

REPENTANCE

At the same time, in a tactful and gentle manner, the mourner needs to know that at any time of distress one has to repent and resolve to live a better life.[87] This in no way means that one caused the death by one's evil actions. It is just one of the purposes of all mourning and distress; people should use them as catalysts to become better human beings.

In truth, according to some, the whole purpose of the mourning ritual is to empathize with the deceased who is undergoing his or her heavenly judgment. When one reflects on that judgment and repents, this can bring great merit to the soul of the deceased.[88]

The *rebbe* of Gur, the Chidushei HaRim, while sitting deep in thought at the deathbed of his daughter Pessiah, suddenly turned to those around him and said, "When one gets a slap on the cheek from Heaven, one must reflect upon and study the reason for the slap."[89]

A mourner should not say, however, "I haven't received all the punishment I deserve," because one should not tempt the Accuser for further punishment.[90]

Certainly, doing *teshuvah*, repenting, will help therapeutically in many ways, and will even help to alleviate guilt feelings, as mentioned above in the story with the Chofetz Chaim.

WHEN ONE IS WEEPING

When a visitor is confronted with a mourner who is crying and weeping, he or she should be careful not to repress these expressions of grief. To say "Now, now, let's be mature and not cry" is not only wrong from a grief psychotherapeutical stance; it simply is a false notion of what maturity is. Just as not crying is no indication of maturity, crying is absolutely no indication of immaturity.

Similarly, words like "Buck up, don't take it so hard" sound like one is minimizing the loss. A mourner *should* take the loss hard. As Rabbi Hirsch expresses it, "The pain when an immediate relative dies cannot be dismissed any more than the physical suffering when a limb is amputated from one's body."[91]

It only makes the mourner feel worse when one seemingly doesn't understand the depth of his or her loss. It is more appropriate to say, "It must be really tough; I know how hard this must be for all of you." In this manner the mourners recognize how much the visitor empathizes with them. One allows them to feel free to express their pent-up grief and to release the flood of emotions that are overwhelming them. This is good grief therapy.

King Solomon tells us, "There is a time to cry."[92] The Talmud tells us, "Whoever cries at the demise of good man, all of his sins are forgiven."[93] "Whoever cries at the demise of a good man, the Almighty counts those tears and places them in His treasure house."[94] "The gates [in heaven] for tears are never locked,"[95] and so on.

All this, however, is referring to *normal* crying and weeping. A mourner should not cry *excessively*. On the verse in Jeremiah (22:10), "Do not cry for the dead . . . ," the Talmud explains that this means that one is not allowed to weep excessively. The first three days are for crying, seven for eulogizing, thirty for not wearing pressed clothes or getting a haircut. After this the Almighty says, "You are not more merciful than I."[96] The Talmud further states there: "Rabbi Judah said in the name of Rav, Whoever indulges in excessive grief will weep over another death. It recounts there that there was a certain woman that lived in the neighborhood of Rabbi Huna; she had seven sons, one of whom died, and she wept for him rather excessively. Rabbi Huna sent word to her not to act in this manner. She paid no attention and he again sent word to her: "If you heed my word all will be well; if not, are you anxious to provide [shrouds] for another?" . . . In the end she and her sons all died.[97]

The point here is to distinguish between the normally expected tears of grief, and those of excess, which call into question the justice of the Almighty and the nonacceptance of His decree. The Talmud says, "When the Second Temple in Jerusalem was destroyed, many Jews began to withdraw from life and sank into a state of depressed mourning for the sons and daughters of Israel who had perished and also for the Temple that had gone up in smoke. They refused to eat and drink. Rabbi Joshua said to them, 'My sons, I know that it is impossible not to mourn, but to mourn excessively is forbidden.'"[98]

> The story is told of a man who had a little daughter, an only and beloved child. He lived for her. She was his life. When she became ill and the efforts of the most skilled physicians failed to cure her, he became like a man possessed, moving heaven and earth to bring about her recovery. All efforts proved unavailing, and the little girl died.
>
> The father's heart was broken. He was totally inconsolable. He became a bitter recluse, shutting himself away from his many friends and refusing every activity that might restore his poise and bring him back to a normal life.
>
> One night he had a dream. He was in heaven and was witnessing a giant pageant of all the little child angels. They were marching in an apparently endless line, past a great white throne. Every white-robed angelic tot carried a candle. He noticed that one child's candle was not lit. Then he saw that the child with the dark candle was his own little girl.
>
> Rushing to her, he took her in his arms, caressed her tenderly, and asked, "How is it, darling, that your candle is not lit?"
>
> The child said, "*Father, they often relight it, but your tears always put it out.*"
>
> Just then he awoke. From that hour on, he was no longer a recluse but began to mingle freely and lovingly with his former friends. No longer would his little darling's candle be extinguished by his tears.[99]

It is natural to grieve over the death of a loved one, but we should also be thankful for the years that God allowed us to have that loved one and realize that all life is a deposit to us from the Almighty, Who can recall that loan when He sees fit.

One of the most touching stories of the *Midrash* relates the following, concerning the death of Rabbi Meir's children:

> The story is told of Rabbi Meir who was sitting at *Minchah* time on *Shabbos* afternoon [in the study hall] and giving a lecture. During that time his two beloved children suddenly passed away. What did their grief-stricken mother do? She placed them both on a bed and covered them with a sheet. When Rabbi Meir returned after *Shabbos* from the study hall, he asked his wife, "Where are my two sons?" She said to him, "They went to the study hall." He said to her, "I expected them to come there but I did not see them." She gave him the cup of wine over which to recite the *havdalah* and he did so. Again he enquired, "Where are my two sons?" She replied, "Sometimes they go to a certain place and they should be returning now." She then served him his meal.

After the meal she said to him, "My master, I have a question to ask you."

He said to her, "Ask your question."

She said to him, "My master, some time ago someone came and asked me to safeguard an object and now he returned and asked for it back. Shall I return it or not?"

He said to her, "My daughter, does not one have to return a deposited object to its real owner?"

Thereupon, she said to him, "Were it not for your opinion, I would not have returned it."

What did she do? She took him by the hand and brought him upstairs to the room. She drew him close to the bed and removed the sheet, and he saw the two of them lying dead on the bed. He began to cry, "My sons, my sons, my teachers, my teachers; my sons in *derech eretz* and my teachers because they enlightened my eyes in Torah."

At that moment she said to him, "My master, did you not just tell me that one must return a deposited object to its original owner? So here, *HaShem* gave [us these children] and now He has taken them back. May the Name of God be blessed."

Rabbi Chanina said on the above, "In this manner she comforted him and appeased his mind. That is why it is written: 'Who can find a woman of valor?'"[100]

Rabbi Hirsch also incorporates this thought into his advice to those who visit the mourners:

Be with him from whom God has taken a member of his family, and make him feel that though the individual dies, the Jewish community never dies. Let his sorrow for the deceased be softened by the sympathy of the community. Stay by him and show him that he is not forsaken. Comfort him, remind him of the teachings of the Torah, *show him how everything is only loaned, and that we have to give thanks for its withdrawal even as we give thanks for its bestowal.* Show him that in both days of joy and of adversity there are opportunities of fulfilling tasks which God's wise love has imposed on us for our own salvation. Console him, and melt the bitter sorrow into silent dedication to God's will. Do not say, however, "What can one do, one must resign oneself," for that is not consolation but blasphemy; it is the murmuring of the helpless against his helplessness, not the recognition of the blessed wisdom of God. Sit silently by until the mourner himself gives vent to his sorrow in words, and leave him as soon as your presence seems to be a disturbance and he shows that he wishes to be alone with his grief" (emphasis mine).[101]

In another passage Rabbi Hirsch writes:

Our sages—how wise they are—tell you not to chain yourself to anything you have, however noble it be, so long as it is transient, or else, when it passes on, you decline with it and you only cast yourself into the grave with him who has passed away. As long as God's love bestows upon you its grandest gifts, use them as God's own for God's purposes. But be ready at every moment to return them, for you do not know when He will demand them. And if He takes away, recognize in the taking, as in the giving, the same loving Fatherly hand; and with what is left to you, in whatever condition you may be, rise to live fulfilling the will of God, pursuing it and blessing Him—until He also calls you away to another existence and to a new life.[102]

GILGUL—REINCARNATION[103]

Perhaps it is appropriate here to introduce the concept of *gilgul*. The great Sephardic writer and kabbalist, Rabbi Chaim Dovid Azulai, actually uses this to explain to us the story of the death of Rabbi Meir's children that was quoted above. For the question can really be asked, "In what way did his wife really comfort him. Could not his young sons have lived much longer and accomplished more in their lifetime?" But the idea of the "deposited object" refers to the reincarnated soul that was deposited in the second body.

Souls are often required to come back to this earth to complete an unfilled mission they had in a previous lifetime, or to rectify some sin or tainted existence that prevents them from enjoying eternal bliss in the World to Come. When this is the case, as soon as the new mission has been accomplished, the soul is recalled, so it can enjoy its eternal existence in its now-repurified condition.

This explains the tragic deaths of those who die young, children or otherwise. It was the tragic death of a groom about to be married that led to Rabbi Azulai's explanation in trying to comfort the father of the groom.

Perhaps the following story adapted from the writings of the great kabbalist Rabbi Chaim Vital, a student of the holy Arizal, will illustrate this concept for us. It demonstrates how little we understand about God's world of souls, His grand master scheme and purpose for each and every soul. And as Rabbi Vital explains, if we only understood a little, we would never suffer, for we would understand how every happening in life is so precisely coordinated by the Almighty, Whose ways are totally beyond our comprehension.

Yosef, a young married man, and his younger brother Dovid left *shul* one Friday night and made their way to their mother Rachel's house to wish her a good *Shabbos*. There was a pleasant warmth in the home. The candles burned peacefully as if saying that *Shabbos Kodesh* had come to the world. Only the empty chair at the head of the table, the chair of their father who had departed from the world two short years earlier, momentarily disturbed the peace. Feelings of yearning and pain filled their hearts. Rachel sat on her chair as usual and was engrossed in a holy book.

"Good *Shabbos,* Mother," said the sons. "Good *Shabbos*," Rachel responded, trying with all her might to hide the tears that streamed from her eyes.

"You're crying again," said Yosef. "There has to be an end to these tears. Today is the holy *Shabbos* and it is forbidden to be sad."

"But you know," said Rachel, "two years ago today, your father Avraham passed away. How can I control myself from crying?"

"Good," said Yosef, "today you have an excuse, but what about yesterday and the day before! Two years have passed already and you cannot find peace. You cry and are constantly in distress; Father is in Heaven and is certainly not happy with you. And the Creator of the World—He is also not happy. In the *Shulchan Aruch* it is written when one may mourn and when one has to stop. If you don't abide by it, you show that you do not agree with the will of the Almighty! Please forgive me, *Imma*, for speaking seemingly in disrespect," Yosef ended his words.

Their mother arose, wiped away her tears and said, "You are right, Yosef. With all my power I want to forget, but I can't." And once again she wiped away her tears.

Yosef wished his mother a good *Shabbos* and went home. Dovid remained with his mother, fulfilling the former role of his late father. He made *kiddush* and made the *motzi*, and all through the *Shabbos* meal they experienced true *Shabbos* rest. Mother even smiled. The children spoke about the weekly *parshah* and *Imma* had much *nachas*. They all went to bed very late.

Rachel was unusually at peace with herself, the likes of which she had not felt since the passing of her beloved husband. She began to think that she was not alone; there are other young widows who were happy, having accepted and made peace with their bitter lot. She recalled the latest *shidduch* they had proposed to her; she shuddered a little, but this night she fell asleep peacefully. And she dreamed.

In her dream she saw men running. She also ran; and they left the city and came to a thick forest. They continued to run in the darkness and suddenly a light shone through and the forest ended. The sun appeared in full brightness and she saw before her a beautiful garden filled with magnificent flowers sending forth an exquisite fragrance. Surrounding the garden were sparkling pools of water. Suddenly she saw before her a Jew with a long silvery beard, dressed in a long white robe. The Jew asked her if she wanted to see her husband, and she immediately followed him with a pounding heart. The old man halted by a large tree filled with beautiful fruit. In the distance she saw a large field, surrounded by a golden fence. In the middle she saw many Jews wearing beautifully colored clothing, sitting in rows and learning Torah. In the middle was a young man who was delivering a Torah lecture.

"Wait here for a while," said the old man. "Soon they will be finished with the lecture and then you will see your husband." She looked in all directions and couldn't believe the wondrous sights. The lecture ended and the man giving the shiur began to walk toward her. Suddenly she recognized the garment of her husband. Her head lifted and she saw her husband standing beside her.

"Avraham," she cried, and she fell on a nearby tree. "It is I, Rachel." Said her husband, "Be calm." For a long time she remained motionless with her eyes closed. When she had composed herself, she opened her eyes and asked, "Why did you leave me when you were so young?"

"You should know," he answered pleasantly, "that the world in which you live is a land where people are sent to complete a certain mission, or to suffer for sins that they did in the past." The true world is right here. Know that I was once in your world before you knew me. I was a Torah luminary and a righteous man, but I didn't want to get married and have children for fear that this would disturb my learning. When I departed the first time from your world they gave me in Gan Eden the head post in a yeshivah, and I began to elevate myself higher and higher. But when it was noted that I had not married and had children, I was returned to your world with the express purpose of fulfilling this task and I took you as my wife. When our seventh child was born, they recalled me to Gan Eden to my former post as head of my yeshivah, where they had all been waiting for me. Great is your merit that I was your husband, for I have a good name here. When the time comes we shall once again live together in happiness in this world."

"But I didn't know that you were such a great scholar," said Rachel. "You never had much time to learn." Said her husband, "I also did not know. But once I came back to your world to rectify my neglect to marry, have children, and support them, when I returned to this world immediately my head was filled with Torah knowledge with no bounds."

His wife continued to speak and she asked, "Why is our son Yosef not successful in his business?" Her husband replied, "You must certainly remember the din Torah that Yosef had with that Jew. Yosef won, but because he caused the other Jew so much pain, they wanted to punish him with a severe punishment. I interceded for him and I requested that they give him four difficult years in business as his punishment. In one more year the period of punishment will be over, and he will begin to be successful."

"And what is with our Dovid? He is already twenty-four years old and they have not yet proposed for him a suitable match. I also do not have the means with which to marry him off."

Her husband chuckled and said, "The reason for this is simple. His life's mate entered the world late. She is now only thirteen years old and she lives in another country. In another five years she will come to your city, marry Dovid, and give him all the expenses that you will need."

Rachel began to tremble as she recalled a very painful memory. With very little strength left she asked her husband, "And why did that terrible accident befall our three-year-old son when he was killed by that drunken *goy*?"

Her husband smiled and said, "Follow me." They came to a garden that was filled with small trees budding on all sides. From Heaven descended pillars of light in different colors. Pretty birds flew from tree to tree and she heard their song. Some were singing, "A light is sown for the righteous and joy for the upright." Others were singing, "So that they will praise you in Glory." Big flies of all colors were flying and singing in her ears, "Peace, peace to the far and the near." Little deer ran in the grass singing, "And I will sing Your might, I shall sing Your praises in the morning." Even the trees were singing, "All the trees of the forest will sing."

Suddenly she saw from above circles of fire interwoven with a host of colors. They descended beside her and stood as pillars. Following them little angels with wings descended and stood beside her. Round about could be heard a beautiful orchestra playing magnificent music. Rachel felt as if her soul was leaving her and that she was about to faint. Immediately her husband took some grass from the garden and placed it on her forehead. Her spirit returned to her. She looked again and saw a *chuppah* [canopy] studded with precious stones dazzling with all colors of the rainbow. From under the *chuppah* came an angel who stopped opposite her. She recognized her slain son, who was laughing before her in great happiness. She fainted again, and again her husband used the grass to revive her. She opened her eyes and saw that she was not mistaken. It was her son, none other.

She asked him, "Why did you leave me at such an early age?"

Her son replied, "All goes according to the reckoning of the Master of the Universe. I was already in the world before you gave birth to me, *Imma*. I was born into a very honorable family. In our city there was a terrible pogrom and the Gentiles killed out all of the Jews. I alone remained alive, six months old. A Gentile woman took me to her home and raised me until I was ransomed by Jews and I returned to live among my own people. I became a great Torah scholar and lived out my years in peace and serenity. When I departed from the world, I was received in the World of Truth with great joy, and I was elevated higher and higher until I could go no further. Since I was nursed by a non-Jewish woman, judgment was pronounced that I be born again and that I nurse from a holy Jewish mother for three years. Then I would be able to return to even greater heights in this World of Truth and Eternity. That's when I was born to you, *Imma*, and it is a great merit for you. When the three years were up, I was returned to my place, for there was nothing else for me to do in your unhappy world."

"But why did you have to depart in such a terrible way?" his mother asked. The son replied, "When I was about to depart the world, a decree went out against the Jews of our town and all were about to be killed, including you and my father. They then bestowed upon me the honor that I could atone for the whole city, and I was killed for their sake in order to save the entire city. That is why I merit all this great honor up here. No one in Heaven has the right to see me except *Abba*, any time he wants to see me." The child laughed pleasantly, departed, and was gone.

Then her husband said to her, "You see that to all of your questions there are answers. The Creator does not create any bad. Now I have to return to my *shiur* [lecture]." He escorted her to the place under the first big tree and said to her, "Here things are very good, but I cannot bear your crying and your tears. You will do me a great favor if you will begin to live in happiness. If they propose to you a proper match, do not be against it." Her husband was gone and the old man reappeared. He took her back to the great forest.

Rachel awoke from her dream as though she was born anew. She lay there for a long time with a smile on her face and continued to see her happy husband and her smiling son. A heavy stone had been rolled off her heart and she accepted comfort. She is now remarried and is living a happy and pleasant life.[104]

On a very personal note, upon returning from the hospital shortly after my son passed away, I remembered the following similar story and offered it to my wife as words of comfort and understanding. I have recounted it many times when the death of young children was involved. The story is told by Rabbi Chaim of Kosov about the Baal Shem Tov HaKodosh.

A childless woman once came to the Baal Shem Tov and with bitter tears pleaded with him for a blessing. The *tzaddik* assured her that in the same year she would bear a son. Soon after her return home, she became pregnant, and nine months later she gave birth to an unusually beautiful baby boy. When he was two years old she brought him to the Baal Shem in order to receive his blessing before he was weaned. As they entered, the Baal Shem bade his attendant take the baby and pass it to him. The *tzaddik* hugged and kissed him, and then bade his attendant to return him to his mother's arms. They made their way home, and on their arrival, the child died.

The woman cried endlessly, and, grief-stricken, she returned to confront the Baal Shem. Due to the bitterness in her heart she cried out to him, "My master has killed the child!"

"Weep not," said the Baal Shem, "and listen carefully to what I am about to tell you."

"A king who was childless once confided in his chief advisor: 'You are my counselor on everything, even on military strategy. Can you not advise me on my predicament—I have no children. Who will inherit my kingdom?'

"No one can help you in this matter except the Jews," said his advisor.

"Very well," replied the king. "If the Jews will help me, I will annul all of their taxes and tributes."

"That will not help you at all," retorted the advisor. "Only this will help. Issue a decree compelling all the Jews in your kingdom to pray to the Almighty that you beget a son this year; if they are unsuccessful, there will be no trace of any Jew thereafter in your kingdom."

The king listened to his advisor and issued a decree threatening that if he would not bear a son that year, he would expel every Jew, man and woman, young and old, from his land. The Jews were struck with terror from the decree. They fasted, recited *tehillim* [psalms], and beseeched the Almighty that He save them from their distress—and their outcry ascended to Heaven.

Now a certain lofty soul in heaven that had heard the Jews' outcry came before God pleadingly and said, "I volunteer to go down to the world below to become the king's son, in order to save the Jews from their impending danger."

And so it was. The queen soon after became pregnant and that year bore a son. And for the Jews—there was boundless light and joy!

When the child was weaned they began to instruct him in his lessons. The boy was blessed with a sharp and brilliant mind, and he immediately grasped all that he was taught. As he grew up he mastered more and more knowledge, and one day he said to his father, "None of my studies has yet given me pleasure. I yearn to study something in which I can delight!"

"If so," replied his father, "I will request the foremost clergyman in my realm to teach you; from his instruction you will most certainly take great pleasure."

The king summoned the priest and requested that he tutor his beloved only son. The priest answered, "I am of course obliged to fulfill my lord's command, but allow me, your majesty, just one request. I spend two hours every day in solitude—that is when I ascend to heaven—and the life of any mortal who visits me then is forfeit. I ask, therefore, that your majesty decree and forbid his son, too, to enter my chamber at that time."

The king promised to honor this request, and the priest began to tutor his son. It wasn't long before the young prince became fluent and an expert in all of the subjects that the priest taught him, for he truly had a brilliant mind. Only one thing gnawed at him: why could he not see what his mentor did in those two mysterious hours when he locked himself in his secret chamber?

He made a duplicate set of keys to the chamber, waited impatiently for the daily period of solitude, opened the door and—to his amazement—found the cleric sitting enwrapped in *tallis* and *tefillin*, studying the

Talmud! The priest, taken totally by surprise, almost fainted from fear at his discovery. But the prince promised him faithfully that he would reveal to no one the dread secret that their chief clergyman and priest was really a Jew.

"Now I shall begin to teach you, too, the Torah," said the beloved mentor to his student. "It is a study in which you will truly delight for it is sweeter than honey." The prince began to learn Torah and indeed sensed that it refreshed his soul.

One day he asked his mentor, the clandestine Jew, "But why is it necessary to deceive everyone?"

His mentor replied, "Most of my years have passed, and I am forced to remain in this position as long as I live."

"Advise me, though," begged the prince, "how I can convert to your faith, for I want to be a Jew. You know, however, that my father cannot bear to live even a single day without seeing me."

"Then say to your father," replied the mentor, "that he asked for a son in order to have an heir to his throne. Tell him that you have not yet seen any part of his kingdom, and that you would like to travel through the land to acquaint yourself with the kingdom and with all of the governors of the various provinces. But since this would hardly be feasible because you will so sorely miss each other, being unable to part for even a short time, you suggest the following. For the duration of one month you propose that you accustom yourselves to meeting only at distant intervals. Thereafter, you will be able to bear being apart, and you can then travel throughout the country for the aforementioned purpose."

The prince hearkened to the advice of his mentor, and the idea was received very favorably by the king. A month later the prince was on his way to visit the various provinces of the kingdom. When they finally came close to the city bordering on the next kingdom, the prince dismissed his carriage driver and sent him home. He explained that he had some urgent business and would be spending a long time in the city and thus would not need his services. As soon as the coachman left, the prince crossed the border into the other kingdom, and soon after he converted to Judaism. He settled in a certain town and spent his days studying Torah diligently in the *beis hamedrash*. He had enough money with which to support himself, for he took his money with him from the palace. He did this for many years, each year of his life, until he died.

When his soul ascended to the World Above, the prosecuting angels could not find a single count on which to accuse him. What could one say about a soul so lofty that its very descent to the lower world was born of self-sacrifice to save the Jewish people from certain peril? What could one say about a soul that had forfeited riches, glory, and a royal crown in order to convert to the faith of Torah and Judaism?

One prosecuting angel, however, opened his mouth and challenged, "But for the first two years of his life he was nursed by a non-Jewess!"

Whereupon the Heavenly Court issued its verdict that this soul must descend to the lower world once again to be nursed by a Jewess for two years.

The Baal Shem Tov, who had now concluded his story, turned to the woman and said, "Why should it grieve you, then, that you were fortunate to merit nursing such a pure and lofty soul for two years?"[105]

The following story refers to the previous discussion of weeping:

The story is told of a bitterly unhappy woman who once came to Reb Aryeh Levin's home. "Let me sit in your house," she pleaded, "and cry and weep before you."

"You may surely sit," he replied, "and even cry and weep—but not before me. Direct your tears to the Holy, Blessed One Who listens to weeping and hears the cries of His beings."

Taking a seat, the woman simply began a lament without end, unable to stop. In between her tears she managed to sob out her story of woe, about her husband who was mortally sick.

"Do not cry so," said Reb Aryeh. "The Holy, Blessed One will surely have mercy and grant a cure." But alas, a few days later the woman returned to tell him that her husband had passed away. And she wept anew with bitter tears.

Reb Aryeh did his best to comfort her, seeking words that would touch her heart. Finally, with some spirit she answered, "Look. I will accept your solace and stop my lament—but only if you tell me what became of the thousands of tears I shed over the tehillim, the Book of Psalms, when I said its words of prayer to the Master of the world, imploring Him to cure my husband when he lay ill. It was all for nothing, wasn't it?"

"I will tell you," said Reb Aryeh gently. "When your life on earth ends and you come before the court of justice in heaven, you will find out how many severe and harsh decrees against the Jewish people were torn up, made null and void, because of those precious holy tears you shed for your husband. Not one teardrop goes to waste. The Holy, Blessed One counts them like pearls and treasures them."

At that the woman burst into weeping again, but now with tears of happiness (that all her suffering and prayer were truly not in vain). Some time later she came back: "Tell me again, dear rabbi, those beautiful words: What happened with those tears of mine that I wept?"[106]

It has also been beautifully expressed in the following manner:

What is this taboo on tears? Men hate to see tears. They shy away from crying women, and frown on tears in their own sex. Tears disfigure and ravage, yes. But modern mankind's distress stems from the abuse of weeping. The tears of the morally weak, the infantile personality, the self-indulgent, and the spiritual thief who uses them to burglarize another's principles are so repelling and so degenerating as to give rise to general condemnation of weepers.

But God Almighty gave us tears. It is unlikely that they are meant merely to chap our cheeks when the wind stings our eyes. Or just to keep the eyeballs moist.

No one really denies their importance. We must breathe, eat, sweat, digest, expel—and weep. Tears border on the sacred; they are the only off-casting of our bodies that flows from spiritual and emotional wounds. They are the only channel to release dammed-up sensibilities, letting out the poisonous streams of anxiety that can infect our whole being. Even those we cause ourselves, due to temper, self-will, self-pity, pride, fear of punishment or terror are a safeguard against more disastrous behavior. . . .

We weep at separations that we would not change, but which cut deep at habits and comforts nonetheless. Beyond such weeping are emotions of faith and hope, and great selflessness. . . . The tears for another, the tears of grief, these are holy tears when shed from a pure heart. . . .

So why be ashamed or nonplused at grief, then, or cheat ourselves in denying its expression? Tears are a necessary adjunct to shock. . . .

In Oriental countries one can still find the delicate little tear vases used by the mourners in bereavement. Their philosophy did not discount the cleansing and draining purposes of crying. And they held that the most sacred tears we have are wept for those who are done with this world and are carried on to the mysteries of the next, leaving us to battle out the finish. Those tear bottles were kept and often were buried with the person mourned, where archaeologists now come across them.[107]

It is clear from all of the above that when the mourners shed tears, these are healthy tears. It helps them express grief rather than repress it. There is no need for people to clam up or cease speaking when they see that their words are causing tears to flow from the mourner.

VISITORS SHEDDING TEARS

At the same time it is entirely appropriate for visitors to shed tears along with the mourners. The Talmud has already been quoted above in reference to shedding tears at the demise of a good man. It also states, "Weep for the mourners and not for their loss, for [the deceased] has gone to eternal rest, but we are suffering."[108]

The following stories are related about Rabbi Aryeh Levin.

Once his student Yaakov David Perlin came to him and found him bent over his table writing a letter, while he wept bitterly. "What happened?" his student asked. "What makes you grieve so?"

Reb Aryeh answered that he was writing a letter of condolence to a known family that had suffered for years in the Soviet Union, since its members had insisted on speaking Hebrew at home, in a land that considered "Zionism" a major crime. Just a while ago, however, they succeeded in getting out and migrated to Israel—and now the parents lost their only son. He served as a medical doctor on the submarine *Dakar*, which was lost in the depths of the sea with no survivors.[109]

When a noted woman, the Israeli jurist, Dr. Gitta Gnehovsky passed away, Reb Aryeh did not hesitate to travel to Bnai Brak to comfort her husband during the *shivah*. The pious rabbi came to the man's home and sat. Suddenly feeling the impact of the family's loss he burst into tears. For a long while he could not control himself and stop weeping. Not a word of comfort or solace could he utter. When the grieving husband saw this, he himself began to cry bitterly.

Realizing that he was only darkening and deepening the gloom, and doing nothing to console the mourners, Reb Aryeh arose and left the house. He returned in about an hour and sat once more with the sorrowing family, forcing himself now to show a cheerful face and say kind words of comfort. No one noticed that only his face was cheerul and optimistic, but his eyes still bore his pain.[110]

I also heard a similar story about Rabbi Chaim Shmulevitz, *ztz'l*. A young scholar in the *kollel* of Mir passed away. When Reb Chaim went to pay a condolence call to the young widow, he was unable to restrain himself and burst out crying. Unable to say anything, he left. Someone who had observed the scene tried to excuse Reb Chaim's behavior by explaining that he was an extremely emotional man.

The widow replied, "There is no need to excuse Reb Chaim. On the contrary, I received more comfort from him than from any of the words that have been spoken to me."[111]

When mourners see the genuine tears of a visitor, it tells them, more than anything that can be expressed in eloquent words, that the visitor shares deeply in their grief, appreciates their loss, and values both the life of the deceased and the feelings of the living. Rabbi Krohn, in his introduction to his marvelous book, *The Maggid Speaks*, describes how they met their wonderful friend, Rabbi Sholom Schwadron, the *Maggid*, six months after the family had sustained the great loss of their father. The family went to the pier in New York to meet the ship that brought Rabbi Schwadron from Israel:

> After waiting a long while, we recognized him among the mass of people leaving the ship, walking slowly, cane over his wrist, and carrying his valise. My two brothers and I started running towards him. In the distance, he saw us, and stopped in his tracks. He resumed walking at a slower pace, moving forward slowly, his head down. We waited for my mother, and then together walked quietly towards him. When he saw

her, the widow of his friend, and mother of seven orphaned children, he nodded his head in greeting, shook his head to and fro, sat down on a bench—and wept.

Tearfully we inched closer to him and after a long few moments, he looked up, tried to say something and motioned helplessly that he could not talk. *The man of a million words had none. The tears on his saddened face spoke instead, and his silence touched us. He knew our pain and he shared it. There could be no greater consolation*" (emphasis mine).[112]

Another story is related about Rabbi Aryeh Levin.

During the Six-Day War a fine young Torah scholar fell in the battle for Jerusalem, leaving behind a young widow with small children. In their days of mourning, Reb Aryeh went to visit them, to offer his consolation. When he arrived at the house, however, his spirit failed him. He did not have the heart, the spiritual strength to enter. So he went home and returned the next day. But the second day, too, he was utterly unable to open the door. However, the young widow heard some slight sound of movement, and she came into the hallway.

Once Reb Aryeh saw her, he burst into tears, simply unable to restrain himself. So the young woman comforted him: "Reb Aryeh, if it was decreed in heaven that I should be a widow and my children orphans, what greater merit could we have been given than this—that my husband fell fighting for Jerusalem?"

Thus the one who came to give consolation was himself given it. A long time later, when he told this to someone and repeated the young woman's words, tears still choked up his voice.[113]

SHARING SORROWS

The following story is related:

When the son of Rabbi Yochanan ben Zakkai died, Rabbi Yochanan's disciples came to comfort him. Rabbi Eliezer entered and said, "Adam, the first man, had a son who died, and he was consoled. You should also accept consolation."

"Not only do I have my personal suffering, but now you also wish to remind me of the first man's suffering," said Rabbi Yochanan.

Rabbi Yehoshua entered and said, "Job had sons and daughters and they all died, and he was consoled."

"Not only do I have my personal suffering, but now you also wish to remind me of Job's suffering," said Rabbi Yochanan.

Rabbi Yosi entered and said, "Aaron had two great sons and they both died on the same day, and he was consoled. You also should accept consolation."

"Not only do I have my personal suffering, but now you also wish to remind me of Aaron's suffering," said Rabbi Yochanan.

Rabbi Shimon entered and said, "David, the king, had a son who died and he was consoled, you also should accept consolation."

"Not only do I have my personal suffering, but now you wish to remind me of David's suffering," said Rabbi Yochanan.

Rabbi Elazar ben Arach entered and said, "I will give you an analogy to your situation. The king entrusted a precious object with one of his subjects. The subject was in a constant state of worry: 'When will I be able to return the object undamaged and unsoiled to the king?' My teacher, you are in a similar situation. You had a son who was a Torah scholar and left this world without sin. Be consoled that you have returned in a perfect state that which the King entrusted to you."

"Elazar, my son, you have indeed properly comforted me," said Rabbi Yochanan.[114]

From the above it is quite apparent that to console others by relating one's own personal tragedies or by referring to the tragedies suffered by others is not the appropriate way to bring the mourners comfort.

Sometimes the mourners may already be aware of tragedies that befell one of the visitors or others, and the presence of those visitors is in itself a comfort. The mourners may themselves realize that if these people were comforted and went on with life, then surely they, too, will eventually be comforted. But it is not necessary to point out the suffering of others, inform the mourners of it, and discuss it with them.

On the other hand, the Talmud relates that when Rabbi Yochanan's tenth son died, he took one of his dead son's teeth, which he made into a bracelet or necklace, and used it for comforting other mourners by saying, "This is the tooth of my tenth son who died. As I was comforted, so you, too, shall be comforted."[115]

As two great rabbis have pointed out, the amazing part of the above incident is that when Rabbi Yochanan was faced with the vast tragedy of the death of his tenth son, he wasn't wrapped up solely in his own grief. Rather, he had the presence of mind and the sensitivity to use his own tragedy as a means of comforting other mourners.[116]

The following is also related about the Gerrer *rebbe*, Rabbi Yitzchok Meir, *ztz'l*. He had thirteen children, all of whom died during his lifetime. When the last one died, his wife turned to him for some words of consolation. He comforted her by saying, *"Our great suffering will serve as a partial consolation for other people who might lose a child. They will comfort themselves by saying, "Reb Yitzchok Meir and his wife lost thirteen children and our loss is not as tragic as theirs."*[117]

The following story also highlights the sensitivity one who has suffered a great loss has for another mourner.

In 1979, the great *rosh hayeshivah*, Rabbi Shneur Kotler, *ztz'l*, suffered the great personal loss of his beloved son, Reb Meir, a very young scholar who left behind a wife and small child.

One afternoon as Rabbi Kotler and his family were sitting *shivah* in Lakewood, New Jersey, following their devastating loss, Rabbi Spira, the Bluzhover *rebbe*, *ztz'l*, came to comfort the mourners. The *rebbe* sat down and began, "*Rosh HaYeshivah*, I am jealous of you."

The hushed crowd of mourners and visitors were shocked at these words. How could anyone be envious of a father who had just suffered such a terrible loss? The *rebbe* continued. "You should know that I once had a beautiful daughter, who herself had a daughter. Both were taken from me and killed during the Holocaust, but I have no idea exactly where or when they were murdered. I therefore have no *Yahrzeit* for my daughter, I can never visit her grave, nor do I have any living reminder of her. You at least have a *Yahrzeit* to commemorate, you will have a gravesite to visit, you have grandchildren from whom you will have, God willing, much *Yiddishe nachas*. I will never have any of these."

A few days later, when *shivah* was over, Rabbi Kotler called Rabbi Spira. "My attitude changed the moment you uttered your words. You gave me a perspective to live with. I thank you for coming to comfort me." And then two anguished yet uplifted hearts bid each other farewell.[118]

The *Midrash* relates the following:

> When Rabbi Bun died, Rabbi Zeira eulogized as follows: "To what can we compare this case? To a king who hired workers for his garden. He observed that one of them worked more expertly and efficiently than all of the others. He called him over and walked with him for many hours in the garden. In the evening when pay time came the king gave him full pay (although he had taken much time off from working while he was walking in the garden with the king). The other workers protested to the king. "We worked a full day, and he worked for only two hours, and you give him full pay?" The king responded, "What are you complaining about? He worked more in two hours than you all worked during the whole day." Similarly Rabbi Bun learned [and accomplished] in twenty-eight years what a diligent student cannot do in one hundred years.[119]

The *Midrash* also relates the following:

> A rabbi lectured to his students under a certain fig tree. Each day the owner of the tree rose early to pick the figs off the tree. "Perhaps he suspects that we shall eat his fruit," they said. "We had better move to another place." They did so. When the owner came the next day he could not find them. He searched and finally found them. "Why did you leave my property?" he enquired. "You have deprived me of the one *mitzvah*

you allowed me to do [to host a Torah lecture of rabbis]." "We thought you suspected us of taking your figs," they replied. "God forbid," said the owner of the tree. "The reason I rose early to pick the fruit is simply because when the sun shines upon them they will rot if I do not pick them quickly." They returned to his property. The next day the owner did not come as usual and they noticed that the fruit had indeed rotted. They said, "The owner of the tree spoke wisely. *And if he knows so well the appropriate time to pick his fruit, surely the Almighty knows the proper time to pluck the righteous from this world.*"[120]

A gentleman's gardener had a beautiful daughter whom he loved dearly. She died at a young age, and the father was sorely distressed and murmured at the dealings of Providence.

   The gardener had an exquisite rose, his favorite flower in one of his master's flower beds. He watched it daily, nurtured it carefully, intending to send it to his master's mansion when it was in full bloom. One morning, horrified, he noticed that it was gone. Someone had obviously plucked it. Angered at what he thought was the misconduct of one of the servants, the gardener began to look for the culprit. How surprised he was to find out that it was the master himself who had been attracted by the beautiful rose and had plucked it to adorn the most elegant room in his mansion. The gardener's anger was changed into great pleasure. He felt happy when he reflected on the fact that his master had thought the flower worthy of such special notice and had given it such a place of honor.

   "Ah, Richard," said the gentleman to his gardener. "You can gladly give up the rose, because I thought it worthy of a special place in my home. And will you forever fret at your Heavenly Father Who has seen fit to pluck your beloved daughter from a world of trial and hardship to be with Himself in a glorious place in Heaven?"[121]

In the Second Book of Samuel we read the following when King David's son was stricken by God:

And David implored God for the child, and David fasted, and he came and lay all night upon the earth. And the elders of his household arose and wished to raise him from the earth; but he would not [rise], neither would he eat bread with them.

   On the seventh day, the child died but the servants of David were afraid to tell him that the child was dead, for they said, "Behold, while the child was yet alive, we spoke to him and he did not listen to our voices; how then shall we now say to him that the child has died; he may harm himself?"

   And David saw that his servants were whispering, and David understood that the child had died. And David said unto his servants: "Is the child dead?" And they said, "He is dead." Then David arose from the earth and washed and anointed himself and changed his clothing; and he came to the House of God and prostrated himself. Then he came to his own house and he asked [for food], and they put bread before him and he ate. Then his servants said to him: "What is this that you have done; while the child was alive you fasted and wept; and when the child died, you arose and ate bread?"

And he said: "While the child was yet alive I fasted and wept, for I said: 'Who knows, maybe God will be gracious unto me, and the child will live.' But now he is dead. Why should I fast? Can I bring him back again [to life]? I shall go to him, but he will not return to me." And David comforted Bathsheba his wife.[122]

The Talmud tells us that David was brought into the apparent sin of David with Bathsheba, only to become a model of repentance for the world.[123] The Dubno *Maggid* explains this and the sale of Joseph by his brothers with the following parable, one that we can use for many occasions when life sends its bruises and wounds upon us.

A king once owned a large, magnificent, and very valuable diamond. One day the diamond accidentally sustained a rather deep scratch. The king summoned his most skilled diamond cutters and enquired whether or not they could remove the imperfection from his treasured jewel. They informed him that even were they to polish it, some mark of the flaw would remain.

After some time, a gifted lapidary came and promised to make the rare jewel even more beautiful than it had been before. "I shall etch upon the diamond beautiful rosebuds, and engrave your honored name within the flowers. And you should know that this work will all begin from the scratch that the jewel sustained.[124]

Many times in life we are struck by events that scratch deeply into our hearts and souls. But we must rise, strengthen ourselves, and create from that scratch the means to elevate ourselves to an even higher sphere of living. Having faith in the Almighty and reflecting on many of the thoughts that we have written thus far can afford us the starting point from which to etch our rosebuds and our everlasting names on the imperfect diamonds of our lives.

We have discussed several areas and thoughts concerning the appropriate ways to respond to the needs of various mourners. In summation, one key word to comforting is "discretion." As always, a visitor should take his cue from the mourners. If they seem anxious to talk about the visitor's own tragic experience or allude to it, the visitor may perhaps use it in a manner to bring comfort to the mourners. Otherwise, generally speaking, one should keep the conversation focused on the deceased, and not on the death of others.

To illustrate this concept of discretion, I would like to relate the following two incidents. When we were sitting *shivah* for our little son Ephraim, *a'h*, a woman who had recently given birth came to be *menachem aveil*. I assume that she was unable to get a babysitter (or at least I shall so judge her favorably), so she brought her infant with her. Naturally all were cooing and coddling over the new baby. I was able to restrain myself from asking her to please leave or at least to take the infant away. But I thought to myself, "How inconsiderate could one be? Here we were, my wife and I, just having lost a baby (two years old), and a woman was coming to be *menachem aveil*, displaying her own baby in front of us to all around?" I'm sure the woman had no idea what hurt she was causing us. But it behooves all who go to a house of mourning to anticipate, if possible, all sensitivities and any situations that could cause discomfort to the mourners.

Recently I gave a lecture on *nichum aveilim*. I mentioned that it was all right to cry in front of the mourners.[125] After the lecture a woman said, "When I was sitting *shivah* for my child, another woman who had recently lost a child came to be *menachem aveil*. First, she looked terrible. It was obvious that she was still very much grieving herself. Secondly, she began to cry uncontrollably. I was deeply disturbed by her visit. I thought to myself, 'Is this what is going to happen to me a few months after *shivah*?' I don't think she should have come to visit me if she knew she was still in that state of mourning."

I agree with her. Discretion must be used. I was talking about shedding empathizing tears and crying with control. I was not referring to uncontrollable hysterical crying that it is inappropriate when going to visit others. Although one should not use excuses for avoiding a *shivah* visit, if one knows that his or her situation is not under control, one should not make the visit.[126]

10

Prayers, Phrases
of Comfort,
and the Seventh Day

PRAYING FOR THE DECEASED

It is appropriate, while in the house of mourning, to utter a [silent] prayer asking *HaShem* to be merciful to the soul of the deceased.[1] The Hebrew names of the deceased and the deceased's father should be used.[2] Hence the prayer would be:

הַמָּקוֹם יְרַחֵם עַל נִשְׁמַת [פְּלוֹנִי בֶּן/בַּת פְּלוֹנִי] וְיִזְכֶּה לִתְחִיַּת הַמֵּתִים

HaMakom yerachem al nishmas [ploni ben/ bas ploni] veyizkeh li'techiyas hameisim.

May *HaShem* be merciful to the soul of _____ [name of deceased] son/daughter of _____[name of deceased's father], and may he/ she merit resurrection.[3]

Many Sephardim use the name of the deceased and that of the deceased's mother.[4]

If one does not know the Hebrew names, it is entirely in order to acquire the names from one of the mourners. If the Hebrew names are not known, the English names may be used.[5]

THE TRADITIONAL PHRASES OF COMFORT

When one is about to terminate his visit,[6] he should recite the traditional phrase of comfort:

הַמָּקוֹם יְנַחֵם אֶתְכֶם בְּתוֹךְ שְׁאָר אֲבֵלֵי צִיוֹן וִירוּשָׁלָיִם

HaMakom yenachem eschem besoch she'ar aveilei Tziyon ve'Yerushalayim.

May [*HaMokom*][7] the Almighty comfort you among the other mourners of Zion and Jerusalem.[8]

This traditional phrase of comfort communicates to the mourners two major ideas. One, it is almost impossible, if not impossible, for any human being to find words that are truly adequate to provide them with comfort at this time. But we have faith in God, and as the Talmud expresses it: "Our Father, the Master of comfort, will surely comfort you."[9] So we pray to Him that He will send you His comfort, as it also says: "[God] Who heals the broken-hearted and binds up their wounds."[10] It is He "Who can turn grief into gladness, and can console and cheer the mourner after their sorrow."[11] It is true that "for a moment He has forsaken you, but with great compassion He will gather you."[12] "He has torn, and He will heal, He has smitten, but He will bind up."[13]

Rabbi Dessler expresses it this way:

> In truth there are no natural means by which a person can be comforted. Even were one to say to the mourner many words of comfort, this would not result in any benefit, according to natural events. The fact that we see despite all this that people are comforted is a result of *HaShem*'s special gift that He goes Himself and comforts the mourners. In this way an actual miracle is performed for each and every mourner, that the Almighty heals him from the agony of mourning through His medicaments which He injects into him—consolations.
>
> Between people there is an accepted phrase that "time will heal." We should know that this is a mistake. On the contrary we find in *chazal* that one does not accept comfort on one who is alive but thought to be dead (as by Yaakov Avinu on Yoseph).[14] It appears therefore that time did not heal at all. What really happens in the course of time is a result of *HaShem*'s decree that the deceased should be forgotten from the heart. Therefore by mistaken mourning (as in the case above) there is no such decree and therefore there is no healing power.
>
> It appears, therefore, that we must teach the mourners that they must willingly accept the healing consolation that *HaShem* sends to them. They should not be stubborn in their mourning as is the way of the rest of the world. They must know that they may not mourn too much, and that they must accept with a willing heart the consolations that are a gift from Him, may He be blessed.[15]

Secondly, we do not wish to minimize your personal grief. But as it says: "The troubles of many is half the consolation" [when many people carry the same burden the load becomes a little easier to bear][16]—so, too, know that we are all mourners, for we mourn the destruction of the Temple; Zion is in distress; Jerusalem is incomplete; and God is still in exile. This, too, should afford you some comfort by knowing that you are not alone in grief. It also sets one's personal sorrow into a larger perspective and reminds the mourners of their heritage and of the great community and nation to which they belong.

Our religious perspective was expressed well in the following statement: "We bereaved are not alone. We belong to the largest company in the world—the company of those who have known suffering. When it seems that our suffering is too great to be borne, let us think of the great family of the heavy-hearted into which our grief has given us entrance and, inevitably, we will feel about us their arms, their sympathy, their understanding."[17]

Perhaps we can also offer the following thought. It is recorded that on July 8, 1941, Moshele, the eldest son of the Belzer *rebbe*, Rabbi Aaron Rokeach, was thrown by a Ukrainian mob into the flames of a blazing synagogue set fire by the mob and German soldiers. A *chasid* came to bring the tragic news to the *rebbe*. The *rebbe* lifted his sorrowful eyes to Heaven and said, "God is merciful; I, too, offered a sacrifice." It is purported that the *rebbe* never again mentioned the death of his son and although the *rebbe* knew the date of his death, he never observed *Yahrzeit*, nor did he ever publicly mourn the death of other members of his family who were killed in the Holocaust. In explanation of this it is said that the *tzaddik* of Belz, who was known for his boundless love and compassion for the Jewish people, said, "How can one mourn the death of an individual, even a beloved son, when one is overwhelmed by the collective pain of a nation mourning its six million dead!"[18]

To each individual mourner who is mourning his individual loss, we, too, say, "Know that we are all publicly mourning the destruction of Zion and the Temple in Jerusalem. Our loss is the loss of a multitude, and nevertheless we have complete faith that God will comfort us and will one day rebuild and restore to us Zion and Jerusalem. In the same fashion, He will certainly bring you comfort on your individual loss."[19]

WHEN THERE IS ONLY ONE MOURNER

The Hebrew word אֶתְכֶם, *eschem*, is masculine plural for the English word *you* and is said to many mourners. If there is only one mourner, some say[20] that the wording should be adjusted to אוֹתְךָ, *oscho*, for a male, and אוֹתָךְ,. *osoch*, for a female. Accordingly, when there are several females who are sitting *shivah* together, the correct word would be אֶתְכֶן, *eschen*, rather than אֶתְכֶם, *eschem*.

Others maintain, however, that the wording should not be changed even if there is only one mourner, but rather the plural form should be retained.[21] This is because one is also reciting the comfort phrase to the soul of the deceased that hovers in the house during *shivah*.[22] The only difference would be if there is only one female mourner. Then the plural form, אֶתְכֶן, *eschen*, would be used even if the deceased was a male, as the word נְשָׁמָה, *neshamah*, is feminine in gender. Another possible explanation for keeping the plural form is because we are extending our comfort to *all other* family members who are mourning for the deceased, *wherever they may be,* even though they are not present here with the singular mourner. Others say we retain the plural form because we are including *this* mourner with all *other* mourners.

SEPHARDIM

The customary phrase used by Sephardic Jews when leaving the mourner's house is: מִן הַשָּׁמַיִם תְּנוּחָמוּ, *Min HaShomayim tenuchamu,* "From Heaven you should be comforted,"[23] or תִּתְנַחֵם מִן הַשָּׁמַיִם, *Tisnachem min HaShomayim,* "You should be comforted from Heaven."[24]

Again the grammatical form of the last word should be changed to the appropriate number and gender of the mourners. Others maintain that since this is part of a verse in the Bible, its form should be kept in all cases.[25]

DO VISITORS STAND OR SIT WHEN RECITING THE PHRASE?

One writer quotes a rabbinic authority who maintained that the custom in Europe was for the visitors to be seated while reciting the comforting phrase.[26] Others maintain, however (and it would seem that this is the more common practice), that the visitors should rise and recite the phrase while standing.[27]

DO THE MOURNERS HAVE TO BE SEATED?

It is customary for the mourners to be seated when the phrase of comfort is recited by the visitors.[28] At this time there is no obligation for them to draw their hats over their eyes; on the contrary, they should look at the comforter.[29] However, if a mourner is standing, one should not tell him to be seated in order that he may recite the phrase.[30] He should rather recite it while the mourner is standing.[31]

REPEATING THE PHRASE

Generally, if mourners are sitting together, it is unnecessary to recite the phrase separately to each mourner; it may be addressed once to all of the mourners.[32] This is generally the custom,[33] although some write that the phrase should be said separately to each mourner.[34] If, however, the mourners are sitting apart or in different areas of the room [or naturally if they are sitting in different rooms, ladies in one and men in another], and not all of the mourners hear the phrase being recited, then the visitor should of course repeat the phrase to the other mourners who were not addressed or did not hear it the first time.[35]

RESPONDING "AMEIN"

The custom seems to be that mourners may respond to the phrase by answering "Amein."[36] Some have written that it is preferable that they do not respond with "Amein."[37]

ONE MAY ADD ANY BLESSINGS OR GOOD WISHES

Although the traditional phrases should of course be recited, one may add anything else that is appropriate. Many[38] add וְלֹא יֹסִיפוּ לְדַאֲבָה עוֹד, *velo yoseefu ledaavah od*, "May you be spared from further sorrow," or the Yiddish equivalent, "*Du zolst mer nisht vissen fun kein tzaar*" (you should know of no more pain and sorrow), which is based on the above Hebrew verse from Jeremiah (31:11). These are sincere sentiments and timely for the moment. As such, I cannot agree with one writer who states, "When I visit a shiva home and hear a visitor tell a mourner in Yiddish, 'You should be spared of future grief,' I wince. I have the feeling that what is really being said is: 'You be the next to die rather than I.' As long as there is life, there will be death, and if there is death, fortunate is that individual who will be grieved and mourned by those left behind."[39]

Many wish the mourners חַיִּים אֲרוּכִים, *chayim aruchim* (may you be blessed with long life).[40] I once heard a rabbi tell a widow the same as above in a beautiful wording: "May you live to bring all of your grand-children to the *chuppah*."[41]

Some write that if the visit is made during the seven weeks of comfort (from *Shabbos Nachamu* until Rosh HaShanah) one should add *tisnachamu bekiflayim*—may you be doubly comforted. During the month of *Elul* one should wish the mourner a *kesivah vachesimah tovah*.[42]

THANKING THE VISITORS

The mourners are permitted to thank the comforters for having come to offer condolences and for paying their respects to the deceased.[43]

AT THE CONCLUSION OF *SHIVAH*

Early *Davening*

Some have the custom of making the *Shacharis* service on the seventh day a little earlier than the usual time it is held during the rest of week.[44] Perhaps this is done in order that the *shivah* will be over earlier. Nevertheless, the convenience of the mourners and of those who come to the services should be given priority.

Telling the Mourners to Rise

After the *Shacharis* service has concluded, the custom is for all the mourners to be seated and all the visitors present to recite together the traditional mourning phrase.

הַמָּקוֹם יְנַחֵם אֶתְכֶם בְּתוֹךְ שְׁאָר אֲבֵלֵי צִיּוֹן וִירוּשָׁלָיִם

HaMakom yenachem eschem besoch she'ar aveilei Tziyon ve'Yerushalayim. "May the Almighty comfort you among the other mourners of Zion and Jerusalem," or according to the Sephardic tradition, תִּתְנַחֵם מִן הַשָּׁמַיִם , *Tisnachem min HaShomayim,* "May you be comforted from Heaven."

Then the mourners should be directed to stand and "rise" from their mourning.[45] As they rise some[46] have the custom of saying:

הַמָּקוֹם יִגְדּוֹר פִּרְצוֹת עַמּוֹ יִשְׂרָאֵל

HaMakom yigdor pirtzos amo Yisrael, "May the Almighty prevent any further breaches among His nation Israel." Then the assembled wish the mourners חַיִּים אֲרוּכִים *chaim aruchim,* long life.[47] Others add:[49]

לֹא יָבֹא עוֹד שִׁמְשֵׁךְ וִירֵחֵךְ לֹא יֵאָסֵף כִּי יי יִהְיֶה לָךְ לְאוֹר עוֹלָם

וְשָׁלְמוּ יְמֵי אֶבְלֵךְ

Lo yavo od shimsheich veereicheich lo yei'aseif kee HaShem yiheyeh loch le'or olam veshalmu yemei evleich, "Your sun shall no longer set, nor shall your moon be darkened; for *HaShem* will be your everlasting light and your days of mourning will end" (Isaiah 60:20) and

כְּאִישׁ אֲשֶׁר אִמּוֹ תְּנַחֲמֶנּוּ כֵּן אָנֹכִי אֲנַחֶמְכֶם וּבִירוּשָׁלַיִם תְּנֻחָמוּ

Ke'ish asher immo tenachamenu, kein Anochee anachemchem, uveYerushalayim tenuchamu. "Like a man whose mother comforts him so shall I [God] comfort you, and in Jerusalem you shall be comforted" (Isaiah 66:13).[49]

A Prayer for the Conclusion of *Shivah*

Some have the custom of saying the following prayer:[50]

אָנָּא יְיָ מֶלֶךְ מָלֵא רַחֲמִים · אֱלֹהֵי הָרוּחוֹת לְכָל־

בָּשָׂר · אֲשֶׁר בְּיָדְךָ נַפְשׁוֹת הַחַיִּים וְהַמֵּתִים · אָנָּא

קַבֵּל בְּחַסְדְּךָ הַגָּדוֹל אֶת־נִשְׁמַת _____

For a Woman, say:–	For a Man, say:–
אֲשֶׁר נֶאֶסְפָה אֶל עַמָּהּ:	אֲשֶׁר נֶאֱסַף אֶל עַמּוֹ:

In the case of a young child omit from חוס to לְפָנָיו

חוּס וַחֲמוֹל עָלָיו · סְלַח
וּמְחַל לְכָל־פְּשָׁעָיו · כִּי אָדָם
אֵין צַדִּיק בָּאָרֶץ אֲשֶׁר יַעֲשֶׂה־
טּוֹב וְלֹא יֶחֱטָא: זְכוֹר
לוֹ צִדְקָתוֹ אֲשֶׁר עָשָׂה
וִיהִי שְׂכָרוֹ אִתּוֹ וּפְעֻלָּתוֹ
לְפָנָיו:
אָנָּא הַסְתֵּר אֶת־נִשְׁמָתוֹ
בְּצֵל כְּנָפֶיךָ · הוֹדִיעֵהוּ אֹרַח
חַיִּים שֹׂבַע שְׂמָחוֹת אֶת־
פָּנֶיךָ נְעִימוֹת בִּימִינְךָ נֶצַח ·
וְתוֹשִׁיעַ לוֹ מֵעֹז מִטּוּב
הַצָּפוּן לַצַּדִּיקִים ·

In the case of a young child omit from חוס to לְפָנֶיהָ

חוּס וַחֲמוֹל עָלֶיהָ ·
סְלַח וּמְחַל לְכָל־פְּשָׁעֶיהָ ·
כִּי אָדָם אֵין צַדִּיק בָּאָרֶץ
אֲשֶׁר יַעֲשֶׂה־טּוֹב וְלֹא
יֶחֱטָא : זְכוֹר לָהּ צִדְקָתָהּ
אֲשֶׁר עָשָׂתָה וִיהִי שְׂכָרָהּ
אִתָּהּ וּפְעֻלָּתָהּ לְפָנֶיהָ:
אָנָּא הַסְתֵּר אֶת־נִשְׁמָתָהּ
בְּצֵל כְּנָפֶיךָ · הוֹדִיעֶהָ אֹרַח
חַיִּים שֹׂבַע שְׂמָחוֹת אֶת־
פָּנֶיךָ נְעִימוֹת בִּימִינְךָ נֶצַח ·
וְתוֹשִׁיעַ לָהּ מֵעֹז מִטּוּב
הַצָּפוּן לַצַּדִּיקִים ·

כְּמוֹ שֶׁכָּתוּב · מָה רַב טוּבְךָ אֲשֶׁר־צָפַנְתָּ לִּירֵאֶיךָ פָּעַלְתָּ
לַחוֹסִים בָּךְ נֶגֶד בְּנֵי אָדָם :
אָנָּא יְיָ הָרוֹפֵא לִשְׁבוּרֵי לֵב וּמְחַבֵּשׁ לְעַצְּבוֹתָם
שַׁלֵּם נִחוּמִים לָאֲבֵלִים ·

[In the case of a female child include the following:–

וּתְהִי פְּטִירַת הַיַּלְדָּה
הַזֹּאת קֵץ לְכָל־צָרָה וְצוּקָה
לְאָבִיהָ וּלְאִמָּהּ:]

[In the case of a male child include the following:–

וּתְהִי פְּטִירַת הַיֶּלֶד הַזֶּה
קֵץ לְכָל־צָרָה וְצוּקָה לְאָבִיו
וּלְאִמּוֹ:]

חַזְּקֵם וְאַמְּצֵם בְּיוֹם אֶבְלָם וִיגוֹנָם וְזָכְרֵם [וּבְנֵי בֵיתָם]
לְחַיִּים טוֹבִים וַאֲרֵכִים · תֵּן בְּלִבָּם יִרְאָתְךָ וְאַהֲבָתְךָ
לְעָבְדְּךָ בְּלֵבָב שָׁלֵם : וּתְהִי אַחֲרִיתָם שָׁלוֹם · אָמֵן :
כְּאִישׁ אֲשֶׁר אִמּוֹ תְּנַחֲמֶנּוּ כֵּן אָנֹכִי אֲנַחֶמְכֶם וּבִירוּשָׁלַיִם
תְּנֻחָמוּ : לֹא־יָבֹא עוֹד שִׁמְשֵׁךְ וִירֵחֵךְ לֹא יֵאָסֵף · כִּי יְיָ
יִהְיֶה־לָּךְ לְאוֹר עוֹלָם · וְשָׁלְמוּ יְמֵי אֶבְלֵךְ : בִּלַּע הַמָּוֶת
לָנֶצַח · וּמָחָה יְיָ אֱלֹהִים דִּמְעָה מֵעַל כָּל־פָּנִים · וְחֶרְפַּת
עַמּוֹ יָסִיר מֵעַל כָּל־הָאָרֶץ · כִּי יְיָ דִּבֵּר :

MEMORIAL PRAYER.

O Lord and King, who art full of compassion, God of the spirits of all flesh, in whose hand are the souls of the living and the dead, receive, we beseech thee, in thy great lovingkindness the soul of _____

For a Man, say:–
who hath been gathered unto his people.
In the case of a young child, omit from "Have mercy" to "before him."

*Have mercy upon him; pardon all his transgressions, for there is

For a Woman, say:–
who hath been gathered unto her people.
In the case of a young child, omit from "Have mercy" to "before her."

*Have mercy upon her; pardon all her transgressions, for there is

none righteous upon earth, who doeth only good, and sinneth not. Remember unto him the righteousness which he wrought, and let his reward be with him, and his recompense before him.*

Oh shelter his soul in the shadow of thy wings. Make known to him the path of life: in thy presence is fulness of joy; at thy right hand, bliss for evermore. Bestow upon him the abounding happiness that is treasured up for the righteous,

none righteous upon earth, who doeth only good, and sinneth not. Remember unto her the righteousness which she wrought, and let her reward be with her, and her recompense before her.*

Oh shelter her soul in the shadow of thy wings. Make known to her the path of life: in thy presence is fulness of joy; at thy right hand, bliss for evermore. Bestow upon her the abounding happiness that is treasured up for for the righteous,

as it is written, Oh how great is thy goodness, which thou has laid up for them that fear thee, which thou hast wrought for them that trust in thee before the children of men!

O Lord, who healest the broken-hearted and bindest up their wounds, grant thy consolation unto the mourners.

[In the case of a male child, include the following:—

May the death of this child mark the end of all anguish and tribulation unto his parents.]

[In the case of a female child, include the following:—

May the death of this child mark the end of all anguish and tribulation unto her parents.]

Oh strengthen and support them in the day of their grief and sorrow; and remember them (and their children) for a long and good life. Put into their hearts the fear and love of thee, that they may serve thee with a perfect heart; and let their latter end be peace. Amen.

Like one whom his mother comforteth, so will I comfort you (saith the Lord), and in Jerusalem shall ye be comforted. Thy sun shall no more go down, neither shall thy moon withdraw itself; for the Lord shall be thine everlasting light, and the days of thy mourning shall be ended. He maketh death to vanish in life eternal; and the Lord God wipeth away tears from off all faces; and the reproach of his people shall he take away from off all the earth: for the Lord hath spoken it.

Perfumed Oil

There was a custom in former days for the visitors to pour perfumed oils on the heads of the mourners after they had risen from *shivah.*[51] This custom was based on the verse: לָשׂוּם לַאֲבֵלֵי צִיּוֹן לָתֵת לָהֶם פְּאֵר תַּחַת אֵפֶר שֶׁמֶן שָׂשׂוֹן תַּחַת אֵבֶל וכוי.

Lasum laaveilei Tziyon laseis lahem pe'eirtachas eifer, shemen sason tachas eivel . . . , "To place upon the mourners of Zion; to give them adornment in place of ashes, and joyous oil in place of mourning . . ." (Isaiah 61:3).

I have not seen this custom mentioned in any of the contemporary books on the laws and customs of mourning, so apparently this custom has been discontinued.

Placing a Stone or a Nail Where the Mourners Sit

Among Lubavitch *Chasidim* there are some who have the custom of either placing a stone or knocking in a nail with a stone on the spot where the mourners sat during *shivah*.[52] This is meant to symbolize the hope that this should be the finality of death.

Light Refreshments

It is customary for all to partake of light refreshments such as cake and whiskey and to say לחיים, *lechaim*, to the mourners.[53]

Accompanying the "*Neshamah*"

Some have the custom that the mourners actually go to the cemetery after the *shivah* has concluded.[54] Others do not go to the cemetery but go outside and simply walk around the block, to escort the *neshamah* (the soul) on its way to the grave.[55] Others suggest that this custom is to symbolize the return to society from which the mourner has withdrawn.[56]

Meeting a Non-Jew First

Some have the custom that the mourners go directly to the home of a non-Jew so that their first outside contact is with a non-Jew. This is based on a talmudic statement that Satan has no power over two different nations, and it is an omen of pleading for the cessation of death to come upon the family.[57]

Some Sephardic Customs

Syrian Jewish Mourning Practices

The conclusion of the *shivah* is marked by an *ariyat* (reading) which takes place at *Minchah* of the final afternoon, when the *Zohar* is read. Appropriate words of eulogy are again offered by the rabbi, and this is followed by

a dinner for the mourners and all who are present. This same *ariyat* ceremony is repeated on the weekend before the thirty days have passed. This
afternoon *ariyat*, which followed the *Minchah* service, is followed by an
Arvit service, a eulogy, and a sweet table.

The members of the family who are mourning go to the cemetery on
the morning after the *ariyat* at both the conclusion of the *shivah* and the
conclusion of the *shloshim* (thirtieth day). At the cemetery, they simply recite
tehillim, spelling out the name of the deceased with the *alfa beta* (Psalm
119).[58]

Moroccan Jewish Mourning Practices

On the beginning of the seventh night, Moroccan Jews hold a *mishmarah*,
which is a *limud* wherein they study *Zohar, Parashat HaShavua*, the *maftir*,
and *Shuvah Yisrael* (Hosea 14:2-10) for a man or *Vatitpalel Chanah* (1
Samuel 2:1) for a woman. Then they read from *Pirkei Avot (Ethics of the
Fathers)*, some *Mishnah*, and they conclude with the reading from the *Zohar*.
On this occasion, words of eulogy are again offered, and the *seudah* in-
cludes the normal food of mourners, such as round cakes, black coffee,
fish, and whiskey. The words of Torah taught usually call upon the mourners to do *teshuvah*, and the occasion is used to arouse the need for self-
improvement in memory of the deceased one. Often, the mourners begin
to lead a life of complete religious observance for at least the year of mourning. Some thenceforth maintain that way of life.

It is the custom of some to go to the cemetery at the end of the *shivah*
period, where they spell out the name of the deceased from the *alfa beta*
(Psalm 119). It is common for some to add the recitations in this psalm
for the Hebrew letters *nun, chet*, and *tet*. Others spell out the Hebrew words
kera Satan ("tear away the Satan"). They then recite the *Hashkavah* again.
A member of the family or a member of the *Chevrah Kaddisha* then takes
in his hand a vessel full of water and washes the hands of the mourners as
they leave the cemetery. Immediately thereafter, he breaks the vessel in
which the water was held so that it cannot be used again. This is to symbolize that death should not return to the family.[59]

Judeo-Spanish Jewish Mourning Practices

On the morning of the seventh day, the *minyan* visits the family once again.
A meal of condolence is again served, and at the conclusion of the meal
and the recitation of the special *birkat hamazon* (including *nachem*), friends
outstretch their hands to the mourners and "lift the mourners up" from
their mourning. A *minyan* then accompanies the mourners to the cemetery,
where the *Mishnah* is again learned and the *hashkavah* is again recited. That

night, a special *limud* entitled *corte de siete* is held at the home of the deceased, and the name of the deceased is spelled out through the *Mishnayot*. The mourners are permitted to participate for the first time in the Torah study session. *Zohar* is studied as well.[60]

Spanish and Portuguese Jewish Mourning Practices

On the last day of the *shivah*, as the mourners are being lifted from their mourning, the following verses are added in Hebrew before the final *kaddish*: "Thy sun shall no more go down, neither shall thy moon wane; for the Lord shall be thy everlasting light and the days of thy mourning shall be ended" (Isaiah 60:20); and it is written, "As one whom his mother comforted, so will I comfort you, and through Jerusalem shall you be comforted" (Isaiah 66:13).[61]

11

After *Shivah*

NICHUM AVEILIM / CHESED

The actual practical *mitzvah* of *nichum aveilim* ceases at the end of *shivah*, although one who was unable to attend the *shivah* and did not call or write to the mourners may still recite the phrase of comfort upon meeting the mourners for the entire mourning period.[1] Nevertheless, the *mitzvah* of *gemillus chesed*, of helping a friend in need, certainly never ceases.[2] Therefore, it is everyone's duty to help the bereaved in any way they can, even, or perhaps especially *after,* the *shivah*.

Many times the mourners, especially widows who are left all alone, or left with young children, feel the loss, loneliness, and despair even more *after* the *shivah*, when they are no longer surrounded by all the caring visitors who gave them support *during* the *shivah*.

It is therefore extremely important for relatives and friends to keep in contact and to be as supportive as possible to the bereaved, perhaps even more so after the *shivah*. This support should be offered for days, weeks, months, or even years, depending on each circumstance.

Each mourner is different, and each relative or friend has a unique relationship with the bereaved one. Therefore, every situation has to be assessed on an individual basis as to what can be done to help in aiding the mourner readjust once again to normalcy and to continue with the goal of carrying on with life without the deceased.

The mourner must know that sometimes, if not always, it is difficult to traverse the path of recovery alone. They need help and should not be embarrassed to ask for help.

The story is told of the little boy who was struggling to lift a heavy stone but could not budge it. The boy's father, who happened to be watching, said to his son, "Are you using all your strength?" "Yes, I am," the boy said with irritation.

"No," the father said calmly. "You're not. You have not asked me to help you."

Time Will Heal

Normal grief runs a natural course. The pain will slowly dissipate; time will heal the wounds, and the mourning will pass.

There is a tradition that tells of King David's search for an inscription to be etched on his ring. His challenge: Inscribe on the ring the same words that will both humble me when I become haughtily intoxicated with success, and, on the other hand, will raise my spirits when I am depressed and melancholy. No one could think of a solution. One day Solomon his son found the answer.

"Inscribe upon the ring these three words, *"Gam zu yaavor,"* "This, too, shall pass." When King David looked upon the inscription he was reminded that both sorrow and joy are not forever. When he was exalted and prideful, he was able to humble himself. When he was despondent and in despair, he took courage from the knowledge that "this, too, shall pass."[3]

But if only a vacuum is left after the grief period is over, self-pity will rush in to fill it, and the mourners may find it difficult to resume once again their normal routine and to continue with life. Some practical suggestions follow, therefore, to aid in the healing process.

SOME GENERAL AND PRACTICAL SUGGESTIONS

Keep in Contact

Keep in contact with the mourner by phone or personal visits. Go over to the mourner's home, reminisce, look at old photo albums or home family videos together. Invite the mourner over to your house for a chat and a cup of coffee, for lunch, and so on.

The following story is related about Rabbi Aryeh Levin:

During one *Chol HaMoed* Succos, Reb Aryeh was approached by a rabbi who was curious to know what he was doing in that neighborhood. Reb Aryeh told him that he was going to visit Mrs. Bengis, the widow of the noted scholar and former head of the *Beth Din*, Rabbi Zelig Reuven Bengis.

"Do me a favor," Reb Aryeh continued, "and come with me."

"For what reason?" asked the rabbi.

Reb Aryeh answered the following:

"It is my custom to visit the widows of worthy rabbis on the days of *Chol HaMoed*. The whole year everyone is busy with work and a widow does not feel her loneliness. On *Chol HaMoed*, however, it is different. People are at leisure, and such women surely think back to the good days when their prominent and respected husbands were alive and all the worthy citizens would come to visit them. They must remember how their houses were filled with visitors and the atmosphere was happy and cheerful. And now, what a contrast! They sit alone, forsaken; and the days of *Yom Tov* turn into a time of sadness. How much they must suffer. For this reason I make it a special point, no matter what, to visit these widows specifically during these days, to cheer them up and bring a little happiness into their sorrowful hearts."[4]

Take the Mourner out of the House

Draw the mourner out of the house—go shopping, take walks in the park, visit museums, take short trips. Offer to take him or her to visit relatives, other friends, grandchildren. A little gentle prodding on your part, encouraging him or her to do any of the above and expediting travel arrangements, can fill the day with much pleasure and help take the mourner's mind off grieving.

Discuss the Possibility of a Job

If the mourner is interested in working, discuss the kind of work that could be done. Speak to employment agencies or private individuals who could use the trained skills, or find jobs that could match the talents of the mourner.

Volunteer Work

If the mourner is not interested in seeking formal employment, think of volunteer work that could be done in places such as schools, hospitals, old-age homes, and clubs. There are also so many *chesed* organizations that need help.

These not only encourage the mourner to leave the home of brooding, but allows him or her to make new contacts and friends, and makes him or her feel useful and responsible, giving a renewed purpose in life. Often the mourner is made aware of the troubles of others. In hospital volunteer work, one may become aware of the various illnesses of others and can even begin to focus on one's blessings in life, despite his or her recent bereavement. The famous utterance "I was feeling miserable over the fact I had no shoes, and then I met a man who had no feet" can be translated into a myriad of life's situations.

There is a legend of a sorrowing woman who came to wise man with the heartrending plea that he return to her her only son, whom she had just lost. He told her that he could comply with her request on one condition. She must bring him a mustard seed taken from a home entirely free from sorrow.

The woman set out on her quest. Years elapsed and she did not return. One day the wise man chanced upon her, but he hardly recognized her, for now she looked so radiant. He greeted her and then enquired why she had never kept their appointment.

"Oh," she said, in a tone of voice indicating that she had completely forgotten about it, "well, this is what happened. In search of the seed, I came into homes so burdened with trouble and sorrow that I could not just walk out. Who better than I could understand how heavy was the burden they bore? Who better than I could offer them the sympathy they needed? So I stayed in each home as long as I could be of service. And," she added apologetically, "please do not be angry, but I never again thought about our appointment."[5]

There is a similar legend of how Alexander the Great consoled his own mother when he knew that his death was near. He wrote her the following letter:

"My mother, remember that all earthly things are transitory and that your son was not a small king but a great one. Therefore you are not to bear yourself like the mother of a little king, but like the mother of a great king.

"After my death command a great hall to be built and command furthermore that on a given day all the princes of the empire shall come to the hall and be merry and of good cheer. Proclaim, however, that none is to come who has suffered any ill, for the joy at the feast shall be a pure and perfect joy and shall not be darkened by the thoughts of any concerning any sorrow that befell him."

When her son died, she acted exactly according to his will. She had a magnificent hall built and she named the day on which the princes were to come to the feast.

When the appointed day came she was prepared for many, many people. Not a single soul came. She asked the wise men of the court, "What is the meaning of this? Why do guests not come to this great hall which I have built?"

The answer she received was this: "Dear Queen, you issued the command that none should come who has suffered any grief or any ill. But there is no such human being in the whole world, and therefore there is no guest who could come."

This consoled the mother of the great king. She was not alone in her grief.[6]

Or as another writer put it so beautifully:

Our sorrow can bring understanding as well as pain, breadth as well as the contraction that comes with pain. Out of love and sorrow can come a compassion that endures. The needs of others hitherto unnoticed, the anxieties of neighbors never before realized, now comes into the ken of our experience, for our sorrow has opened our life to the needs of others. A bereavement that brings us into the lives of our fellow-men writes a fitting epilogue to a love that had taught us kindliness and forbearance, and had given us so much joy.

Sorrow can enlarge the domain of our life, so that we may now understand the triviality of the things many pursue. We have in our hands a noble and refined measure for judging the events and objects we daily see. What is important is not luxury but love; not wealth but wisdom; not gold but goodness.

And our sorrow may so clear out our vision that we may, more brightly, see the God, of Whom it was said, "The Lord is nigh unto them that are of a broken heart" (Psalms 34:19). Beyond the hurry and turmoil of life rises the Eternal. There is God in a world in which love like ours could bloom. There is God in a world in which human beings could experience tenderness. There is God in a world in which two lives can be bound together by a tie stronger than death.

Out of that vision will come a sense of obligation. A duty, solemn, sacred and significant, rests upon us. To spread the love we have known to others. To share the joy which has been ours. To ease the pains which man's thoughtlessness or malice inflicts. We have a task to perform. There is work to be done and in work there is consolation.

Out of love may come sorrow. But out of sorrow can come light for others who dwell in darkness. And out of the light we bring to others will come light for ourselves—the light of solace, of strength, of transfiguring and consecrating purpose."[7]

Invitations for Special Times

Invite the mourner [and family] for *Shabbos*, *Yom Tov*, a *seder*, a Purim *seudah*, for Chanukah lighting, to eat in the *succah*, and so on. These times, in particular, can bring sadness to the lonely person who remembers nostalgically these good times that were shared with the deceased.

Help with Decisions

Help the mourner to cope with day-to-day decisions.

What should be done with the deceased's clothes and effects? Help take them out of the house, and give them to a clothe-the-needy charity.

Help them with finances—arranging financial aid, setting up accounts, filling out insurance forms, tax forms, widow benefits, and so on. Many community resources help with these matters. Help find out who they are. Go with the mourner to the consultation if necessary.

Do things need fixing around the house? Is there need for an electrician, a plumber, a carpenter, a painter? Help them choose the right professional.

Study and Play Together

Go over to the house or invite the mourner to your house to study together, to play a game (Scrabble, chess, Ping-Pong). Help them establish a new hobby, such as drawing, painting, gardening, sewing, stamp-collecting. Bring them good books to read or take them to the library.

Shiurim, Study Groups, Lectures

Bring them to *shiurim,* lectures, and study groups. Enroll them in an interesting course in a community center.

Help the Children with Schoolwork

If a young widow is left behind with children, much of the above is applicable to both her and the children. In addition, one can make sure that the children befriend the children of the deceased, play with them, invite them over, take them along on outings and trips, and so on. Perhaps they also need help in doing homework, studying for tests, and generally keeping up with schoolwork.

Ensuring the Livelihood of the Survivors

Perhaps one of the most delicate but the most important help that can be given is in a situation where the widow and family are having financial difficulties. They may be too proud to request help from others, but financial difficulties are hard to bear even under the best of circumstances, certainly when one has been left a widow and has to care for a large family.

Discreetly finding out the situation and, if necessary, approaching others to help contribute to some sort of fund to assist the family is a *mitzvah* of inestimable value.[8]

WHEN GRIEF IS PROBLEMATIC

Many of the problems encountered in unnatural and unhealthy grief are avoided in a situation where the family has a deep religious faith and commitment. The whole Jewish system, from the time of death through the funeral and burial and on through the *shivah*, is a magnificent structure of guidance and assistance to the mourners to enable them to bear their burden of grief in this most trying time of their lives.

It takes into consideration all of the symptons of grief that were mentioned in chapter 4. It encourages full expression of grief, but it gently allows for the various progressions and the eventual weaning away from grieving. It addresses itself so poignantly and sensitively to the loneliness and bewilderment that the mourners experience, and it offers them such strong personal and communal support that is apparent throughout the whole *mitzvah* of *nichum aveilim*.

Yet, there are many situations, and many differing degrees of faith and religious commitment. And there are those who are far removed from any spiritual connection with the supporting structure of our religion, heritage, and culture. We are obligated to show sensitivity and to perform *chesed* to all within our fold.

It is important to be aware, therefore, of the possibility of problems that may be encountered in certain grief situations.

When Is Grief Problematic?*

When grief continues in an intense form a couple of years after death, or when the mourning process is delayed or inhibited for an extended period of time, chances are that the bereaved person's response is problematic and may require professional help. Problematic mourning occurs when the bereaved do not get past the early phases of the mourning process.

Mourning can become problematic when, after a considerable amount of time, there still is:

- A lack of acceptance of the death;
- An avoidance of experiencing the pain of grief;
- A resistance to continuing on with daily living;
- A lack of desire to form new relationships.

People at Risk

If any of the following factors are present in the lives of your friends or relatives who are mourning, be aware that they might be developing an unhealthy grief response. This is not to say that they will definitely have difficulty, but rather that research and clinical findings indicate they are

---

*This section has been reprinted with the kind permission of the Benjamin Family Foundation from their pamphlet *Nichum Aveilim: Comforting the Mourners*, by Dr. Michelle Goodman.

more likely to experience problems. Here are some circumstances that place
an individual at higher risk:

   • The person was highly dependent on the deceased and had invested
all reason for living in them and now lacks a purpose in life;
   • There was no opportunity to anticipate the death;
   • Lack of social or family support and lack of a supportive environ-
ment in which to grieve;
   • Other current or ongoing crises happening before, at the time of,
or following the death;
   • Unresolved previous deaths, especially in early years (e.g., Holo-
caust survivors);
   • Multiple losses in a short period of time;
   • Traumatic deaths: deaths caused by suicide, accidents, homicide,
or self-neglect;
   • The bereaved person's belief that they are responsible in part or
totally for the death;
   • The person is in poor mental and/or physical health and lacks the
stamina to handle grief.

Symptoms of Problematic Mourning

If you suspect that a friend or relative is dealing with their grief in an
unhealthy way, you can confirm this by checking for the following
behaviors:

   • A person cannot speak without experiencing intense and fresh grief
many years after the death;
   • Some relatively minor event triggers off an intense reaction and/or
there is an overreaction to another person's trouble;
   • A person is unwilling to move possessions of the deceased;
   • The bereaved develop physical symptoms similar to those experienced by the deceased person before death or there is evidence of a com-
pulsion to imitate the dead person;
   • Exaggerated grief—excessive depression, anger, or some other fea-
ture usually associated with normal grief manifested in an exaggerated way;
   • A person refuses to believe that someone else can comfort them;
   • Radical changes in lifestyle and in relationships—the person becomes
withdrawn and despite considerable encouragement, does not reestablish
social ties;
   • A person is overactive, does not acknowledge the loss, and is
euphoric—unusually happy;
   • Unusual fears about illness or death develop or the person has increased health-related complaints and develops illness;

• A long history of depression marked by persistent guilt, lowered self-esteem, and self-destuctive impulses.

Finding Professional Help

When helping a bereaved loved one, it is important to recognize when your help is not enough. There are professionals who are trained to help when you cannot. Your role can be one of:

• Recommending to the bereaved that they need professional assistance;
• Convincing them that they are not crazy but that their mental health is at risk if they do not seek help;
• Suggesting the names of professionals who specialize in the area of bereavement; and
• If the bereaved are open to seeking help, assisting them in making arrangements and offering to take them to their first appointment.

Often, people feel that others will stigmatize them as weak and inadequate when they cannot cope with their problems by themselves. They feel that seeking professional help is a sign of failure. If they refuse to seek professional help, try to encourage them to see their rabbi or family physician. If they continue to refuse to see anyone, consult with a professional who can offer suggestions on what to do next. What you may find is that your friend or relative will reach out for help when ready.

Remember, if grief is problematic, professional help is necessary. However, other kinds of help can be beneficial for anyone who is experiencing difficulty in coping. You might encourage friends and relatives to become involved in a support group with others who are in a similar situation. Support groups are helpful in reassuring the bereaved that what they are experiencing is normal and that they are not alone. A visit with a congregational rabbi might help them work through spiritual as well as emotional issues. Seeking professional help is not a sign of weakness but a sign that the bereaved individual is ready and willing to move beyond the pain and would like assistance in doing so.[9]

* * *

"For His anger lasts for only a moment; there is life if He so wills it. In the evening weeping may linger, and come morning—a cry of joy! . . . You have turned my mourning into dancing for me. You have untied my sackcloth and girded me with joy" (Psalms 30).

בִּלַּע הַמָּוֶת לָנֶצַח וּמָחָה ה' אֱלֹקִים דִּמְעָה מֵעַל כָּל־פָּנִים

"God will destroy death forever and will banish tears from all faces" (Isaiah 25:8).

Appendix I

Special Grace after Meals Recited, According to Some Customs, in the Mourner's Home

Before reciting the grace after meals in the mourner's home, some use the following wording if the *zimun* (group response) will be said:

נְבָרֵךְ מְנַחֵם אֲבֵלִים שֶׁאָכַלְנוּ מִשֶּׁלוֹ, 'Let us bless the One Who comforts mourners, [and] of Whose we have eaten.'

According to some customs, especially among Sephardic Jews, the following passages are substituted for the third and fourth blessings. Many authorities write, however, that nowadays the custom is to recite the usual text of the grace after meals.

נַחֵם ה' אֱלֹהֵינוּ, אֶת אֲבֵלֵי יְרוּשָׁלַיִם, וְאֶת הָאֲבֵלִים הַמִּתְאַבְּלִים בָּאֵבֶל הַזֶּה: נַחֲמֵם מֵאֶבְלָם וְשַׂמְּחֵם מִיגוֹנָם, כָּאָמוּר: כְּאִישׁ אֲשֶׁר אִמּוֹ תְּנַחֲמֶנּוּ, כֵּן אָנֹכִי אֲנַחֶמְכֶם וּבִירוּשָׁלַיִם תְּנֻחָמוּ: בָּרוּךְ אַתָּה, ה', מְנַחֵם צִיּוֹן בְּבִנְיַן יְרוּשָׁלָיִם. אָמֵן.

"O comfort, HaShem our God, the mourners of Jerusalem and those who mourn this sad event. Console them from their mourning and gladden them from their grief, as it is said (Isaiah 66:13), 'Like a man whose mother consoles him, so I will console you, and in Jerusalem you will be consoled.' Blessed are You, HaShem, Comforter of Zion through the rebuilding of Jerusalem." "Amein."

בָּרוּךְ אַתָּה ה' אֱלֹהֵינוּ מֶלֶךְ הָעוֹלָם, הָאֵל, אָבִינוּ מַלְכֵּנוּ, אַדִּירֵנוּ, בּוֹרְאֵנוּ, גּוֹאֲלֵנוּ, יוֹצְרֵנוּ, קְדוֹשֵׁנוּ, קְדוֹשׁ יַעֲקֹב, רוֹעֵנוּ רוֹעֵה יִשְׂרָאֵל, הַמֶּלֶךְ הַטּוֹב וְהַמֵּטִיב לַכֹּל, שֶׁבְּכָל יוֹם וָיוֹם הוּא הֵיטִיב, הוּא מֵטִיב,

הוּא יֵיטִיב לָנוּ. הַמֶּלֶךְ הַחַי, הַטּוֹב וְהַמֵּטִיב, אֵל אֱמֶת, דַּיַּן אֱמֶת, שׁוֹפֵט בְּצֶדֶק, לוֹקֵחַ נְפָשׁוֹת בְּמִשְׁפָּט, וְשַׁלִּיט בְּעוֹלָמוֹ לַעֲשׂוֹת בּוֹ כִּרְצוֹנוֹ. כִּי כָל דְּרָכָיו בְּמִשְׁפָּט, וַאֲנַחְנוּ עַמּוֹ וַעֲבָדָיו. וְעַל הַכֹּל אֲנַחְנוּ חַיָּבִים לְהוֹדוֹת לוֹ וּלְבָרְכוֹ. גּוֹדֵר פִּרְצוֹת יִשְׂרָאֵל, הוּא יִגְדּוֹר אֶת הַפִּרְצָה הַזֹּאת, מֵעָלֵינוּ וּמֵעַל הָאָבֵל הַזֶּה, לְחַיִּים וּלְשָׁלוֹם וְכָל טוֹב וּמִכָּל טוֹב לְעוֹלָם אַל יְחַסְּרֵנוּ.

'Blessed are You, HaShem our God, King of the Universe, the Almighty, our Father, our King, our Sovereign, our Creator, our Redeemer, our Maker, our Holy One, Holy One of Jacob, our Shepherd, the Shepherd of Israel, the good and beneficent King, for every single day He did good, does good, and will do good to us. He is the living King, Who is good and Who does good for all, God of truth, Judge of truth, Who judges with righteousness, Who takes souls with justice, Who rules His universe to do with it as He wishes, for all His ways are with justice and we are His nation and His servants. For everything we are obliged to thank Him and to bless Him. He Who repairs the breaches of Israel, may He repair this breach from us and from this mourner for life, for peace, and for all good; and of all good things may he never deprive us.'

Appendix II

Studying Tractates of *Mishnah*

It brings great merit to the soul when tractates of *Mishnah* are studied in honor of the deceased. (See pages 78-79.) The following chart may be reproduced and used for filling in names of those who volunteer to learn the tractates.

לעילוי נשמת _____

לסיים בלי נדר עד: יום השלשים _____ יום היארצייט _____

לכל המשתתפים: נא למלאות את השם והכתובת
כדי שנוכל להמציא לו תזכיר על מה שקיבל.

מועד

_____	שבת	(כד)
_____	עירובין	(י)
_____	פסחים	(י)
_____	שקלים	(ח)
_____	יומא	(ח)
_____	סוכה	(ה)
_____	ביצה	(ה)
_____	ר"ה	(ד)
_____	תענית	(ד)
_____	מגילה	(ד)
_____	מו"ק	(ג)
_____	חגיגה	(ג)

זרעים (סכום הפרקים)   השם

_____	(ט)	ברכות
_____	(ח)	פאה
_____	(ז)	דמאי
_____	(ט)	כלאים
_____	(י)	שביעית
_____	(יא)	תרומות
_____	(ה)	מעשרות
_____	(ה)	מע"ש
_____	(ד)	חלה
_____	(ג)	ערלה
_____	(ד)	ביכורים

נשים

יבמות (טז) _____
_____

כתובות (יג) _____
נדרים (יא) _____
נזיר (ט) _____
סוטה (ט) _____
גיטין (ט) _____
קידושין (ד) _____

נזיקין (סכום הפרקים)   השם

ב״ק (י) _____
ב״מ (י) _____
ב״ב (י) _____
סנהדרין (יא) _____
מכות (ג) _____
שבועות (ח) _____
עדיות (ח) _____
ע״ז (ה) _____
אבות (ה) _____
הוריות (ג) _____

קדשים

זבחים (יד) _____
מנחות (יג) _____
חולין (יב) _____

בכורות (ט) _____
ערכין (ט) _____
תמורה (ז) _____
כריתות (ו) _____
מעילה (ו) _____
תמיד (ז) _____
מדות (ה) _____
קנים (ג) _____

טהרות

כלים (ל) _____
_____
_____

אהלות (יח) _____
_____

נגעים (יד) _____
פרה (יב) _____
טהרות (י) _____
מקואות (י) _____
נדה (י) _____
מכשירין (ו) _____
זבים (ה) _____
טבול יום (ד) _____
ידים (ד) _____
עוקצים (ג) _____

Appendix III

Mishna L'Neshoma

משנה לנשמה

A Rov of the last generation told a group of his *talmidim* and relatives, shortly before he passed away. "As long as I was alive, I tried to avoid asking for assistance from anyone. Soon, however, I will need your help. Please send me packages." The "packages" to which he referred were of a spiritual nature — a gift which allows the *niftar* (deceased) to constantly progress to more elevated heights in the World-to-Come. These "packages" come in the form of Torah and *mitzvos* which are performed for the merit of the *niftar*.

It has long been the accepted custom in *Klal Yisroel* to study *Mishnayos* for the *Neshoma* (soul) of the *niftar*. The word *Mishna* — משנה — contains the same Hebrew letters as "*Neshama*" — נשמה, which hints at the profound spiritual effects and priceless treasure which a *Neshoma* attains through study of *Mishnayos*. That so much can be accomplished by so small an expenditure, is truly incredible.

Toward this end, a service called *Mishna L'Neshoma* has been established to provide this enduring *Chesed-shel-Emes* to a *niftar*, by supplying the items enumerated below to anyone requesting them, so that the learning of *Mishnayos* proceeds smoothly.

*   *   *

The following are available free upon request:

a) *Mishnayos* Card — to be placed in the home of the mourner or in the *Bais Hamedrosh* of the *niftar*, etc., for relatives and acquaintances to be able to sign up to learn specific *Masechtos*. The card has space for entering addresses of participants, so that contact can be made with the participants in matters relating to the learning of the *Mishnayos*, *Siyum*, etc.

b) 65 cards with the *T'filah* (prayer) to be said after the *Mishnayos* learning, one to be given to each participant.

c) 65 reminder cards to be mailed to participants.

*   *   *

If there is a niftar for whom no one is learning Mishnayos, we will be more than happy to learn Mishnayos for the niftar, on the Yahrtzeit date. Just send us his/her name and his/her father's name (i.e., Avrohom ben Yaakov, Avrohom being the niftar and Yaakov his father), and the day of the Yahrtzeit-Hebrew date. If Hebrew date is unknown, send English date and year, indicating time of death — daytime or night-time. Send this information to the address below.

*   *   *

Note: Full permission is granted to anyone who wishes to duplicate any of the items provided by the service. For further information, or if you wish to volunteer to have *Mishnayos* cards picked up from your home contact us.

*   *   *

Mishna L'Neshoma was established to perpetuate the memory of Reb Dovid Mayer Barnetzky, zt'l, who, throughout his short lifetime, selflessly extended himself to others with all types of *Chasodim shel Emes*.

Mishna L'Neshoma, 421-6th Street, Lakewood, NJ 08701. Tel: (201) 363-3302

MISHNAYOS CARDS CAN BE OBTAINED FROM:

CALIFORNIA:
LOS ANGELES . . . . (213) 651-5672
SAN FRANCISCO . . . . (DAY) (415) 752-7333
(EVE) (415) 665-8779

COLORADO:
DENVER . . . . (303) 573-0471
WEST HARTFORD . . . . (DAY) (203) 722-6815
(EVE) (203) 523-1888

FLORIDA:
NORTH MIAMI . . . . (305) 651-2747

GEORGIA:
ATLANTA . . . . (404) 633-0551

ILLINOIS:
CHICAGO . . . . (312) 267-0980

MARYLAND:
BALTIMORE . . . . (301) 764-6020

MASSACHUSETTS:
WORCESTER . . . . (508) 754-3681

MICHIGAN:
OAK PARK . . . . (313) 542-9243

MINNESOTA:
ST. PAUL . . . . (612) 698-3858

NEW JERSEY:
DEAL . . . . (201) 229-7108
LAKEWOOD . . . . (201) 363-2476

NEW YORK:
BORO PARK . . . . (718) 436-4067
CROWN HEIGHTS . . . . (718) 774-0741 / 1840
EAST SIDE . . . . , ... (212) 982-2330
FLATBUSH . . . . (718) 376-9078
FOREST HILLS . . . . (718) 699-4033
KEW GARDENS . . . . (718) 805-2246
LONG BEACH . . . . (516) 432-4928
MONSEY-SPRING VALLEY . . . . . . (914) 356-4841
STATEN ISLAND . . . . (718) 494-1487
WILLIAMSBURG . . . . (718) 384-4867

OHIO:
CINCINNATI . . . . (513) 761-0329
WICKLIFFE . . . . (216) 943-3895

PENNSYLVANIA:
MCKEESPORT . . . . (412) 678-2264
PHILADELPHIA . . . . (215) 742-6231
PITTSBURGH . . . . (412) 421-8996
SCRANTON . . . . (DAY) (717) 346-1747
(EVE) (717) 346-3948

TENNESSEE:
MEMPHIS . . . . (901) 683-7485
NASHVILLE . . . . (615) 292-6614

TEXAS:
DALLAS . . . . (214) 239-7248

VIRGINIA:
RICHMOND . . . . (804) 740-2000

WISCONSIN:
MILWAUKEE . . . . (414) 444-5733

CANADA:
MONTREAL . . . . (514) 738-6126
TORONTO . . . . (416) 783-5773

Appendix IV

Prayer for the Deceased after the Study of *Mishnah*

לימוד משניות מסכת _____

_____ לעילוי נשמת _____

_____ יום היארצייט _____ לסיים בלי נדר עד: יום השלשים _____

תפלה על הנפטר אחר תלמוד

אָנָּא ה' מָלֵא רַחֲמִים אֲשֶׁר בְּיָדְךָ נֶפֶשׁ כָּל חַי וְרוּחַ כָּל בְּשַׂר אִישׁ יִהְיֶה נָא לְרָצוֹן לְפָנֶיךָ תּוֹרָתֵנוּ וּתְפִלָּתֵנוּ בַּעֲבוּר נִשְׁמַת _____ וּגְמֹל נָא עִמָּה בְּחַסְדְּךָ הַגָּדוֹל לִפְאֹחַ לָהּ שַׁעֲרֵי רַחֲמִים וָחֶסֶד וְשַׁעֲרֵי גַן־עֵדֶן וִּתְקַבֵּל אוֹתָהּ בְּאַהֲבָה וּבְחִבָּה וְשָׁלַח לָהּ מַלְאָכֶיךָ הַקְּדוֹשִׁים וְהַטְהוֹרִים לְהוֹלִיכָהּ וּלְהוֹשִׁיבָהּ תַּחַת עֵץ הַחַיִּים אֵצֶל נִשְׁמוֹת הַצַּדִּיקִים וְהַצִּדְקָנִיּוֹת חֲסִידִים וַחֲסִידוֹת לֵהָנוֹת מִזִּיו שְׁכִינָתֶךָ לְהַשְׂבִּיעָהּ מְטּוּבְךָ הַצָּפוּן לַצַּדִּיקִים, וְהַגּוּף יָנוּחַ בַּקֶּבֶר בִּמְנוּחָה נְכוֹנָה בְּחֶדְוָה וּבְשִׂמְחָה וְשָׁלוֹם כְּדִכְתִיב יָבֹא שָׁלוֹם יָנוּחוּ עַל מִשְׁכְּבוֹתָם הוֹלֵךְ נְכוֹחוֹ,וּכְתִיב יַעְלְזוּ חֲסִידִים בְּכָבוֹד יְרַנְּנוּ עַל מִשְׁכְּבוֹתָם,וּכְתִיב אִם־תִּשְׁכַּב לֹא תִפְחָד וְשָׁכַבְתָּ וְעָרְבָה שְׁנָתֶךָ. וְתִשָּׁמֵר אוֹתוֹ (לנקבה אוֹתָהּ) מֵחִבּוּט הַקֶּבֶר וּמֵרִמָּה וְתוֹלֵעָה. וְתִסְלַח וְתִמְחֹל לוֹ עַל כָּל פְּשָׁעָיו (לנקבה לָהּ עַל כָּל פְּשָׁעֶיהָ) כִּי אָדָם אֵין צַדִּיק בָּאָרֶץ אֲשֶׁר יַעֲשֶׂה טוֹב וְלֹא יֶחֱטָא. וְזָכֹר לוֹ זְכֻיּוֹתָיו וְצִדְקוֹתָיו אֲשֶׁר עָשָׂה (לנקבה לָהּ זְכֻיּוֹתֶיהָ וְצִדְקוֹתֶיהָ אֲשֶׁר עָשְׂתָה) וְתַשְׁפַּע צ לוֹ מִנִּשְׁמָתוֹ לְדַשֵּׁן עַצְמוֹתָיו (לנקבה לָהּ מִנִּשְׁמָתָה לְדַשֵּׁן עַצְמוֹתֶיהָ) בַּקֶּבֶר מֵרֹב טוֹב הַצָּפוּן לַצַּדִּיקִים דִּכְתִיב מָה רַב טוּבְךָ אֲשֶׁר צָפַנְתָּ לִּירֵאֶיךָ, וּכְתִיב שׁוֹמֵר כָּל עַצְמוֹתָיו אַחַת מֵהֵנָּה לֹא נִשְׁבָּרָה. וְיִשְׁכֹּן (לנקבה וְתִשְׁכֹּן) בֶּטַח בָּדָד וְשַׁאֲנַן מִפַּחַד רָעָה וְאַל יִרְאֶה (לנקבה תִרְאֶה) פְּנֵי גֵיהִנָּם וְנִשְׁמָתוֹ (לנקבה וְנִשְׁמָתָהּ) תְּהֵא צְרוּרָה בִּצְרוֹר הַחַיִּים וּלְהַחֲיוֹתוֹ (לנקבה וּלְהַחֲיוֹתָהּ) בִּתְחִיַּת הַמֵּתִים עִם כָּל מֵתֵי עַמְּךָ יִשְׂרָאֵל בְּרַחֲמִים אָמֵן

Notes

Note: Several sources quoted throughout the book refer more directly to the *mitzvah* of *bikkur cholim* (visiting the sick). Based on *Rambam, Mishneh Torah, Hilchos Aveil* 14:7, citations have been used where appropriate *a fortiori* to the laws of *nichum aveilim* (comforting the mourner). See also Rabbi Moshe Stern, *Responsa Be'er Moshe* (New York, 1975), vol. 4, no. 107; Rabbi Yaakov Breisch, *Responsa Chelkas Yaakov* (Bnei Brak, 1966), vol. 3, no. 38, and others.

INTRODUCTION

1. See *Megillah* 16b.
2. See Rashi ad loc.

CHAPTER 1

1. *Breishis Rabbah* 8; *Yalkut Shimoni, Tehillim,* 834.
2. *Sotah* 14a.
3. *Devarim* 13:5, 28:9, and *Sotah* 14a.
4. A rule of logic meaning with yet stronger reasoning; more conclusively.
5. *Vayikra* 19:18. See also *Bamidbar* 16:29 and *Nedarim* 39b. Cf. also *Rashi, Tosfos, Nimukei Yosef,* and *Shittah Mekubetzes–Nedarim* 39b.
6. *Sifra, Kedoshim.*
7. *Shabbos* 31a.

8. *Rambam, Mishneh Torah, Hilchos Aveil* 14:1.

9. See Rabbi Yisrael Berger, *Sefer Eser Tzichtzachus* (Pietrikow, 1910), p. 52, quoted in Rabbi Zelig Pliskin, *Love Your Neighbor* (New York, 1977), p. 306; Meir Meisels, *Judaism Thought and Legend* (Kfar Chabad, n.d.), p. 15, in name of *Hasidic Tales*.

10. *Michah* 6:8.

11. Rabbi Yisrael Meir Kagan, *Sefer Ahavas Chesed* (Warsaw, 1888), pt. 2, chap. 1.

12. *Hoshea* 6:6.

13. *Yalkut Shimoni, Hoshea,* 522.

14. *Tehillim* 89:3.

15. *Hoshea* 10:12.

16. *Succah* 49b.

17. *Succah* 49b; *Pe'ah* 1:1.

18. *Pirkei Avos* 1:2.

19. *Yevamos* 79a.

20. *Kesubos* 8b.

21. See p. 11, this volume.

22. Rabbi Moshe Yechiel Epstein, *Be'er Moshe* (Jerusalem: Ho'Ivri Publishing, 1966), *Shemos*, p. 521, 16.

23. *Shemos* 18:20.

24. *Bava Metzia* 30b.

25. *Kiddushin* 2b. See also *Mechilta, Shemos* 18:20.

26. *Sotah* 4a.

27. Rabbi Kagan, *Sefer Ahavas Chesed,* pt. 2, chap. 12.

28. Rabbi Isaiah Horowitz, *Shnei Luchos HaBris* (Amsterdam, 1649), end of tractate *Pesachim.*

29. See Rabbi Yisrael Meir Kagan, *Shemiras HaLashon* (New York: A. Y. Friedman, 1952), gate 1, chap. 2. See *Zohar, Parshas Emor.*

30. *Avos d'Rabbi Nosson* 16:5.

31. *Pirkei d'Rabbi Eliezer,* chap. 17. See also tractate *Sofrim,* end of chap. 19.

CHAPTER 2

1. *Rambam, Mishneh Torah, Hilchos Aveil* 14:1; *Meiri, Nedarim* 39b; *Rashi, Sanhedrin* 70b. See also *Rambam, Sefer HaMitzvos, Shoresh Sheni* (Constantinople, 1510; Warsaw, 1871; Jerusalem: Pardes Publishers, n.d.), Rabbi Moshe Stern, *Responsa Be'er Moshe* (New York, 1962), vol. 2, no. 104; Rabbi Yisrael Landau, *Responsa Beis Yisrael* (New York, 1976), *Yoreh De'ah,* no. 138; Rabbi Avraham Freolich, *Sheroshim b'Semochos* (Jerusalem, 1980), *shoresh* 10. See also Rabbi Chaim Bernstein, *Yakra d'Chaya* (Bnei Brak, 1979), pp. 11-12, that really all *Rishonim* and *Acharonim* agree that there is also a *mitzvah d'Oraisa* involved in *nichum aveilim.* See also Rabbi Yissachar Frand, *Oholei Yissachar* (Baltimore, 1986), pp. 135-139.

2. Cf. Rabbi Shimon Kaira *Baal Hilchos Gedolos* (Venice, 1548; Jerusalem, 1972), positive *mitzvos,* 36; *Ramban,* commentary to *Sefer HaMitzvos, shoresh* 1, response 3; *Rabbeinu Yonah, Berachos,* chap. 3, on the *Mishnah* (17b); Rabbi

Yitzchak of Corbeil, *Sefer Mitzvos Kattan* (Constantinople, 1510), 47; Rabbi Eliezer of Metz, *Yereim* (Venice, 1565), 219; Rav Achai Gaon, *Sheiltos* (Venice, 1546), 93; Rabbi Chaim Medini, *Sdei Chemed* (Warsaw, 1890), vol. 1, *Maareches habeis*, 116; Rabbi Chaim Palagi, *Responsa Chikekei Lev* (Salonica, 1840-1849), vol.1, no. 17; Rabbi Abraham Steinberg, *Responsa Machazeh Avraham* (New York, 1972), *Yoreh De'ah*, no. 14; Rabbi Eliezer Valdenberg, *Ramat Rachel* (Jerusalem, 1984), no. 2. See also Rabbi Tzvi Chajes, *Maharitz Chiyus, Nedarim*, 39; Rabbi Yosef Shaul Nathanson, *Responsa Sho'eil uMeishiv* (New York, 1954), vol. 1, *Mahadura* 3, no. 244. See also Rabbi Bernstein, *Yakra d'Chaya*, pp. 11-12.

3. See chap. 1, n. 3.

4. *Breishis* 25:11 and *Rashi*; *Sotah* 14a.

5. *Breishis* 35:9 and *Rashi*.

6. *Shemos* 18:20.

7. *Bava Metzia* 30b.

8. *Shemos* 18:20 and *Bava Metzia*, ibid.; *Rambam, Mishneh Torah, Aveil*, chap.14; *Pirkei d'Rabbi Eliezer*, chap.17; Rabbi Yitzchak Abohab, *Menoras HaMa'or* (Constantinople, 1514), *Ner* 3, *k'lal* 8, *chelek* 2, chap. 2; Rabbi Yisrael Kagan, *Ahavas Chesed*, pt. 3, chap. 3. Cf. Rabbi Chaim Shapira, *Divrei Torah* (Munkacz, 1922), vol. 3, no. 100.

9. See Rabbi Eliezer Papo, *Peleh Yo'eitz* (Constantinople, 1825), vol. 2, *Nechamah*, p. 25b. See also Rabbi Zelig Pliskin, *Love Your Neighbor* (New York, 1977), pp. 114-116, for many stories of the rabbis in this respect.

10. Rabbi Yitzchak Blauser, *Or Yisrael*, p. 112.

11. *Taanis* 22a.

12. See Rabbi Horowitz, *Shaloh HaKadosh*.

13. *Devarim* 22:2.

14. *Bava Kamma* 81b; *Sanhedrin* 73a; *Bartenurah, Nedarim*, chap. 4:4.

15. Cf. *Bava Metzia, Mishnah*, 33a. Also, see story on page 111, this volume.

16. *Mishnah, Pe'ah* 1:1; *Shabbos* 127a-b.

17. Rabbi Sharya Deblitzky, *Zichron Betzalel* (Bnei Brak, 1977), p. 118, from *Rambam, Mishneh Torah, Aveil* 13:2, and from *Shach, Yoreh De'ah* 340:51; Rabbi Gershon Marber, *Darkei HaChaim* (Lublin, 1927), chap. 4, 2. Cf. *Shulchan Aruch, Yoreh De'ah* 335:2. See later, p. 41.

18. *Shulchan Aruch, Yoreh De'ah* (loc. cit.). See later, p. 41, that when the mourner indicates he no longer appreciates the visit, the visitor must leave—*Moed Kattan* 27b; *Shulchan Aruch, Yoreh De'ah* 376:1.

19. Rabbi Shlomo Ibn Aderes, *Responsa Rashba* (Bologna, 1539), vol. 1, no. 18. Cf. Rabbi Malkiel Tennenbaum, *Responsa Divrei Malkiel* (Jerusalem, 1987), vol. 3, no. 6; Rabbi Isaac Sternhell, *Responsa Kochavei Yitzchak* (New York, 1969), vol. 1, no. 2; Rabbi Yosef Schwartz, *Ginzei Yosef* (Oradea, 1930), no. 50, 3.

20. Rabbi Binyamin ben Mattisyahu, *Responsa Binyamin Ze'ev* (Venice, 1539), vol. 1, no. 169.

21. Rabbi Yitzchak of Vienna, *Or Zarua* (Jerusalem, 1867), Laws of *Birchas HaMotzi*, vol. 1, 140.

22. Rabbi Yitzchak Lampronti, *Pachad Yitzchak* (Bnei Brak, n.d.), *erech nichum*, in name of Raavad. See also Rabbi Chaim Tzvi Hollander, *Sefer Zevach Mishpachah* (Chicago, 1976), p. 138, for other possible reasons.

23. See Rabbi Aaron Levine, *Zichron Meir al Aveilus* (Toronto: Zichron Meir, 1985), vol. 1, pp. 99-100, and n. 127.

24. See *Yalkut Shimoni, Koheles,* 973; *Rambam, Mishneh Torah, Hilchos Aveil,* chap. 14, 7; See Rabbi Avraham de Boton, *Lechem Mishneh,* and Rabbi Yosef Caro, *Kesef Mishneh* (ad loc.), that this would mean after the *chuppah* (and *chasunah*) so it would refer to attending *Sheva Brachos* or being *menachem aveil.*

25. *Mishnah, Pe'ah* 1:1; *Shabbos* 127a.

26. *Tanna d'Bei Eliyahu Rabbah.*

27. *Sifri, Parshas Ki-Seitzei.*

28. *Pirkei d'Rabbi Eliezer,* chap. 33.

29. Rabbi Meir of Rothenburg, *Responsa Maharam m'Rothenberg* (Cremona, 1557), cited in Rabbi Sholom Cherniak, *Mishmeres Shalom* (Warsaw, 1928), letter *tzaddi,* 10. Cf. Rabbi Dovid Assaf, *Yalkut Dos v'Din* (Palestine, 1944), p. 87.

30. *Shulchan Aruch, Yoreh De'ah* 247:4.

31. *Vayikra Rabbah* 34.

32. *Pirkei d'Rabbi Eliezer,* chap. 17.

33. *Koheles Rabbah* 7, *Tinyana,* 4.

34. Ibid., *Tinyana* 5.

35. Rabbi Shimon Frankfurter, *Sefer HaChaim* (Amsterdam, 1703), p. 246.

CHAPTER 3

1. *Koheles* 7:2. See also *Alshich* quoted in Rabbi Avraham Sperling, *Taamei HaMinhagim u'Mekorei HaDinim* (Lvov, 1896), p. 414; Rabbi Moses Isserles, *Remoh, Yoreh De'ah* 403:10.

2. *Koheles* 7:4.

3. *Sefer Histalkut HaNefesh.*

4. *Zohar, Parshas Vayechi,* p. 223b.

5. *Pirkei Avos* 4:22.

6. *Kesuvos* 8b.

7. *Breishis* 3:19.

8. *Pirkei Avos* 4:16.

9. Rabbi Yechiel Michel Tuchachinsky, *Gesher HaChaim* (Jerusalem, 1947), vol. 3, chap. 1, pp. 5-6). See Rabbi Maurice Lamm, *The Jewish Way in Death and Mourning* (New York: Jonathan David, 1969), pp. 222-224.

10. *Midrash Tanchuma, Parshas Pekudei,* 3. See also *Niddah* 16b.

11. Attributed to Colonel David "Mickey" Marcus, cited in William B. Silverman and Kenneth M. Cinnamon, *When Mourning Comes* (Northvale, NJ: Jason Aronson, 1990), beginning of book.

12. *Yom Kippur Machzor,* evening *piyut.*

13. *Devarim* 32:39.

14. *Moed Kattan* 27b.

15. Rabbi Aaron Berechiah, *Maavar Yabok, Sifsei Renanos* (Mantua, 1626), chap. 19.

16. *Shabbos* 151b.

17. Isaiah 25:8.

CHAPTER 4

1. A list of books on this subject has been included in the bibliography.

2. *Pirkei Avos* 5:22.

3. *Eichah Rabbah*, chap. 2, 13.

4. Geoffrey Gorer, *Death, Grief, and Mourning in Contemporary Britain* (London: Cresset, 1965), p. 113.

5. Jack D. Spiro, *A Time to Mourn* (New York: Bloch, 1985), pp. 145-146.

6. *Sanhedrin* 46b.

7. *Berachos* 58a.

8. Sol L. Nemzoff, *Understanding Bereavement and Grief*, ed. Norman Linzer (New York: Yeshiva University Press, 1977), p. 36.

9. Alfred Weiner, *Understanding Bereavement and Grief*, op. cit., p. 42.

10. Eric Lindenmann, "The Symptomatology and Management of Acute Grief," *American Journal of Psychiatry* 101 (1944): 141-148.

11. See later, p. 154, for the legend of King Solomon. Cf. also *Berachos* 58b and *Moed Kattan* 8b.

12. Rabbi Samson Raphael Hirsch, *Horeb* (London: Soncino Press, 1962), vol. 1, pp. 204-205.

13. See also chapter 8, pp. 72-73, and chapter 9, p. 88, regarding the "private *shivah*."

14. Gorer, *Death, Grief, and Mourning in Contemporary Britain*, ibid.

15. Colin Murray Parkes, *Bereavement* (New York: International University Press, 1965), p. 159.

16. Gorer, *Death, Grief, and Mourning in Contemporary Britain*, op. cit., p. 123.

CHAPTER 5

1. *Pirkei Avos* 4:18. *Rashi* explains because in his time of sorrow he will not accept words of comfort. *Rabbeinu Yonah* goes further and explains that words of comfort offered at such a time may anger the mourner and cause him to utter inappropriate responses.

2. Rabbi Nissim Ashkenazi, *Responsa Maasei Avraham* (Smyrna, 1855), no. 60.

3. Simcha Raz, *A Tzaddik in Our Time* (Jerusalem: Feldheim, 1976), p. 180.

4. See Rabbi Aaron Levine, *Zichron Meir al Aveilus* (Toronto: Zichron Meir, 1985), vol. 1, pp. 320-322.

5. See Rabbi Yekutiel Greenwald, *Kol Bo al Aveilus* (New York: Feldheim, 1973), p. 262, 11.

6. See chapter 6, this volume.

7. See Rabbi Eliezer Deutsch, *Responsa Duda'ei HaSadeh* (Satmar, 1929), no. 47, and many other *poskim*.

8. See p. 78, this volume.

9. See p. 78, this volume.

10. See Levine, *Zichron Meir al Aveilus*, vol. 1, p. 167 n. 54; p. 397 n. 26a.

11. See Rabbi Maurice Lamm, *The Jewish Way of Death and Mourning* (New York: Jonathan David, 1969), pp. 26-35.

12. See Levine, *Zichron Meir al Aveilus*, pp. 389-390.

13. Ibid., pp. 445-446. See later, pp. 141.

14. Ibid., p. 452.

15. See chapter 6.

16. Rabbi Shlomo Kluger, *Responsa Tuv Taam v'Daas* (Podgorza, 1900), *Mahadura* 3, vol. 2, no. 239.

17. Rabbi Tuchachinsky, *Gesher HaChaim*, vol. 1, p. 209, in footnote; Rabbi Aharon Rotter, *Shaarei Aharon* (Bnei Brak, 1968), p. 82.

18. Rabbi Sholom Cherniak, *Mishmeres Shalom* (Warsaw, 1928) citing *Daas u'Mezimah* from *Vayikra Rabbah* (see *Yedei Moshe*); Rabbi Sholom Schwadron, *Daas Torah* (Jerusalem: Machon Daas Torah, 1980), *Yoreh De'ah* 376, citing *Midrash Tanchuma, Parshas Mikeitz*. See also Rabbi Tuchachinsky, *Gesher HaChaim,* vol. 1, p. 209, note.

19. See p. 72, this volume.

20. See chapter 8, nn. 12 and 13, this volume.

21. Rabbi Abraham Lipshitz, *Yalkut Avraham* (Munkacz, 1931), *Yoreh De'ah* 376, p. 118; Rabbi Wolf Leiter, *Responsa Beis Dovid* (Vienna, 1932), no. 6.

22. See *Kesubos* 8b; *Rambam, Mishneh Torah, Hilchos Aveil*, chap. 13, 5; Rabbi Yaakov Moelin, *Responsa Maharil* (Venice, 1549), no. 23; Rabbi Lipshitz, *Yalkut Avraham*, op. cit.

23. Rabbi Tuchachinsky, *Gesher HaChaim*, op. cit., and p. 210; Rabbi Schwadron, *Daas Torah*, op. cit.; Rabbi Avraham Yaffe-Schlesinger, *Responsa Be'er Sarim* (Jerusalem, 1986), vol. 3, no. 75; Rabbi Rotter, *Shaarei Aharon*, p. 82, in the name of Steipler Gaon; Rabbi Gavriel Zinner, *Nitei Gavriel* (New York, 1993), p. 372, n. 5, citing *Minhagei Chazon Ish*.

24. Rabbi Zinner, *Nitei Gavriel*, p. 372, 2.

25. Rabbi Chaim Binyamin Goldberg, *Pnei Baruch* (Jerusalem, 1986), p. 126, end of n. 11; Rabbis Nissim and Chaim Rabi, *Yakra d'Chaya* (Jerusalem, 1980), p. 64, in name of Rabbi S. Dablitsky.

26. Cf. Rabbi Yaakov Culi, *Yalkut Me'Am Loez* (Constantinople, 1733), *Parshas Vayeira*; Rabbi Yosef Yuspa Nordlinger Hahn, *Yosef Ometz* (Frankfurt am Main, 1723), p. 329; Rabbi Zinner, *Nitei Gavriel ,* p. 366, 3.

27. Raz, *A Tzaddik in Our Time*, p. 173.

28. Rabbi Tuchachinsky, *Gesher HaChaim,* vol. 1, p. 210.

29. Rabbi Aaron Berechiah of Modena, *Maavar Yabok* (Mantua, 1626), sec. *Imrei Noam*, chap. 37. See also sources quoted on p. 192 n. 44; Rabbi Tzidkiyah ben Avraham HaRofei, *Shibolei HaLeket* (Venice, 1546), *Semochos* 20. See also p. 87, this volume.

30. See also p. 76, this volume, regarding the custom of waiting for the mourner to initiate the conversation.

31. The reason for those who deter a night visit seems to be based on *Maavar Yabok*, op. cit., chap. 35, who writes that stern judgments are called upon mourners at night. But almost universally there are no objections in the *Poskim* to a night visit. See Rabbi Schwartz, *Responsa Ginzei Yosef*, 72; Rabbi Yosef Schwartz, *VaYelaket Yosef* (Munkacz, 1899-1917), vol. 12, no. 180; Rabbi Tuchachinsky, *Gesher*

HaChaim, p. 209. Rabbi Greenwald, *Kol Bo al Aveilus*, p. 297, also points out that in Job 2:13 we find that he was visited at night, too, and we learn numerous laws of mourning from Job.

32. *Moed Kattan* 27b; *Shulchan Aruch, Yoreh De'ah* 376:1.

33. See above chapter 2, n. 17. See also *Imrei Emes Likutim* that the Gerrer Rebbe used to visit the mourner every day (cited in Rabbi Zinner, *Nitei Gavriel*, p. 366 n. 3).

34. Rabbi Herbert C. Dobrinsky, *A Treasury of Sephardic Laws and Customs* (New York: Ktav/Yeshiva University Press, 1986), p. 73.

35. Rabbi Zinner, *Nitei Gavriel*, op. cit.

36. Rabbi Moshe Rivkes, *Be'er HaGolah* (Amsterdam, 1662), *Yoreh De'ah* 393.10, Rabbi Meir Eisenstadt, *Responsa Panim Meiros* (Amsterdam, 1715), vol. 2, nos. 40 and 124; Rabbi Tuchachinsky, *Gesher HaChaim*, p. 209, 3.

37. Rabbi Avraham Tzvi Hirsch Eisenstadt, *Pischei Teshuvah* (gloss to *Shulchan Aruch*), *Yoreh De'ah* 400.1, citing Rabbi Shmuel Segal Landau, *Responsa Shivas Tziyon* (Prague, 1787), no. 60; Rabbi Yisrael Landau, *Responsa Beis Yisrael* (New York, 1976), *Yoreh De'ah*, no. 139.

38. See chapter 1, this volume. Also see Rabbi Rivkes, *Be'er HaGolah*, loc. cit.

39. Rabbi Yosef Yuspa Nordlinger Hahn, *Yosef Ometz*, p. 330.

40. Rabbi Landau, *Responsa Beis Yisrael*, op. cit.

41. Rabbi Yisrael Meir Kagan, *Mishnah Berurah* (Warsaw, 1892-1898), *Orach Chaim* 548, 25, citing Rabbi Yosef Teomom, *Pri Megadim* (gloss to *Shulchan Aruch*). See also Rabbi Greenwald, *Kol Bo al Aveilus*, p. 298, for further clarification.

42. See Rabbi Greenwald, *Kol Bo al Aveilus*, ibid.; Rabbi Tuchachinsky, *Gesher HaChaim*, p. 259, 5; Rabbi Eisenstadt, *Responsa Panim Meiros*, vol. 2, 40.

43. Rabbi David ben Samuel HaLevi, *Turei Zahav* (gloss to *Shulchan Aruch*), *Orach Chaim* 696, 2; Rabbi Yehuda Ashkenazi, *Be'er Hetev* (gloss to *Shulchan Aruch*), *Orach Chaim* 696, 8; Rabbi Chaim Margolis, *Shaarei Teshuvah* (gloss to *Shulchan Aruch*), *Orach Chaim* 696, 6. Regarding *Shushan Purim*, see *Shaarei Teshuvah* 696, 9. See also Rabbi Chaim Elazar Shapira, *Nimukei Orach Chaim* (Tyrnau, 1930), 696.

44. Rabbi Landau, *Responsa Beis Yisrael*, nos. 139 and 150.

45. See Rabbi Kagan, *Mishnah Berurah, Orach Chaim* 287, 3, citing *Pri Megadim, Eishel Avraham*. The *Mishnah Berurah* adds that nevertheless he may go to the mourner privately to say *Shabbos hi mi'lenachem*. . . . See also *Turei Zahav, Orach Chaim* 526.

46. Rabbi Aaron Felder, *Yesodei Semochos* (New York: CIS Publications, 1992), p. 101, 3c, quoting HaGaon Rabbi Moshe Feinstein.

47. Rabbi Tuchachinsky, *Gesher HaChaim*, pp. 265-266, even though *Pri Megadim (Mishbetzos Zahav), Orach Chaim* 541, is unsure of this.

48. *Shabbos* 12a—only with difficulty did they permit comforting mourners on *Shabbos*. *Rashi* explains there because this will cause the mourners distress on *Shabbos*; Rabbi Avraham Gombiner, *Magen Avraham* (gloss to *Shulchan Aruch*), *Orach Chaim* 287, quotes the reason of Rabbi Alfasi that it may cause them to cry. See also *Succah* 41b; *Pirkei d'Rabbi Eliezer*, chap. 17; Rabbi Yitzchak of Vienna, *Or Zorua* (Zhitomir, 1862), *Shabbos* 51; Rabbi Yaakov ben Asher, *Tur* (New York: Otzar Hasefarim Turim, 1959), *Yoreh De'ah* 393; Rabbi Kagan, *Mishnah Berurah, Orach Chaim* 287, 2. In the event that one went, he should either change the phrase of

comfort to *Shabbos hi mi'le'nachem u'nechamah kerovah lovo* or simply *HaMokom yenachemcha* (*Mishnah Berurah*), or rather omit any phrase of comfort whatsoever (*Matei Yehudah* 287, 1).

49. *Shulchan Aruch, Orach Chaim* 287, 548:6; *Yoreh De'ah* 399:2.

50. Rabbi Yechiel Michel Epstein, *Aruch HaShulchan* (Warsaw, 1894), *Orach Chaim* 287:3; Rabbi Tuchachinsky, *Gesher HaChaim*, p. 208; Rabbi Gershon Ephraim Marber, *Darkei HaChaim* (Lublin, 1927), p. 33, 13 and 14; Rabbi Shapira, *Nimukei Orach Chaim*, no. 287; Rabbi Bezalel Stern, *Responsa B'Tzeil HaChochmah* (Jerusalem, 1967), vol. 2, no. 44.

51. Rabbi Tuchachinsky, *Gesher HaChaim*, loc. cit.; Rabbi Stern, *Responsa B'Tzeil HaChochmah*, loc. cit.

52. See Rabbi David HaLevi, *Turei Zahav*, in name of Rabbi Yoel Sirkis, *Bayis Chadash*; Rabbi Gombiner, *Magen Avraham*, in name of Rabbi Yehoshua Falk Katz, *Derishah* (gloss to *Tur, Shulchan Aruch*); Rabbi Kagan, *Mishnah Berurah*, loc. cit., 3. See *Tur, Yoreh De'ah* 393, who permits saying *HaMokom yenachemcha,* and *Derishah*; Rabbi Chaim Dovid HaLevi, *Mekor Chaim HaShaleim* (Tel Aviv, 1967–1974), vol. 3, p. 179.

53. See Dobrinsky, *A Treasury of Sephardic Laws and Customs*, p. 74. See also *Rambam, Mishneh Torah, Hilchos Aveil*, chap. 13, 2.

54. See Dobrinsky, loc. cit., p. 83.

55. Dobrinsky, loc. cit., p. 74. See also Rabbi Yaakov Chaim Soffer, *Kaf HaChaim* (Jerusalem, 1963), *Orach Chaim* 287, 2.

56. Dobrinsky, op. cit., p. 93.

57. See Rabbi Soffer, *Kaf HaChaim,* op. cit., 3.

58. Rabbi Tuchachinsky, *Gesher HaChaim*, p. 209.

59. HaGaon Rabbi Moshe Feinstein *ztz'l*, cited in Rabbi Aaron Felder, *Yesodei Semochos*, loc. cit., p. 101, 1c. See also Rabbi Ephraim Greenblatt, *Responsa Rivevos Ephraim* (New York, 1980), vol. 3, pp. 424–425. Cf. Rabbi Epstein, *Aruch HaShulchan, Orach Chaim* 557, 3.

60. *Moed Kattan* 21b; *Shulchan Aruch, Yoreh De'ah* 385:2; Rabbi Tuchachinsky, *Gesher HaChaim* p. 212, 10.

61. *Moed Kattan* 21b; *Shulchan Aruch, Yoreh De'ah* 385:2. Rabbi Epstein, *Aruch HaShulchan, Yoreh De'ah* 385:3, states that nowadays we do not follow this custom.

62. *Moed Kattan* 21b.

63. *Moed Kattan* 21b; *Shulchan Aruch, Yoreh De'ah* 385:3.

CHAPTER 6

1. See Rabbi Gershon Marber, *Darkei HaChaim* (Lublin, 1927), appendix to *siman* 5, 1; Rabbi Israel Feldman, *Sefer Likutei Yaffe* (New York, 1974), chap. 14; *Binyan Yehoshua* (*Maseches Semochos*).

2. See Rabbi Aaron Levine, *Zichron Meir al Aveilus* (Toronto: Zichron Meir, 1985), vol. 1, p. 188 and n. 42a.

3. *Moed Kattan* 27b; *Shulchan Aruch, Yoreh De'ah* 378:1.

4. See 2 Samuel 3:35 in regard to King David. This is also the source for the term *havraah*. See Rabbi Tzidkiyah HaRofei, *Shibolei HaLeket* (Venice, 1546), *Semochos* 23.

5. *Bava Basra* 16b.

6. *Eichah Rabbah* on v. 4.

7. See Rabbi Chaim Medini, *Sdei Chemed* (Warsaw, 1890), vol. 4, *Klalim maareches samech*, 53. See also *Sanhedrin* 63.

8. Ezekiel 24:17.

9. *Moed Kattan* 27b; *Shulchan Aruch, Yoreh De'ah* 378:1.

10. Rabbi Yerucham ben Meshulam, *Toldos Adam v'Chavah* (Constantinople, 1516), *Chelek Chavah, nesiv 28, chelek sheni*; see also Rabbi Yosef Caro, *Beis Yosef* (gloss to *Tur Shulchan Aruch*); Rabbi Yehoshua Falk Katz, *Perishah* (gloss to *Tur*); Rabbi Abraham Danziger, *Chochmas Adam* 163:5.

11. Rabbi Mordechai Yaffe, *Levush* (Lublin, 1590), *Hilchos Aveilus* 378, 1. See also Rabbi Yitzchak of Vienna, *Or Zorua* (Zhitomir, 1862), pt. 2, 130.

12. See Rabbi Moses Feinstein, *Responsa Igros Moshe* (New York, 1973), *Yoreh De'ah*, vol. 2, no. 168.

13. Rabbi Samson Raphael Hirsch, *Horeb* (London: Soncino Press, 1962), vol. 1, pp. 213-214.

14. Rabbi Yehudah Ayache, *Shevet Yehudah* (Livorno, 1783), 378, 1.

15. Rabbi Meir Simchah of Dvinsk, *Meshech Chochmah* (Riga, 1927), end of *Parshas Vayechi*.

16. Rabbi Chaim HaLevi, *Mekor Chaim HaShaleim* (Tel Aviv, 1967 1974), vol. 5, p. 394.

17. See Rabbi Aaron Berechiah of Modena, *Maavar Yabok* (Mantua, 1626), *Chelek Sefas Emes*, chaps. 28 and 35.

18. See *Yerushalmi Berachos* 3:1; *Tur, Yoreh De'ah* 378; *Mordechai* cited in *Beis Yosef*.

19. *Hagahos HaRosh* to *Moed Kattan*, chap. 3, letter 89, citing *Or Zorua*; Rabbi Sholom Cherniak, *Mishmeres Shalom* (Warsaw, 1928), in name of *Rikanti* 574. This would certainly seem the case according to reason no. 3.

20. Rabbi Yitzchak of Vienna, *Or Zorua*; Rabbi Asher ben Yechiel, *Rosh*; Rabbeinu Yerucham, *Toldos Adam v'Chavah*; *Shulchan Aruch*; Rabbi Tuchachinsky, *Gesher HaChaim*, p. 199, and many others.

21. *Tosafos, Moed Kattan* 20a and 27b; Rabbi Alfasi, *Rif*, and others. See Rabbi Cherniak, *Mishmeres Shalom, Erech Havraah*, 4; Rabbi Eliyahu Frankel, *Responsa Nachalas Avi* (Bulgaria, 1937), no. 77, commenting on *Rambam, Mishneh Torah Hilchos Aveil*, chap. 4, 8.

22. Rabbi Yishmael HaKohen, *Responsa Zera Emes* (Livorno, 1796), vol. 2, no. 156.

23. Rabbi Shlomo Luria, *HaGahos Chochmas Shlomo* (gloss to *Shulchan Aruch*), *Yoreh De'ah* 378; see Rabbi Epstein, *Aruch HaShulchan, Yoreh De'ah* 378, 2; Rabbi Shimon Sidan, *Shevet Shimon* (Pressburg, 1884), *Beis Aveil* 378; Rabbi Moshe Tzvi Noah, *Nachamu Ami*, chap. 15, 2; Rabbi Malkiel Tennenbaum, *Responsa Divrei Malkiel* (Jerusalem, 1987), vol. 2, no. 27.

24. See Rabbi Ovadiah Yosef, *Responsa Yabia Omer* (Jerusalem, 1986), vol. 2, *Yoreh De'ah*, no. 25; Rabbi Tuchachinsky, *Gesher HaChaim*, p. 201, 4 and n. 2; Rabbi Yehudah Ayache, *Shevet Yehudah* 378; Rabbi Eliezer Valdenberg, *Even Yaakov* (Jerusalem, 1962), no. 51.

25. Rabbi Yosef Yuspa Nordlinger Hahn, *Yosef Ometz* (Frankfurt am Main: 1723); *Binyan Yehoshua*, end of *Maseches Semochos*, cited from *Lashon Chachamim*

in *Lechem HaPanim* to Rabbi Solomon Ganzfried, *Kitzur Shulchan Aruch* (Lvov, 1860), 196; Rabbi Medini, *Sdei Chemed*, vol. 1, *Maareches Alef,* letter *kuf; Teil Talpiyos,* year 5668, p. 49.

26. Rabbi Yekutiel Greenwald, *Kol Bo al Aveilus* (New York: Feldheim, 1973), p. 273; Rabbi Tennenbaum, *Responsa Divrei Malkiel,* vol. 2, no. 97; Rabbi HaLevi, *Mekor Chaim,* vol. 5, p. 396, 15. See also Rabbi Yechiel Michal Gold, *Darkei Chaim, v'Shalom* (Munkacz, 1940), 982; Rabbi Valdenberg, *Even Yaakov,* no. 51; *Binyan Yehoshua,* op. cit.

27. For the law follows leniency in matters of mourning—*Moed Kattan* 20a. See also Levine, *Zichron Meir al Aveilus,* p. 244 n. 8a. See later, n. 56.

28. *Shulchan Aruch, Yoreh De'ah* 378:1.

29. *Talmud Yerushalmi* cited in *Beis Yosef, Yoreh De'ah* 378.

30. See *Shulchan Aruch, Yoreh De'ah* 378:2 "Similarly, if one employs a scribe or other employee, if he provides his meals as part of his salary, and the scribe or employee becomes a mourner, he cannot eat the employer's food for the meal of condolence. But if one is supporting a poor person or an orphan, or is giving unconditional support to his own son or daughter, and the person supported becomes a mourner, he may eat the food of the master of the house for the meal of condolence." Conversely, whether such a son may feed his father the *seudas havraah* is questionable. See below, n. 38.

31. Rabbi Yosef Schwartz, *Hadras Kodesh* (Oradea, 1930), *Likutei Dinim,* p. 46.

32. *Shulchan Aruch, Yoreh De'ah* 378:2.

33. *Tur, Yoreh De'ah* 378; Rabbi Epstein, *Aruch HaShulchan, Yoreh De'ah* 378, 3; Rabbi Tuchachinsky, *Gesher HaChaim,* p. 201, 7.

34. Rabbi Yosef Molko, *Shulchan Govoha* (Salonika, 1756), *Yoreh De'ah* 378; Rabbi Yitzchak Yossef, *Yalkut Yossef* (Jerusalem, 1989), vol. 7, p. 101, 2. See also Rabbi Tuchachinsky, *Gesher HaChaim* for explanation—pp. 201-202.

35. Rabbi Tuchachinsky, *Gesher HaChaim,* ibid. See also Rabbi Eliezer Valdenberg, *Responsa Tzitz Eliezer* (Jerusalem, 1988), vol. 17, no. 45, 1; Rabbi Moshe Donath, *Devorei Emes* (Berdiczew, 1931), *Yoreh De'ah* 378.

36. *Shulchan Aruch, Yoreh De'ah* 378:2; and *Sifsei Kohen (Shach).*

37. A fortiori from the law above.

38. See Rabbi Menachem of Adrianopoli, *Menachem Aveilim* (Symrna, 1880), letter *heh,* 6, that he may, and Rabbi Valdenberg, *Responsa Tzitz Eliezer,* loc. cit., 2, citing *Chasam Sofer,* that he may not. Rabbi Aaron Felder, *Yesodei Semochos,* p. 80, 4c, also quotes HaGaon Rabbi Moshe Feinstein that he may not. See also Rabbi Tuchachinsky, *Gesher HaChaim,* p. 201, 6, and Rabbi Noah, *Nachamu Ami,* p. 42, 13 and n. 15; Rabbi Gavriel Zinner, *Nitei Gavriel* (New York, 1993), p. 360 n. 38, in the name of *Zikaron l'Yom Acharon* and *takanos* of *Chevrah Kaddisha* of Frankfurt—that he may.

39. *Moed Kattan* 20b; *Shulchan Aruch, Yoreh De'ah* 374:4.

40. See *Shulchan Aruch, Yoreh De'ah* 396:3. See also Rabbi Shmuel Landau, *Responsa Shivas Tziyon,* no. 61; Rabbi Avraham Schreiber-Sofer, *Responsa Ksav Sofer* (Pressburg, 1879), *Yoreh De'ah,* no. 172, and others.

41. See Rabbi Greenwald, *Kol Bo al Aveilus,* p. 273; *Tanya Rabbasi* (Mantua, 1514), *Hilchos Aveil* 67, beginning "*vetinok*" (only in this respect so as not to inconvenience the neighbors).

42. The *Shulchan Aruch* clearly states this even in respect to the *seudas havraah—Shulchan Aruch, Yoreh De'ah* 378:6. See Rabbi Tuchachinsky, *Gesher HaChaim*, p. 202, 8, and others.

43. See many sources cited in Levine, *Zichron Meir al Aveilus*, p. 245. See also Rabbi Valdenberg, *Responsa Tzitz Eliezer,* vol. 9, no. 28; Rabbi Moshe Stern, *Responsa Be'er Moshe* (New York, 1973), vol. 1, no. 64; Rabbi Shmuel Wosner, *Responsa Shevet HaLevi* (New York, 1981), vol. 3, *Yoreh De'ah,* no. 143; Rabbi Yitzchok Weiss, *Responsa Minchas Yitzchok* (London, 1967), vol. 4, no. 123; Rabbi Ovadiah Yossef, *Responsa Yabia Omer,* vol. 6, *Yoreh De'ah* 34, 4.

44. See Rabbi Yitzchak Yossef, *Yalkut Yossef,* vol. 7, pp. 97-100, and sources in above footnotes.

45. Rabbeinu Yerucham, *Toldos Adam v'Chavah*; Rabbi Chiya Pontrimoli, *Responsa Tzapichis b'Dvash* (Salonika, 1848), no. 69; Rabbi Nesanel Fried, *Pnei Meivin* (Munkacz, 1913), vol. 2, p. 273; Rabbi Medini, *Sdei Chemed, Maareches Aveilus*, 103; Rabbi Schwartz, *VaYelaket Yosef* (year 13, n. 75); Rabbi Chaim Luria, *Responsa Meishiv Halachah* (Lodz, 1922), no. 448; Rabbi Schwartz, *Hadras Kodesh, Likutei Dinim*, p. 92.

46. See Levine, *Zichron Meir al Aveilus*, vol. 1, p. 60 n. 128d.

47. See *Shulchan Aruch, Yoreh De'ah* 345:1; Rabbi Shlomo Kluger, *Responsa Tuv Taam v'Daas* (Podgorza, 1900), vol. 3, no. 202; Rabbi Moshe Schreiber-Sofer, *Responsa Chasam Sofer* (New York, 1958), *Yoreh De'ah* 326.

48. The opinion of the *Maharikash* cited in Rabbi Yitzchak Palagi, *Yaffe l'Lev* (Symrna, 1872), vol. 3, *Yoreh De'ah* 345:5, and of Rabbi Medini, *Sdei Chemed, loc.* cit., is that one does serve the *seudas havraah*. See also Rabbi Chayim Palagi, *Responsa Chaim b'Yad* (Smyrna, 1873), no. 110. Therefore with the addition of the *Shulchan Aruch, Yoreh De'ah* 345:1 and *Chasam Sofer* (above, n. 47), where the mourners wish to be served, there is no question that this should be done.

49. See *Shulchan Aruch, Yoreh De'ah* 377:3. Rabbi Schwartz, *Hadras Kodesh,* p. 92; Rabbi Yaakov Lorberbaum, *Siddur Derech HaChaim* (Berlin, 1860), Laws of *Aveilus*, 11; Rabbi Schwartz, *VaYelaket Yosef,* loc. cit.

50. *Shulchan Aruch, Yoreh De'ah*, loc. cit., 2.

51. Rabbi Epstein, *Aruch HaShulchan, Yoreh De'ah* 378:6; cf. *Shulchan Aruch, Yoreh De'ah* 340:23.

52. Cf. *Shulchan Aruch,* loc. cit.; Levine, *Zichron Meir al Aveilus*, p. 202 n. 84; Rabbi Tuchachinsky, *Gesher HaChaim*, p. 202, 9.

53. Rabbi Tuchachinsky, *Gesher HaChaim*, p. 200, 2.

54. Ibid. See there, n. 1.

55. See *Shulchan Aruch, Yoreh De'ah* 378:12, 402:3; Rabbi Epstein, *Aruch HaShulchan* 12.

56. *Shulchan Aruch*, ibid.

57. *Shulchan Aruch,* op. cit. 342.

58. Rabbi Marber, *Darkei HaChaim*, p. 36, 13. This is obvious. The *seudas havraah* takes precedence over feeding a bride and groom where one has the means to do both. See Rabbi Danziger, *Chochmas Adam* 155:26.

59. See *Shulchan Aruch, Yoreh De'ah* 342, and commentaries.

60. Rabbi Tuchachinsky, *Gesher HaChaim*, p. 200, 3.

61. See *Shulchan Aruch, Yoreh De'ah*, 378:1 and *Sifsei Kohen (Shach),* ad loc., 2. See also Rabbi Katz, *Perishah*, 3.

62. *Turei Zahav (Taz), Yoreh De'ah* 378, 1. Certainly where it is difficult to fast one may rely on this, but if possible should restrict himself to lighter refreshments. See n. 64.

63. Rabbi Achaye, *Shevet Yehudah, Yoreh De'ah* 378; Rabbi Lorberbaum, *Siddur Derech HaChaim* (laws of *seudas havraah*, 1; Rabbi Danziger, *Chochmas Adam* 169:5; Rabbi Ganzfried, *Kitzur Shulchan Aruch* 205:2; Rabbis Rabi, *Yakra d'Chaya*, p. 67, citing Rabbi S. Dablitzky, especially when it is already later on in the afternoon.

64. Rabbi Schwartz, *Hadras Kodesh*, p. 92. See also Rabbi Danziger, *Chochmas Adam* 163, 5.

65. Rabbi Zinner, *Nitei Gavriel*, p. 365, 18, and n. 28.

66. Rabbi Yaakov ben Asher, *Tur,* in name of most *poskim.* See Rabbi Isserles, *Remoh, Yoreh De'ah* 378, 3. See also Rabbi David Ibn Zimrah, *Responsa Radvaz* (Warsaw, 1883), vol. 1, no. 424, that even if burial took place close to the night, he may still eat his own meal when night arrives.

67. See Rabbi Medini, *Sdei Chemed,* loc. cit., 102, citing Rabbi Chaim Palagi, *Responsa Chaim b'Yad*, no. 121; Rabbi Yitzchak Palagi, *Responsa Yaffe l'Lev, Yoreh De'ah* 378.

68. Rabbi Ezekiel. Landau, *Responsa Noda b'Yehudah*, vol. 1, *Yoreh De'ah,* no. 98. See also Rabbi Eisenstadt, *Pischei Teshuvah, Yoreh De'ah* 378, 2, and Rabbi Tuchachinsky, *Gesher HaChaim*, p. 200, 2.

69. Rabbi Tuchachinsky, *Gesher HaChaim,* end of p. 199, and p. 200.

70. See *Shulchan Aruch, Yoreh De'ah* 378:5; Rabbi Palagi, *Responsa Chaim b'Yad*, end of no. 119; Rabbi Tuchachinsky, *Gesher HaChaim,* p. 202, 11. In Rabbi Goldberg, *Pnei Baruch,* p. 81, 6, he adds, "But he may not eat till night." And so writes Rabbi Ganzfried, *Kitzur Shulchan Aruch*, 205:6. See also Rabbis Moshe Leib and Shmuel Tziltz, *Responsa Milei d'Avos* (Tel Aviv, 1972), vol. 3, no. 11. See next note.

71. See Rabbi Medini, *Sdei Chemed,* loc. cit., 100, citing Rabbi Avraham ben Shmuel Alkelai, *Zechor l'Avraham* (Salonika, 1798), p. 169b; Rabbi Danziger, *Chochmas Adam,* loc. cit., 9; Rabbi Felder, *Yesodei Semochos,* p. 88, 6b; Rabbi Marber, *Darkei HaChaim,* p. 36 in note, *biur.* See also Rabbi Zinner, *Nitei Gavriel*, p. 362 n. 9.

72. Rabbi Yosef David Azulai, *Birkei Yosef* (Livorno, 1774-1776), *Yoreh De'ah* 378, 4, citing Rabbi Shmuel Florentine, *Beis HaRoeh*, p. 57, and Rabbi Yosef ben Dovid Philosof, *Beis Dovid*, p. 199.

73. Rabbi Greenwald, *Kol Bo al Aveilus*, pp. 272-273, citing Rabbi Alkelai, *Zechor l'Avraham*; Rabbi Yehudah Shmuel Ashkenazi, *Siddur Beis Oved*, p. 452, 5. See also Rabbi Tuchachinsky, *Gesher HaChaim,* p. 200 n. 1.

74. See sources cited in nn. 70 and 71.

75. See Rabbi Caro, *Beis Yosef, Yoreh De'ah* 378; Rabbi Yehuda Ashkenazi, *Be'er Hetev* to *Shulchan Aruch, Orach Chaim* 471: 9, citing Rabbi Luria, *Maharshal.* See also Rabbi Kagan, *Shaar Hatziyun,* ad loc., 26; Rabbi Teomim, *Pri Megadim, Mishbetzos Zahav* 468, 10; Rabbi Marber, *Darkei HaChaim*, pp. 35-36 nn. 1 and 2. See also Rabbi Zinner, *Nitei Gavriel,* pp. 523-524 n. 15, for dissenting opinions.

76. See Rabbi Menachem of Andrianopoli, *Menachem Aveilim, Maareches Havraah,* 5.

77. *Shulchan Aruch, Yoreh De'ah* 378:11; 401:4. Some say that if he heard a *shemua kerovah* on *Shabbos*, then he should be served a *seudas havraah*–Rabbi Caro,

Beis Yosef 393; Rabbi Danziger, *Chochmas Adam* 163, 15. Others disagree—see *Shulchan Aruch, Yoreh De'ah* 378:11; *Sifsei Kohen,* 11; *Be'er Hetev,* 6; Rabbi Tuchachinsky, *Gesher HaChaim,* p. 303, 12. The *Shulchan Aruch,* loc. cit., however, rules that he should be given the *seudas havraah* on *Motzoei Shabbos.* See Rabbi Isserles, *Remoh,* ad loc., who says that this is not the custom. See also Rabbi Yossef, *Responsa Yabia Omer,* vol. 4, *Yoreh De'ah,* no. 26.

78. See Rabbi Yossef, *Responsa Yabia Omer,* loc. cit., citing sources. The mourner may make *havdalah* on his own wine before partaking of the *seudas havraah—Lechem HaPanim* to Rabbi Ganzfried, *Kitzur Shulchan Aruch,* 156, 10.

79. See Rabbi Isserles, *Remoh,* loc. cit.; *Responsa Beis Dovid,* no. 199.

80. *Shulchan Aruch, Orach Chaim* 547:8, *Yoreh De'ah* 401:4, and *Chidushei Rabbi Akivah Eiger,* ad loc. See also Rabbi Yossef, *Responsa Yabia Omer,* loc. cit., quoting many sources that there is no *seudas havraah* on *Chol HaMoed.* Rabbi Tuchachinsky, *Gesher HaChaim,* p. 202, 10, also cites sources to this effect but concludes that we follow the opinion of most of the *poskim* and we do serve the meal on *Chol HaMoed.* See also *Siddur Beis Oveid,* p. 452, 10. See also Rabbi Feinstein, *Responsa Igros Moshe, Yoreh De'ah,* vol. 2, no. 168.

81. See p. 55, this volume.

82. Rabbi Yossef, *Responsa Yabia Omer,* loc. cit., citing sources; Rabbi Yishmael HaKohen, *Responsa Zera Emes, Yoreh De'ah,* vol. 2, no. 156; *Siddur Beis Oved,* loc. cit.; Rabbi Danziger, *Chochmas Adam, Kuntras Matzeivas Moshe,* 2, in reference to Purim; Rabbi Tuchachinsky, *Gesher HaChaim,* p. 202, 10. Rabbi Medini, *Sdei Chemed,* loc. cit., 101, however, quotes Rabbi Palagi, *Responsa Chaim b'Yad,* no. 125, 73, that there are no changes.

83. Rabbi Cherniak, *Mishmeres Shalom, Erech Havraah,* 9; Rabbi Marber, *Darkei HaChaim,* p. 36, 12; cf. *Shulchan Aruch, Orach Chaim* 547:8; *Yoreh De'ah* 401:4; Rabbi Ganzfried, *Kitzur Shulchan Aruch,* 205, 8.

84. See Rabbi Yossef, *Responsa Yabia Omer,* loc. cit., and no. 25; Rabbi Greenwald, *Kol Bo al Aveilus,* p. 273. Rabbi Tuchachinsky, *Gesher HaChaim,* loc. cit., states that the reason and the source for this *minhag* are not known to us.

85. Rabbis Rabi, *Sefer Yakra d'Chaya,* p. 68, 5.

86. Rabbi Zinner, *Nitei Gavriel,* p. 365, based on *Shulchan Aruch, Orach Chaim* 640:5. Only men are obligated to do so.

87. *Shulchan Aruch, Yoreh De'ah* 401:4; *Beis Yosef, Orach Chaim* 420.

88. See sources in n. 82.

89. See Rabbi Noah, *Nachamu Ami,* p. 41, 12; Rabbi Marber, *Darkei HaChaim,* p. 36, 14.

90. Rabbi Noah, *Nachamu Ami,* loc. cit. and n. 14. There is an opinion in *Sefer Sdei Chaim,* p. 38, 17, that maintains that one should be served the *seudah* in this situation.

91. See Rabbi Schwartz, *Hadras Kodesh,* p. 92, citing *Ikrei Hadat,* 36, 8.

92. Rabbi Yishmael HaKohen, *Responsa Zera Emes,* vol. 2, *Yoreh De'ah,* 145.

93. Rabbi Tuchachinsky, *Gesher HaChaim,* p. 201, and others; see also p. 184n. 101.

94. Rabbi Yishmael HaKohen, *Responsa Zera Emes,* loc. cit., no. 146; Rabbi Tuchachinsky, *Gesher HaChaim,* p. 200, 4.

95. See *Ramban, Toras HaAdam* (Constantinople, 1519), *Shaar HaAveilus;*

Rabbi Tennenbaum, *Responsa Divrei Malkiel*, vol. 2, no. 97; Rabbi Yossef, *Responsa Yabia Omer*, vol. 4, *Yoreh De'ah*, no. 26.

96. See Rabbi Isserles, *Remoh, Shulchan Aruch, Orach Chaim* 167:5. Rabbi Greenwald, *Kol Bo al Aveilus*, vol. 2, pp. 96-97, in response to a query from Dr. DeSola Pool as to why the *minhag* in Turkey is not to dip the bread in salt, lists four possible reasons why this is so.

97. See *Bava Basra* 16b; *Shulchan Aruch, Yoreh De'ah* 378:9; *Pirkei d'Rabbi Eliezer*, chap. 35. See also Rabbi Yitzchak Lipitz, *Sefer Mataamim* (Warsaw, 1889), *Aveil*, 5, in name of *Chidah*.

98. *Bava Basra*, loc. cit.; *Shulchan Aruch, Yoreh De'ah*, loc. cit.; *Ramban, Toras HaAdam*; *Kol Bo* (author unknown) (Naples, 1590), *Hilchos Aveilus*, 114; Rabbi Tzidkiah HaRofei, *Shibolei HaLeket, Semochos*, 23.

I have not found anyone who writes that one should dip the bread (or egg) in ashes as we do on *erev* Tishah B'Av as a sign of mourning, and the two are often compared to each other in many practices—see *Responsa Rabbi Akivah Eiger, Tinyana*, no. 24. Obviously there is a difference. Rabbi Gombiner, *Magen Avraham, Orach Chaim*, 551, 38, states that public mourning is more stringent than private mourning. See also Rabbi Nachman Kahane, *Orchos Chaim–Spinka* (Siget, 1898), *Orach Chaim* 552, and *Beis Yosef* and Rabbi Elijah of Vilna, *Biur HaGra* (gloss to *Shulchan Aruch*), ad loc.

99. Rabbi Meir HaKohen, *Hagahos Maimoniyos* (13th century, gloss to *Rambam, Mishneh Torah, Hilchos Taanis*, chap. 5).

100. Rabbi Elazar Roke'ach of Worms, *Roke'ach* (Fano, 1505), 313, cited in Rabbi Cherniak, *Mishmeres Sholom, Havraah*, 13; Rabbi Isserles, *Remoh, Orach Chaim* 552:5, citing Rabbi Meir HaKohen, *Hagahos Maimoniyos*, loc. cit.

101. See sources above. See also Rabbi Michael Guttman, *Maftei'ach l'Talmud, Aveil Yom Rishon–Havraah* (Csongrad, 1906), p. 180.

102. See p. 77, this volume.

103. See n. 101.

104. See Rabbi Palagi, *Responsa Chaim b'Yad*, no. 125, 73, for other reasons.

105. Rabbi Avraham Hershowitz, *Otzar Kol Minhagei Yeshurun*, p. 301. Rabbi Chaim Press in *Concern for the Living* (Jerusalem: Targum/Feldheim, 1990), p. 83, writes: "Still others point out that roundness bespeaks the endless cycle of life; when one generation dies, another rises to take its place, and mourning eventually yields to rejoicing." See also Rabbi Tuchachinsky's parable, p. 15, this volume.

106. Rabbi Moshe Sofer, *Chasam Sofer.*

107. *Maharikash.*

108. Rabbi Aharon HaKohen of Lunel, *Orchos Chaim* (Berlin, 1899), *Hilchos Aveil*, 13. Rabbi Tzidkiah HaRofei, *Shibolei HaLeket, Semochos* 23, also cites the custom but offers no reason.

109. *Shulchan Aruch, Yoreh De'ah* 378:9.

110. See Rabbi Meir HaKohen, *Hagahos Maimoniyos, Hilchos Aveil*, end of chap. 7. See also discussion in Rabbi Medini, *Sdei Chemed*, loc. cit., no. 104; Rabbi Eliyahu Rigoler, *Responsa Yad Eliyahu* (Warsaw, 1900), no. 68, 4, citing *Yerushalmi, Sotah* 8:3; Rabbi Palagi, *Responsa Yaffe l'Lev, Yoreh De'ah* 378, 5. Rabbi Epstein, *Aruch HaShulchan, Yoreh De'ah* 378:10, writes that there is no obligation to serve wine. See also Rabbi Schwadron, *Daas Torah, Yoreh De'ah* 378, 8, citing *Darkei*

Moshe. See also Rabbi Aaron Berechia of Modena, *Maavar Yabok,* section *Sfas Emes,* chap. 26.

111. *Kesubos* 8b. See also *Customs of the City of Worms,* p. 313.

112. *Sanhedrin* 70a; *Eruvin* 65a. See also Rabbi Menachem of Adrianopoli, *Menachem Aveilim* citing *Nachalas Binyamin,* for another interesting reason for serving wine.

113. *Shulchan Aruch, Yoreh De'ah* 378:8; Rabbi Epstein, *Aruch HaShulchan,* loc. cit. See also Rabbis Rabi, *Yakra d'Chaya,* p. 68, 7, in the name of Rabbi S. Dablitzky, that the requirement for moderation when drinking wine applies all of *shivah.*

114. This applies even to those who normally hold that even drinking of his own is not permitted (see above, n. 25)—Rabbi Tuchachinsky, *Gesher HaChaim,* p. 201, 5.

115. See Rabbi Dovid Ibn Zimrah, *Responsa Radvaz,* vol. 6, 2, 254, cited in *Sdei Chemed,* loc. cit., no. 104.

116. See sources in nn. 109 and 110.

117. See Rabbi Meir Melamed, *Responsa Mishpat Tzedek* (Salonika, 1617), vol. 2, no. 57, cited in *Sdei Chemed,* loc. cit.; Rabbi Avraham Adadi, *Responsa Vayikra Avraham* (Livorno, 1865), *Kuntras Makom Shenahagu,* 12. See also Rabbi Dobrinsky, *A Treasury of Sephardic Laws and Customs,* p. 83—this is the practice today of Moroccan Jews. Judeo-Spanish Jews, however, have no such restriction (loc. cit., p. 91).

118. Rabbi Palagi, *Responsa Chaim b'Yad,* no. 125, 75. The custom of the city of Tunis, however, was not to eat fish at all during *shivah.*

119. See Rabbi Palagi, *Responsa Yaffe l'Lev* , loc. cit.

120. Dobrinsky, *A Treasury of Sephardic Laws and Customs,* loc. cit.

121. Rabbi Tuchachinsky, *Gesher HaChaim,* top of p. 201; Rabbi Noah, *Nachamu Ami,* p. 41 n. 1, writes that this is simply to quench their thirst.

122. Rabbi Tzidkiah HaRofei, *Shibolei HaLeket, Semochos,* 23.

123. See Rabbi Yosef Molko, *Shulchan Govoha,* cited in *Gesher HaChaim,* pp. 201-202. It would seem even from the Talmud and the *Shulchan Aruch* that this was formally the custom—see *Moed Kattan* 24a that on *Chol HaMoed* one only serves the mourners, implying that on regular days others (nonmourners) were served the meal, too; *Shulchan Aruch, Yoreh De'ah* 378:9—"Too many people should not eat with the *aveil* . . ."; see also *Tur, Yoreh De'ah* 378, in name of *Ramban; Shibolei HaLeket, Semochos,* 23.

124. See Rabbi Tuchachinsky, *Gesher HaChaim,* loc. cit.; Rabbi Avraham Binyamin Zilberberg, *Responsa Mishnas Binyamin* (New York, 1948), no. 46. The main reason for this is simply to avoid having a more joyful atmosphere, as the case would be if others eat with the mourners—*Shach, Yoreh De'ah* 378, 9. See also Rabbi Adadi, *Responsa Vayikra Avraham,* loc. cit.; Rabbi Dobrinsky, *A Treasury of Sephardic Laws and Customs,* p. 83, that Moroccan Jews do not eat with the mourners for this reason and also to comply with the custom of not taking anything from the mourner's house during *shivah.* See later, p. 79.

125. See p. 88, this volume.

126. See *Shulchan Aruch, Orach Chaim* 167:18; *Rambam, Mishneh Torah, Hilchos Aveil,* chap. 7, 5. On *Shabbos,* however, the mourner should cut his own

bread, as one is not allowed to publicize mourning on *Shabbos–Mishnah Berurah, Orach Chaim* 168, 89.

127. See Rabbi Meir HaKohen, *Hagahos Maimoniyos, Hilchos Aivel*, chap. 4, citing *Berachos* and *Moed Kattan*. See Rabbi David Abudraham, *Abudraham* (Lisbon, 1489), *betzias hapas*, p. 316.

128. Rabbi Palagi, *Responsa Yaffe l'Lev, Yoreh De'ah* 378, 6.

129. *Shulchan Aruch, Yoreh De'ah* 13. See Rabbi Danziger, *Chochmas Adam*, 163, 16, and Rabbi Zinner, *Nitei Gavriel*, p. 359, 15.

130. See *Shulchan Aruch, Yoreh De'ah* 387:1; *Shach*, ad loc.; Rabbi Epstein, *Aruch HaShulchan, Yoreh De'ah* 387, 3; Rabbi Tuchachinsky, *Gesher HaChaim*, p. 212, 11.

131. See *Moed Kattan* 26b; *Tur* and *Beis Yosef, Yoreh De'ah* 378; Rabbi Yishmael HaKohen, *Responsa Zera Emes*, vol. 3, p. 194.

132. Rabbi Schwartz, *Hadras Kodesh*, p. 92.

133. *Koheles Rabbah* 93:4.

134. See *Shach, Yoreh De'ah* 379, 6; Rabbi Luria, *Hagahos Chochmas Shlomo, Yoreh De'ah* 378. See also his work, *Kinas Sofrim;* Rabbi Shlomo Kluger, *Responsa HaElef Lecha Shlomo, Yoreh De'ah*, no. 318; Rabbi Danziger, *Chochmas Adam*, 163, 21; Rabbi Greenwald, *Kol Bo al Aveilus*, p. 277, 13; Rabbi Tuchachinsky, *Gesher HaChaim*, vol. 1, p. 203, 14; vol. 2, p. 161. Most of the above rule, however, that if three mourners did sit together, they should not abandon the *zimun*.

135. See Rabbi Valdenberg, *Responsa Tzitz Eliezer*, vol. 11, no. 71, and *Even Yaakov*, no. 53 and sources cited there. See also Rabbi Chaim Pinchas Luria, *Responsa Meishiv Halachah* (Lodz, 1922), vol. 1, no. 357.

136. See *Shulchan Aruch, Yoreh De'ah* 379; *Siddur Beis Oved*, p. 453; Rabbi Dobrinsky, *A Treasury of Sephardic Laws and Customs*, pp. 104-105. See also Appendix I, this volume. However, on *Shabbos* if nonmourners are eating with the mourners, the special additions are omitted–*Shulchan Aruch*, loc. cit., 4, and *Shach*, 5.

137. Rabbi Moshe Rivkes, *Be'er HaGolah, Yoreh De'ah* 379; *Responsa Maharam*, no. 676 cited in Rabbi Goldberg, *Pnei Baruch*, p. 113; Rabbi Tuchachinsky, *Gesher HaChaim*, p. 203, 13. See also Rabbi Alkelai, *Zechor l'Avraham, Yoreh De'ah*, letter *beis* cited in Rabbi Greenwald, *Kol Bo al Aveilus*, p. 280, 9, that the *minhag* is not to say any *Horachaman* in the mourner's house.

138. See p. 49, this volume.

139. See Rabbi HaLevi, *Mekor Chayim HaSholeim*, vol. 5, p. 396 n. 58, especially Sephardic Jewry.

140. See *Beis Yosef, Yoreh De'ah* 378; Rabbeinu Yerucham, *Toldos Adam v'Chavah, Chelek Chavah, 28, Chelek Sheni, Orchos Chaim (Hilchos Aivel, 13),* all in the name of the *Rosh* (either from Lunil or Pliza, but not the *Piskei HoRosh–*see n. 300 to Schlezinger edition of *Orchos Chaim* [Berlin, 1899]).

141. Rabbi Isserles, *Remoh, Yoreh De'ah* 385:3. See Rabbi Breisch, *Responsa Chelkas Yaakov*, vol. 2, 169.

142. Rabbi Feinstein, *Responsa Igros Moshe, Yoreh De'ah*, vol. 2, no. 168; Rabbi Greenwald, *Kol Bo al Aveilus*, vol. 2, p. 103; Rabbi Moshe Tomashoff, *Responsa Avnei Shoham* (New York, 1947), vol. 4, *Yoreh De'ah*, no. 57.

143. See p. 79, this volume.

144. See p. 149, this volume.
145. See Rabbi Palagi, *Responsa Chaim b'Yad,* no. 125, 7.
146. Rabbi Yitzchak Alfiah, *HaKuntras HaYechiali, Bais Olomim,* chap. 15, 26.
See also Rabbi Dobrinsky, *A Treasury of Sephardic Laws and Customs,* chap. 5.

CHAPTER 7

1. See Rabbi Chaim Bernstein, *Yakra d'Chaya* (Bnei Brak, 1979), p. 12, from *Rambam, Sefer HaMitzvos.*
2. Rabbi Aaron Berechiah of Modena, *Maavar Yabok* (Mantua, 1626), section *Sfas Emes,* chap. 37.
3. Cf. Rabbi Bernstein, *Yakra d'Chaya,* pp. 83-84.
4. See Rabbi Yisroel Dovid Harfenes, *Responsa VaYevarech Dovid* (New York, 1989), vol. 2, p. 252.
5. See *Moed Kattan* 9a-b; cf. Rabbi Yehudah HeChasid, *Sefer Chasidim* (Bologna, 1538), no. 1486—see Rabbi Reuven Margoliyos, *Mekor Chesed to Sefer Chasidim* (Jerusalem, Mossad HaRav Kook, 1957), p. 1004; Rabbi Yosef Chaim Sonnenfeld, *Responsa Salmas Chaim* (Bnei Brak, 1982), *Yoreh De'ah* 128.
6. Cf. Rabbi Aaron Berechiah, *Maavar Yabok, Sifsei Tzedek,* chap. 3; Rabbi Yaakov Chaim Sofer, *Zera Chaim* (Jerusalem, 1988), chap. 12. See Rabbi Harfenes, *Responsa VaYevarech Dovid,* loc. cit.
7. Talmud, *Moed Kattan* (several places), and other tractates.
8. Cf. Rabbi Yaakov Culi, *Yalkut Me'Am Loez* (Constantinople 1733), *Parshas Vayeira.*
9. Cf. *Moed Kattan* 27b.
10. *Vayikra* 19:15.
11. *Pirkei Avos* 1: 6.
12. *Shabbos* 127b.
13. Ibid.
14. Simcha Raz, *A Tzaddik in Our Time* (Jerusalem: Feldheim, 1976), pp. 86-87.
15. Cf. *Nedarim* 39b and commentaries; *Shulchan Aruch, Yoreh De'ah* 335:2; Rabbi Yitzchok Weiss, *Responsa Minchas Yitzchok* (London, 1958), vol. 2, no. 84; Rabbi Moses Feinstein, *Responsa Igros Moshe* (New York, 1959), vol. 1, *Yoreh De'ah,* no. 222. See also Rabbi Chaim Palagi, *Responsa Chaim b'Yad* (Smyrna, 1873), no. 125, 9.
16. See chapter 2, nn. 3-5.
17. *Pesikta Rabbasi, Parshas Lech Lecha.*
18. Rabbi Shlomo Cohen, *P'eir HaDor* (Bnei Brak: Netzach, 1970), vol. 4, p. 50.
19. *Succah* 52a; See Rabbi Aaron Levine, *Zichron Meir al Aveilus* (Toronto: Zichron Meir, 1985), p. 341, n. 74.
20. See Rabbi Moshe Stern, *Responsa Be'er Moshe* (New York, 1975), vol. 4, no. 107.
21. Ibid.; Rabbi Yechiel Michel Tuchachinsky, *Gesher HaChaim* (Jerusalem, 1947), p. 208; Rabbi Yaakov Breisch, *Responsa Chelkas Yaakov* (Bnei Brak, 1966),

vol. 3, no. 38; Rabbi Solomon Braun, *She'arim Metzuyanim b'Halachah* (Jerusalem: Feldheim, 1970), vol. 4, p. 306; Rabbi Chananya Teitelbaum, *Responsa Levushei Yom Tov*, no. 38.

22. See sources cited above in n. 20. See also *Kol Bo* (author unknown) (Naples, 1590), *Hilchos Aveil*, 114, p. 88.

23. Ibid.

24. Cf. Rabbi Moses Isserles, *Remoh* (gloss to *Shulchan Aruch*), *Yoreh De'ah* 335:2; *Darkei Moshe* (gloss to *Tur*) (Berlin, 1702-1703), *Yoreh De'ah* 335:1; Rabbi Yaakov Moelin, *Responsa Maharil* (Venice, 1549), no. 197.

25. Rabbi Yoel Sirkis, *Bayis Chadash (Bach)* (gloss to *Tur*) (Cracow, 1635), *Yoreh De'ah* 335; Rabbi Shabsai HaKohen, *Sifsei Kohen (Shach)* (gloss to *Shulchan Aruch*) (Cracow, 1646); Rabbi Abraham Danziger, *Chochmas Adam* (Vilna, 1814), 151, 1; Rabbi Yechiel Michel Epstein, *Aruch HaShulchan* (Warsaw, 1898), *Yoreh De'ah* 335, 6; Rabbi Eliezer Valdenberg, *Ramat Rachel* (Jerusalem, 1984), no. 9, citing Rabbi Yehudah Ayache, *Shevet Yehudah* (Livorno, 1783); Rabbi Moshe Mos, *Mattei Moshe* (Cracow, 1591), *Gemillus Chasadim*, chap. 4; Rabbi Hillel Hertz, *Beis Hillel* (gloss to *Shulchan Aruch*) (Dehrenfurt, 1691), *Yoreh De'ah* 362: 6; Rabbi Bernstein, *Yakra d'Chaya*, pp. 44-45, n. 5.

26. Rabbi Epstein, *Aruch HaShulchan, Yoreh De'ah* 335, 6.

27. Rabbi Yisrael Meir Kagan, *Ahavas Chesed* (Warsaw, 1888), *Mitzvas Halvaah*, chap. 3, 1.

28. Ibid. See also *Shulchan Aruch, Yoreh De'ah* 251:1-2.

29. Rabbi Kagan, *Ahavas Chesed*, loc. cit. See also *Shulchan Aruch, Choshen Mishpat* 266:2 and 388.

30. Rabbi Kagan, *Ahavas Chesed*, loc. cit.

31. Cf. Rabbi Bernstein, *Yakra d'Chaya*, p. 48 n. 10; Levine, *Zichron Meir al Aveilus*, pp. 58-59 and n. 128a, citing numerous references; Rabbi Stern, *Responsa Be'er Moshe*, vol. 5, no. 151; Rabbi Valdenberg, *Responsa Tzitz Eliezer*, vol. 10, no. 41; Rabbi Ovadiah Yossef, *Responsa Yabia Omer* (Jerusalem, 1986), vol. 6, *Yoreh De'ah*, no. 36.

32. Cf. Rabbi Stern, *Responsa Be'er Moshe*, loc. cit.

33. Rabbi Maurice Lamm, *The Jewish Way in Death and Mourning* (New York: Jonathan David, 1969), p. 140, 5.

34. Rabbi Yekutiel Greenwald, *Kol Bo al Aveilus* (New York: Feldheim, 1973), p. 298, citing *Shibolei HaLeket*; Rabbi Sholom Cherniak, *Mishmeres Sholom* (Warsaw, 1928), citing *Tanya Rabbasi*.

35. Rabbi Jules Lipschutz in *Rabbinical Council of America Manual* (New York: Rabbinical Council of America, 1978), p. 159.

36. See Levine, *Zichron Meir al Aveilus*, pp. 59-60 n. 128d, citing many references.

37. See references in above note.

38. Ibid. See also *Rashi* to *1 Kings* 17:1.

39. Cf. Rabbi Yehudah HeChasid, *Sefer Chasidim* (Bologna, 1538), no. 361, and commentary of Rabbi Abraham Price, *Mishnas Avraham* (New York, 1960); Rabbi Yaakov Culi, *Yalkut Me'Am Loez* (Constantinople, 1733), *Parshas Vayeira*; Rabbi Kagan, *Ahavas Chesed*, Oschry translation, pp. 202-203.

40. See *Shulchan Aruch, Yoreh De'ah* 342 and commentaries.

41. Ibid.

42. Rabbi Bezalel Stern, *Responsa Betzeil HaChochmah* (Jerusalem, 1967), vol. 2, no. 44.

43. See pp. 80-85, this volume.

44. See Rabbi Greenwald, *Kol Bo al Aveilus*, p. 297, as it is written that King David comforted his wife (*2 Samuel* 12:24); Rabbi Gavriel Zinner, *Nitei Gavriel* (New York, 1993), p. 367 n. 7, citing *Rabbeinu Yonah*, chap. 3, *Berachos*; Rabbi Gershon Marber, *Darkei HaChaim* (Lublin, 1927), appendix to *siman* 4. See also Rabbi Yaakov Reischer, *Responsa Shevus Yaakov* (Lvov, 1861), vol. 3, no. 98, from where it would seem that he should then say *HaMokom yenachem eschem "v'osonu" besoch*, etc. Perhaps one should also use this addition when comforting a mourner on Tishah B'Av.

45. See Rabbi Berel Wein, *Chikrei Halachah* (Jerusalem: Mossad Harav Kook, 1976), pp. 44-46, discussing whether the law of *ger toshav* applies today. See also Rabbi Aaron Levine, *How to Perform the Great Mitzvah of Bikkur Cholim* (Toronto: Zichron Meir, 1987), p. 139 n. 105.

46. See *Devarim* 10:19; *Rambam, Mishneh Torah, Hilchos De'os*, chap. 6:4; *Bava Metzia* 58b and 59b.

47. See *Gittin* 61a; Yerushalmi, *Avodah Zarah* 1:3; *Shulchan Aruch, Yoreh De'ah* 335:9; Levine, *Zichron Meir al Aveilus*, p. 37 n. 15b; p. 74 n. 45; p. 337 n. 35; pp. 393-394 n. 16, for additional references; Rabbi Chaim Palagi, *Responsa Chaim b'Yad* (Smyrna, 1873), no. 33.

48. See *Shabbos* 152a; *Shulchan Aruch, Yoreh De'ah* 376:3; *Rambam, Yad HaChazakah, Hilchos Aveil*, chap. 13:4; Rabbi Yaakov Zolty, *Responsa Mishnas Yaavetz* (Jerusalem, 1984), *Yoreh De'ah*, no. 37. Rabbi Moses Isserles, *Remoh* (gloss to *Shulchan Aruch*) (Sulzbach, 1692), *Yoreh De'ah* 376, writes, however, that he has not seen this custom practiced.

49. *Shabbos* 152a-b. See *Rambam, Mishneh Torah, Hilchos Aveil*, chap. 14:7.

50. Cf. Rabbi Isserles, *Remoh, Yoreh De'ah* 384:3; Rabbi Chaim Dovid HaLevi, *Mekor Chaim HaShaleim* (Tel Aviv, 1974), vol. 5, p. 397, 21.

51. Rabbi Yosef Caro, *Beis Yosef* (gloss to *Tur*) (Venice-Sabbioneta, 1550-1559), *Yoreh De'ah* 393, citing *Kol Bo* (author unknown) (Naples, 1590), *Hilchos Aveil* 114, p. 88, that it is only necessary to do so for the first service after burial.

52. See Rabbi Zinner, *Nitei Gavriel*, p. 367, 5, and n. 6.

53. See chapter 2, n. 18. See also pp. 72 and 88.

CHAPTER 8

1. See p. 23.

2. See *Zohar, Parshas Korach*, p. 176b; Rabbi Shmuel Wosner, *Responsa Shevet HaLevi* (New York, 1981), vol. 2, *Yoreh De'ah*, no. 213. See also *Rashi, Sefer HaPardes* (Constantinople, 1802), *Hilchos Aveil*, p. 290, and Rabbi Simchah of Vitry, *Machzor Vitry* (Berlin, 1889), *Hilchos Aveil*, p. 244, no. 276.

3. See Rabbi Yehoshua Falk Katz, *Perishah* (gloss to *Tur*) (Lublin, 1635), *Yoreh De'ah*.

4. See p. 124, this volume.

5. Rabbi Maurice Lamm, *The Jewish Way in Death and Mourning* (New York: Jonathan David, 1969), pp. 136-137.

6. See p. 73, this volume.

7. See chapter 2, n. 18.

8. Peter Marris in *Understanding Bereavement and Grief* (New York: Yeshiva University Press, 1977), p. 29.

9. See also p. 33, this volume.

10. Interestingly in *Koheles Rabbah* 7, *Tinyana* 4, it states: "Rabbi Simon said, 'We find that those who went to the party house did not have their names publicized; those who went to the house of mourning did have their names publicized,' etc."

11. See p. 62, this volume.

12. *Moed Kattan* 15a; *Shulchan Aruch, Yoreh De'ah* 385:1.

13. *Shulchan Aruch,* loc. cit.

14. Rabbi Yechiel Michel Epstein, *Aruch HaShulchan* (Warsaw, 1898), *Yoreh De'ah* 343, 4; 385, 4. See also Rabbi Chanoch Grossberg, *Chazon l'Moed* (Jerusalem, 1975), p. 29 n. 13, and Rabbi Eliezer Valdenberg, *Even Yaakov* (Jerusalem, 1962), no. 55, for clarification, certainly not in an audible manner. HaGaon Rabbi Moshe Feinstein *ztz'l* would not even extend his hand in greeting while in the mourner's home—see Rabbi Ephraim Greenblatt, *Responsa Rivevos Ephraim* (New York, 1980), vol. 3, no. 375. See also Rabbi Ovadiah Yossef, *Responsa Yabia Omer* (Jerusalem, 1986), vol. 2, no. 31.

15. See Rabbi Yosef ben Moshe, *Leket Yosher* (Berlin, 1903), p. 110; Rabbi Zechariah Mendel, *Be'er Hetev* (gloss to *Shulchan Aruch*), *Yoreh De'ah* 385, 2; Rabbi Yekutiel Greenwald, *Kol Bo al Aveilus* (New York: Feldheim, 1947), pp. 103-104; Rabbi Moshe Stern, *Responsa Be'er Moshe* (New York, 1975), vol. 4, no. 106.

16. Rabbi Stern, *Responsa Be'er Moshe,* loc. cit.

17. *Shulchan Aruch, Yoreh De'ah* 385:1; Rabbi Yechiel Michel Tuchachinsky, *Gesher HaChaim* (Jerusalem, 1947), p. 224, 7:1.

18. See above, n. 14.

19. Some are even strict and refrain from this, depending on the *minhag.* See Rabbi Tuchachinsky, *Gesher HaChaim,* loc. cit., 4.

20. See Rabbi Yaakov ben Asher, *Tur* (Pieve de Sachi, 1475), *Yoreh De'ah* 376, and Rabbi Yehoshua Falk Katz, *Perishah* (gloss to *Tur*) (Lublin, 1635), ad loc., 2; Rabbi Yom Tov Ibn Ashvili, *Ritva,* to *Moed Kattan* 27b. Rabbi Yosef Chaim Sonnenfeld, *Responsa Salmas Chaim* (Bnei Brak, 1982), no. 422, even forbids this.

21. See *Moed Kattan* 21b; Rabbi Moses Isserles, *Remoh* (Sulzbach, 1692), *Yoreh De'ah* 381:1. Rabbi Tuchachinsky, *Gesher HaChaim,* p. 224, 7:3.

22. See Rabbi Tzvi Pesach Frank, *Responsa Har Tzvi* (Jerusalem, 1964), *Yoreh De'ah,* no. 290; Rabbi Yechiel Yaakov Weinberg, *Responsa Seridei Eish* (Jerusalem: Mossad haRav Kook, 1977), vol. 2, no. 135; Rabbi Ovadiah Hadayah, *Responsa Yaskil Avdi* (Jerusalem, 1983), vol. 6, *Yoreh De'ah,* no. 25; Rabbi Ovadiah Yossef, *Responsa Yabi Omer,* vol. 4, *Yoreh De'ah,* no. 35, 10; Rabbi Chanoch Grossberg, *Chazon l'Moed* (Jerusalem, 1975), p. 29, 18. See also Rabbi Yitzchok Hutner, *Pachad Yitzchak, Igros u'Kesavim* (New York, 1981), no. 255 (see p. 84, where I have quoted this letter).

23. See Rabbi Stern, *Responsa Be'er Moshe,* vol. 4, no. 107, who objects generally because this may be construed by others as giving "shalom" and certainly where it may lead to improper behavior. See also Rabbi Grossberg, *Chazon l'Moed,* loc. cit.—*mokom shenohagu;* Rabbi Ephraim Greenblatt, *Responsa Rivevos Ephraim,* vol. 3, 375—one should not introduce this in a place where it is not customary to do so.

24. Rabbi Tuchachinsky, *Gesher HaChaim,* p. 226, 7. There he quotes Rabbi Yekutiel Greenwald, *Ach l'Tzarah* (St. Louis, 1939), p. 265, citing *Tov Leches* and *Hadras Kodesh,* that one may even make a public *Mi Shebeirach* in shul for the mourner. See also Rabbi Sonnenfeld, *Responsa Salmas Chaim,* no. 425; Rabbi Stern, *Responsa Be'er Moshe,* vol. 6, no. 106; Rabbi Yossef, *Responsa Yabia Omer,* loc. cit.

25. See Rabbi Aaron Felder, *Yesodei Semochos* (New York: CIS Publications, 1992), p. 101, 7; Rabbi Tuchachinsky, *Gesher HaChaim ,* loc. cit.

26. See p. 58, this volume; also see Rabbi Isserles, *Remoh, Yoreh De'ah* 385:3.

27. See chapter 6, nn. 139 and 140, this volume.

28. See chapter 6, n. 142, this volume.

29. See Rabbi Eliezer Valdenberg, *Responsa Tzitz Eliezer* (Jerusalem, 1984), vol. 8, no. 33:4; Rabbi Felder, *Yesodei Semochos,* p. 96, 2a.

30. See p. 78, this volume.

31. See p. 80, this volume.

32. See Rabbi Yitzchak Alfiah, *HaKuntras HaYechiali* (Jerusalem, 1928), section *Beis Olomim,* chap. 15, p. 55a.

33. *Moed Kattan* 27b; Rabbi Isserles, *Remoh, Yoreh De'ah* 376:1.

34. Rabbi Yossef, *Responsa Yabia Omer,* vol. 3, *Yoreh De'ah,* no. 27; Rabbi Tuchachinsky, *Gesher HaChaim* (according to most poskim)

35. See Rabbi Epstein, *Aruch HaShulchan, Yoreh De'ah* 376, 4; Rabbi Valdenberg, *Even Yaakov,* no. 43; additional sources quoted in Rabbi Yossef, *Responsa Yabia Omer,* loc. cit.

36. Sources above quoting Rabbi Eliezer Fleckles, *Responsa Teshuvah m'Ahuvah* (Prague, 1821), vol. 3, no. 412.

37. *Moed Kattan* 27b; Rabbi Isserles, *Remoh,* loc. cit. See Levine, *Zichron Meir al Aveilus,* p. 97 and notes, for further discussion.

38. Rabbi Sholom Schwadron, *Daas Torah* (Jerusalem: Machon Daas Torah, 1980), *Yoreh De'ah* 376:2, citing *Nimukei Yosef.* See Rabbi Hillel Posek, *Responsa Hillel Omer* (Tel Aviv, 1957), *Yoreh De'ah,* no. 236, that it would also be permitted to say: "Sit, because standing is difficult for you," etc., where the visitor clarifies his words. Rabbi Uri Mayerfeld, *shlita,* suggested to me that perhaps the prohibition is only when one uses the Hebrew word *shev,* as this connotes *remaining* in one's previous state; perhaps the English word *sit* would not be prohibited.

39. See Rabbi Yitzchak Palagi, *Responsa Yaffe l'Lev* (Smyrna, 1872), vol. 3, *Yoreh De'ah* 376; Rabbi Valdenberg, *Even Yaakov,* no. 43.

40. *Moed Kattan* 28b; *Shulchan Aruch, Yoreh De'ah* 376:1.

41. *Moed Kattan,* loc. cit.

42. Rabbi Yaakov ben Asher, *Tur* (Pieve de Sachi, 1475), *Yoreh De'ah* 376; Rabbi Moshe Rivkes, *Be'er HaGolah* (Amsterdam, 1666), *Yoreh De'ah* 376, citing *Ramban, Toras HaAdam* (Constantinople, 1519), in the name of Rav Hai Gaon.

See Rabbi Moshe Noah, *Nachamu Ami* (Petach Tikvah, 1978), p. 67, 2, that this is the custom of the Sephardim.

43. *Berachos* 6b. According to Rabbi Epstein, *Aruch HaShulchan, Yoreh De'ah* 376:1, this is the reason why one may not initiate conversation, for the *aveil* must first express his acceptance of the Heavenly decree. See also Rabbi Israel Lau's essay in *B'Nesivei Chesed v'Emes* (Annual Journal of the *Chevra Kaddisha* of Tel Aviv, edited by Dr. Yitzchak Alfasi, Tel Aviv, 5753), pp. 13-16, and the other reason brought there that the *aveil* must first show his distress before one can begin to comfort him.

44. Rabbi Tzidkiah HaRofei, *Shibolei HaLeket* (Venice, 1546), *Semochos*, 20. See Rabbi Yitzchak Arieli, *Einayim l'Mishpat* (Jerusalem: Holvri, 1971) on *Berachos* 6b, citing *Teshuvas Gaonim*.

45. *Teshuvas Gaonim,* loc. cit.

46. See Rabbi Katz, *Perishah, Yoreh De'ah* 393, 3; Rabbi Chaim Beneviste, *Kenesses HaGedolah* (Leghorn, 1658), *Yoreh De'ah* 376, 7.

47. Rabbi Maurice Lamm, *The Jewish Way in Death and Mourning* (New York: Jonathan David, 1969), p. 138.

48. See Rabbi Shlomo Cohen, *P'eir HaDor* (Bnei Brak: Netzach, 1970), vol. 4, p. 51, in note citing from Rabbi Karelitz, the Chazon Ish; Rabbi Aryeh Ginzberg, *Responsa Divrei Chachomim* (New York, 1986), p. 230, citing from HaGaon Rabbi Moshe Feinstein; Rabbi Yitzchak Yossef, *Yalkut Yossef* (Jerusalem, 1989), vol. 7, p. 119, in note, citing from HaGaon Rabbi Ovadiah Yossef; Rabbi Valdenberg, *Responsa Tzitz Eliezer*, vol. 17, no. 45, 4.

49. See Rabbi Gavriel Zinner, *Nitei Gavriel* (New York, 1993), p. 377, 7, and n. 8.

50. Rabbi Menachem Mendel Schneerson, *Responsa Yagdil Torah* (New York, 1981), p. 294.

51. Rabbi Aharon Rotter, *Shaarei Aharon* (Bnei Brak, 1968), p. 82; Rabbi Valdenberg, *Responsa Tzitz Eliezer,* op. cit. See also essay of Rabbi Lau in *Binesivei Chesed v'Emes*, op. cit., that preferably the mourner should at least nod his head in indication that the visitor may speak.

52. Rabbis Nissim and Chaim Rabi, *Yakra d'Chaya* (Jerusalem: Nesiv Binyamin, 1980), p. 64, in name of Rabbi S. Dablitsky.

53. See p. 141, this volume. See also Rabbi Rotter, *Shaarei Aharon,* op. cit.; Rabbi Noah, *Nachamu Ami,* p. 67 n. 3, citing HaGaon Rabbi Shlomo Zalman Auerbach. Another proof to this would seemingly be from the *shurah* in the cemetery, where this phrase is uttered by the comforters without any initiated conversation on the part of the mourners, although a distinction can be made.

54. See Rabbi Aaron Levine, *The Complete Yizkor Handbook* (Toronto: Zichron Meir, 1987), chap. 4.

55. See Rabbi Yitzchak Alfiah, *HaKuntras HaYechiali*, loc. cit., pp. 53-55. The Hebrew letters of the word משנה, *mishnah*, spell the Hebrew word נשמה, *neshamah* (soul). See also *Tanna d'Bei Eliyahu Zutta*, chap. 12. See also Rabbi Margoliyos in *Sefer HaYahrzeit* (Jerusalem, 1975), *maamar LeOlam havei rotz lemishnah.*

56. A copy of the forms can be found in Appendix II.

57. Rabbi Moshe Kaufman, *Lechem HaPanim* (gloss to *Shulchan Aruch*) (Hanau, 1716), *Yoreh De'ah* 376, in the name of *Maanei Lashon*, cited in Rabbi

Tzvi Hirsch of Vilna, *Beis Lechem Yehudah* (gloss to *Shulchan Aruch*) (Zolkiew, 1733), *Yoreh De'ah* 376. See also Rabbi Eliyah Shapiro, *Eliyah Rabbah* (Sulzbach, 1752), *Orach Chaim* 224, 7; *Chidushei Rabbi Akivah Eiger*, ad loc.; Rabbi Epstein, *Aruch HaShulchan*, ad loc., 11. The reason for this is because of *ruach tumah,* an unfavorable spiritual uncleanliness that rests upon the belongings of the deceased.

58. Rabbi Menachem Azariah Meir Kastilnovo, *Misgeres HaShulchan* (Livorno, 1840), *Yoreh De'ah* 376, 3; cited also in Rabbi Valdenberg, *Even Yaakov*, no. 44, 3.

59. See Rabbi Valdenberg, *Even Yaakov*, loc. cit.

60. Rabbi Yosef Yuspa Nordlinger Hahn, a contemporary of the Shaloh HaKadosh, *Yosef Ometz* (Frankfurt am Main, 1723), p. 330, in name of his rebbe, Rabbi Segal. See also Rabbi Yosef Kashman Segal, *Noheg Katzon Yosef* (Hanau, 1718), p. 54, 4, also quoted by Rabbi Chaim Palagi, *Responsa Chaim b'Yad,* no. 125, 17.

61. See Rabbi Yossef, *Responsa Yabia Omer,* vol. 4, *Yoreh De'ah* 35, 4.

62. *Pesachim* 110b. See also Levine, *Zichron Meir al Aveilus,* pp. 18-20 and notes, for a further discussion of this principle and other examples in connection with mourning customs.

63. See Rabbi Epstein, *Aruch HaShulchan, Yoreh De'ah* 376, 11; Rabbi Tuchachinsky, *Gesher HaChaim,* p. 213; Rabbi Felder, *Yesodei Semochos,* p. 96, sec. 6, 1a. In the latter the author adds, "Even when a mourner wishes to loan a *sefer,* the offer should not be accepted. In the event that one's possessions were left in a place where *shivah* is being observed, they may be retrieved only if it is extremely necessary, and provided no mourners benefit financially from its being removed," citing HaGaon Rabbi Feinstein. In 1b he adds, "One may retrieve one's own possessions from a mourner's home only if the mourner would not gain financially from its being removed," citing *Noam* (Jerusalem: Machon Torah Shleimah, 1973), vol. 16, *Shaar HaHalachah,* p. 107. The latter two ideas are not related to the first notion, but rather to the prohibition on a mourner not to conduct business during the *shivah* period—see *Shulchan Aruch, Yoreh De'ah* 380.

64. See Rabbi Herbert Dobrinsky, *A Treasury of Sephardic Laws and Customs* (New York: Ktav/Yeshiva University, 1986), p. 83.

65. See above, n. 63.

66. Based on *Shabbos* 152a-b, and *Rambam, Mishneh Torah, Hilchos Aveil,* chap. 14:7, that the soul of the deceased is also comforted by the visit. In addition, from *Moed Kattan* 21b, in reference to Rabbi Akivah, it seems clear that it is more of an honor when a personal visit is made. See sources in next note. See also Rabbi Greenwald, *Kol Bo al Aveilus,* vol. 2, p. 9; Rabbi, *Responsa Minchas Dovid,* nos. 72 and 73, cited in Rabbi Binyamin Goldberg, *Pnei Baruch* (Jerusalem, 1986), p. 128 n. 24; Rabbi Yitzchak Hutner, *Pachad Yitzchak Igros u'Kesavim* (New York, 1981), p. 56, 2.

67. See Rabbi Feinstein, *Responsa Igros Moshe, Orach Chaim,* vol. 4, no. 40, 11; Rabbi Stern, *Responsa Be'er Moshe,* vol. 2, no. 106; Rabbi Greenblatt, *Responsa Rivevos Ephraim,* vol. 3, nos. 84 and 377. For many additional sources on this subject see Levine, *Zichron Meir al Aveilus,* vol. 1, pp. 98-99, n. 121.

68. See source quoted in Rabbi Greenblatt, *Responsa Rivevos Ephraim,* loc. cit.; Rabbi Felder, *Yesodei Semochos,* p. 102, 8b.

69. See p. 72, this volume.

70. See above, n. 15.

71. Rabbi Feinstein, *Responsa Igros Moshe, Orach Chaim,* vol. 4, no. 40, 11.

72. Rabbi Schneerson, *Responsa Yagdil Torah,* p. 293.

73. See p. 78, this volume.

74. See p. 43, this volume.

75. See Rabbi Hutner, *Pachad Yitzchak Igros u'Kesavim*—many condolence letters, especially nos. 242, 243, 252, 255.

76. *Eruvin* 70b.

77. Please refer also to the two famous letters reprinted in Chapter 9, pp. 112-119.

CHAPTER 9

1. See pp. 73-74, 74-75, 76-78.

2. See p. 77, this volume.

3. Sidney Greenberg, in *Understanding Bereavement and Grief* (New York: Ktav/Yeshiva University, 1977), p. 96. See also Rabbi Chaim Palagi, *Responsa Chaim b'Yad* (Smyrna, 1873), no. 125, 7.

4. Simcha Steven Paull, *Guidelines to Understanding the Tradition of Shiva* (Toronto: The Benjamin Family Foundation, 1987), p. 15.

5. Rabbi Yitzchak Alfiah, *HaKuntras HaYechiali* (Jerusalem, 1928), sec. *Beis Olomim,* pp. 55a, b.

6. See *Kol Bo* (author unknown) (Naples, 1590), *Hilchos Aveil,* p. 88. The verse in Proverbs 12:25, reads, "When a man has a worry in his heart he should express it [to others]." See also Rabbi Eliezer Papo, *Peleh Yo'eitz* (Constantinople, 1825), vol. 1, *Aveilus,* p. 13.

7. Jack D. Spiro, *A Time to Mourn, Judaism and the Psychology of Bereavement* (New York: Bloch, 1985), pp. 114-116, and many other studies.

8. Rabbi Sydney Greenberg, *A Treasury of Comfort* (North Hollywood, CA: Wilshire Book Company, 1975), p. 146.

9. Ibid., p, 147.

10. See Introduction, this volume.

11. *Bava Basra* 16b.

12. *Breishis* 30:2.

13. *Ramban,* ad loc., citing *Breishis Rabbah, Parshas Vayeitzei,* 71, 7.

14. See Dr. Meir Wikler's article, "The Psychodynamics of Grief," *Jewish Observer* 18:2 (January 1985): 20.

15. See Rabbi Moshe Mos, *Mattei Moshe* (Cracow, 1591), *Erech Gemillus Chasadim,* pt. 6; Rabbi Yechiel Michel Epstein, *Aruch HaShulchan* (Warsaw, 1898), *Yoreh De'ah* 376, 1. See also *Zohar, Parshas Korach*; Rabbi Aaron Berechiah of Modena, *Maavar Yabok* (Mantua, 1626), sec. *Sifsei Renanos,* chap. 19.

16. Rabbi Moses Isserles, *Remoh* (gloss to *Shulchan Aruch*) (Sulzbach, 1692), *Yoreh De'ah* 376:2. See Rabbi Zechariah Mendel, *Be'er Hetev* (gloss to *Shulchan Aruch*), and Rabbi David HaLevi, *Turei Zahav (Taz)* (gloss to *Shulchan Aruch*) (Lublin, 1646), ad loc., on words of Rabbi Shlomo Luria, *Yam Shel Shlomo* to *Bava Kamma* (Prague, 1616).

17. See *Rashi* in name of *Toras Kohanim*; *Vayikra Rabbah* 12:2.

18. Rabbi Aharon Yaakov Greenberg, *Iturei Torah* (Tel Aviv: Yavneh, 1967),

Vayikra, p. 53, told to me by Rabbi Elias Schwartz at the 1993 Torah Umesorah Principals' Convention.

19. Quoted in a letter by Rabbi Don Segal cited in Rabbi Yisraeil Byfus, *Yalkut Lekach Tov, Pirkei Emunah u'Nechamah* (Kfar Chassidim: Tashbar HoRav, 1993), p. 110.

20. Simcha Raz, *A Tzaddik in Our Time* (Jerusalem: Feldheim, 1976), p. 172.

21. Harold Kushner, *When Bad Things Happen to Good People* (New York: Shocken, 1981), pp. 9–10. See Rabbi Aaron HaLevi of Barcelona, *Sefer HaChinuch* (Jerusalem: Eshkol, n.d.), *mitzvah* 264.

22. Kushner, *When Bad Things Happen to Good People,* loc. cit., pp. 19–23. The Talmud also says one should not say this—see *Bava Metzia* 58b. See Rabbi Moshe Gross, *Otzar HaAggadah* (Jerusalem: Mossad Harav Kook, 1977), *Yisurin,* vol. 1, pp. 475–476, numerous citations.

23. Kushner, loc. cit., pp. 21–22.

24. Kushner, loc. cit., p. 26. See *Shemos Rabbah* 34, 1.

25. Kushner, loc. cit., p. 27.

26. Ibid., p. 28.

27. Ibid., p. 53.

28. *Pirkei Avos* 4:19.

29. *Berachos* 7a.

30. Isaiah 64:3.

31. *Pirkei Avos* 4:22.

32. Rabbi Eliyahu Dessler, *Michtav m'Eliyahu* (Jerusalem, 1983), vol. 1, p. 4.

33. *Pirkei Avos,* end of chap. 5.

34. See also Introduction, this volume.

35. See Rabbi Gross, *Otzar HaAggadah,* loc. cit., vol. 3, pp. 1381–1389, numerous citations.

36. Ibid. See sources, *Sanhedrin* 90b–92a.

37. Maimonides, Principle 13. See daily *siddur,* end of *Shacharis.*

38. *Mishnah, Sanhedrin* 90a; Rambam, *Mishneh Torah, Hilchos Teshuvah,* chap. 3:5 and 6.

39. *Sanhedrin* 91a.

40. Rabbi Maurice Lamm in Sol L. Nemzoff, *Understanding Bereavement and Grief* (New York: Ktav/Yeshiva University Press, 1977), pp. 87–88.

41. See pp. 15–16, this volume.

42. Lamm, pp. 85–86.

43. *Yerushalmi, Sanhedrin* 6:10.

44. See Rabbi Shmuel Greineman, *Chofetz Chaim al HaTorah* (Bnei Brak, n.d.), p. 285, in *Maasei l'Melech.*

45. See p. 29, this volume.

46. *Berachos* 60b. See also Rabbi Eliezer Papo, *Peleh Yo'eitz* (Constantinople, 1825), vol. 2, *Nechamah,* p. 26a.

47. *Berachos* 48b, 54a. See also Rabbi Aaron Berechiah of Modena, *Maavar Yabok,* sec. *Sifsei Renanos,* chap. 19.

48. *Berachos* 60b.

49. See commentary of Rabbi Ezekiel Landau, *Tziyon l'Nefesh Chayah (Tzlach)* (New York: A. Y. Friedman, 1956), ad. loc.

50. *Chayei HaMussar,* vol. 2, p. 64, cited in Rabbi Zelig Pliskin, *A Gateway to Happiness* (Jerusalem, 1983), p. 367.

51. *Toras Avraham,* intro., p. 14, cited in Rabbi Pliskin, *A Gateway to Happiness,* ibid.

52. Rabbi M. Yoshor, *HaChofetz Chaim, Chayav u'Paalo* (Tel Aviv: Netzach, 1958), vol. 1, p. 248.

53. G. Naftali, *Nichum Aveilim* (Jerusalem: Yetzirah, n.d.), p. 17.

54. See Isaiah chap. 54.

55. G. Naftali, *Nichum Aveilim,* op. cit., p. 99.

56. Rabbi Moshe Chaim Luzzatto, *Messilas Yesharim (Path of the Just),* English ed. (Jerusalem: Feldheim, 1966), chap. 19.

57. Irving J. Rosenbaum, *The Holocaust and Halakhah* (New York: Ktav, 1976), pp. 86-87.

58. *Pirkei Avos* 2:4.

59. See Rosenbaum, *The Holocaust and Halakhah;* Yaffa Eliach, *Hasidic Tales of the Holocaust;* Mordekhai Eliav, *Ani Maamin* (Jerusalem: Mossad Harav Kook, 1965); Moshe Prager, *Eleh Shelo Nichne'u* (Bnei Brak: Netzach, 1963), and others.

60. Brenner, *The Faith and Doubt of Holocaust Survivors.*

61. I heard this parable as stated in the name of the Dubno Maggid. In truth he is the source, although as printed in his work, *Kochav miYaakov* (Warsaw, 1880), *Parshas Acharei Mos,* the parable is only with one person, not two brothers. The parable has been also said by Rabbi Elchonon Wasserman (see *Reb Elchonon* [New York: Mesorah, 1982], pp. 411-412), who used it directly to explain the horrors of the Holocaust.

62. See also Rabbi Yaakov Culi, *Yalkut Me'Am Loez* (Constantinople, 1773), *Parshas Shoftim,* p. 81, for another version of the same story.

63. Rabbi Yissachar Frand, cassette tape. See n. 72.

64. *Pirkei Avos* 4:11.

65. *Berachos* 5a.

66. Told by Rabbi Yudlevitz, cited in Rabbi Yisrael Byfus, *Yalkut Lekach Tov* (Kfar Chasidim: Tashbar HoRav, 1990), vol. 1, *Breishis,* pp. 142-144.

67. See Isaiah 55:9.

68. *Pesikta Rabbasi d'Rav Kahana (Parah); Rashi, Parshas Chukas, Bamidbar* 19:2.

69. *Devarim* 14:1.

70. Kushner, *When Bad Things Happen to Good People,* loc. cit., pp. 42-43.

71. Job 42:1-6.

72. The above thoughts have been gleaned from Rabbi Yissachar Frand's tape no. 24, "A Torah Response to When Bad Things Happen to Good People."

73. *Pesikta Rabbasi,* chap. 26.

74. *Moed Kattan* 27b.

75. Rabbi Moshe Rosenstein, *Ahavas Meishorim* (New York 1958), p. 185, cited in Rabbi Pliskin, *A Gateway to Happiness,* p. 364.

76. Rabbi Chaim Ibn Atar, *Or HaChaim* (Venice, 1744), *Devarim* 14:1.

77. *Moed Kattan* 25b. See Jeremiah 22:10.

78. Simcha Raz, *A Tzaddik in Our Time,* pp. 172-173.

79. *Koheles Rabbah* 7, 4.

80. Quoted by Rabbi Shlomo Wolbe, in *Alei Shur* (Be'er Yaakov, 1968), pp. 303-305.

81. Translated from original, Dovid Leib Zunz, *Gedulas Yehonoson* (Jerusalem, 1968), pp. 142-146.

82. See Rabbi Moshe Savar, *Michlol HaMaamarim u'Pisgamim* (Jerusalem: Mossad HaRav Kook, 1961), vol. 3, p. 1754, citing *Shaarei Torah*.

83. See Rabbi Pliskin, *A Gateway to Happiness*, pp. 368-369.

84. Dr. Meir Wikler, *Jewish Observer*, January 1985, pp. 20-21.

85. Rabbi M. Yoshor, *HaChofetz Chaim* (Tel Aviv: Netzach, 1958), vol. 3, p. 1018.

86. Simcha Raz, *A Tzaddik in Our Time*, p. 174.

87. Rabbeinu Yerucham, *Toldos Adam v'Chavah* (Constantinople, 1516), *Chelek Chavah, Nesiv 28; Sefer HaChinuch, mitzvah 264.*

88. See Rabbi Yerucham Levovitz, *Sefer Daas Chochmah u'Mussar* (New York, 1969), vol. 3, p. 230.

89. G. Nuful, *Nichum Aveilim*, p. 33.

90. Rabbi Moses Isserles, *Remoh* (gloss to *Shulchan Aruch*) (Sulzbach, 1692), *Yoreh De'ah* 376:2. See *Berachos* 60a.

91. Rabbi Samson Raphael Hirsch, *Horeb* (London: Soncino Press, 1962), vol. 1, p. 205.

92. *Koheles* 3:4.

93. *Shabbos* 105b.

94. Ibid.

95. *Berachos* 32b.

96. *Moed Kattan* 27b.

97. Ibid.

98. *Bava Basra* 60b.

99. William B. Silverman and Kenneth M. Cinnamon, *When Mourning Comes* (Northvale, NJ: Jason Aronson, 1990), p. 18.

100. *Midrash Mishlei, Shochar Tov* 31b; *Yalkut Shimoni, Mishlei* 31, 964.

101. Rabbi Hirsch, *Horeb*, vol. 2, pp. 433-434.

102. Ibid., vol. 1, p. 214.

103. See Rabbi Chaim Vital, *Sefer HaGilgulim* and other sources.

104. Rabbi Yom Tov Erlich, adapted from the writings of Rabbi Chaim Vital, cited in Rabbi Yisrael Byfus, *Yalkut Lekach Tov* (Kfar Chasidim: Tashbar HoRav, 1990), vol. 5, *Devarim I*, pp. 284-287. See also *Yalkut Shimoni, Breishis* 2:20.

105. Rabbi Shlomo Yosef Zevin, *Sippurei Chasidim al HaTorah* (Jerusalem: Beis Hillel, n.d.), *Parshas Shemos*, pp. 138-140.

106. Simcha Raz, *A Tzaddik in Our Time* , p. 176.

107. Grace Perkins Oursler and April Armstrong, *When Sorrow Comes* (New York: Doubleday, 1950), cited by Sidney Greenberg, *A Treasury of Comfort* (North Hollywood, CA: Wilshire Book Company, 1975), pp. 125-126.

108. *Moed Kattan* 25b.

109. Simcha Raz, *A Tzaddik in Our Time*, pp. 176-177.

110. Ibid., pp. 174-175.

111. Heard from Rabbi Elazar Moshe Rabinowitz.

112. Rabbi Paysach Krohn, *The Maggid Speaks* (New York: Mesorah, 1987), pp. 30-31.

113. Simcha Raz, *A Tzaddik in Our Time,* pp. 179–180.

114. *Avos d'Reb Nosson,* chap. 14.

115. *Berachos* 5b.

116. Rabbi Elya Lopian, *Lev Eliyahu* (Jerusalem, 1972), vol. 1, p. 60; Rabbi Yitzchok Waldshein cited in *Chayei HaMussar* (Bnei Brak: Hotzoas Chochmah U'Mussar, 1963), vol. 1, pp.12–13.

117. Rabbi Yoetz Reketz, *Siach Sarfei Kodesh* (Lodz, 1931), vol. 3, p. 78.

118. See Yaffa Eliach, *Hasidic Tales of the Holocaust,* pp. 231–232, and Rabbi Paysach Krohn, *In the Footsteps of the Maggid* (New York: Mesorah, 1992), pp. 162–163.

119. *Koheles Rabbah* 5.

120. *Shir HaShirim Rabbah* 6.

121. Author unknown. See Sidney Greenberg, *A Treasury of Comfort,* p. 159.

122. *2 Samuel* 12:16–24.

123. *Avodah Zarah* 4b. See also *Sanhedrin* 107a.

124. Rabbi Yaakov Kranz, *Ohel Yaakov* (Jozefow, 1830), *Parshas Vayigash* 45:5.

125. See p. 133, this volume.

126. See Chapter 11, this volume, for additional stories and words of comfort.

CHAPTER 10

1. Rabbi Aaron Berechiah of Modena, *Maavar Yabok* (Mantua, 1626), sec. *Imrei Noam,* chap. 35. See, however, Rabbi Gavriel Zinner, *Nitei Gavriel* (New York, 1993), p. 376, end of n. 3, citing Lubavitcher Rebbe.

2. Cf. Rabbi Mordechai Leib Winkler, *Responsa Levushei Mordechai* (Budapest, 1917–1924), *Tinyana, Yoreh De'ah,* no. 149; Rabbi Eliezer Chaim Deutsch, *Responsa Dudaei HaSadeh* (Satmar, 1929), no. 95; Rabbi Yosef Schwartz, *Vayitzbor Yosef* (Oradea, 1936), no. 82, 3; Rabbi Yechiel Michel Tuchachinsky, *Gesher HaChaim* (Jerusalem, 1947), p. 338, 10.

3. See *Ramban, Toras HaAdam* (Constantinople, 1519); Rabbi Yaakov ben Asher, *Tur* (Pieve de Sachi, 1475), *Yoreh De'ah* 376.

4. Cf. Rabbi Yaakov Chaim Soffer, *Kaf HaChaim* (Jerusalem, 1963), *Orach Chaim* 284, 37; Rabbi Yehudah Leib Tzirelson, *Responsa Gevul Yehudah* (Pietrikow, 1906), *Orach Chaim,* 2; Rabbi Abraham Stern, *Responsa Kisvei Eish* (Jerusalem, 1964), vol. 1, no. 6.

5. See Rabbi Aaron Levine, *The Complete Yizkor Handbook* (Toronto: Zichron Meir, 1987), p. 58, p. 176 n. 189, and *Sefer Teffilah k'Hilchasah,* p. 233 n. 96.

6. See Rabbi Ephraim Greenblatt, *Responsa Rivevos Ephraim* (New York, 1980), vol. 3, p. 424, from Rabbi Soffer, *Kaf HaChaim.* See also the discussion there as to whether it would be more appropriate to recite the phrase in the middle of the visit.

7. See Rabbi Yaakov Chaim Tzemach, *Sefer Negid u'Metzaveh* (Constantinople, 1726), *Aveilus,* and Rabbi Eliezer Valdenberg, *Responsa Tzitz Eliezer* (Jerusalem, 1988), vol. 17, no. 7, as to why the word *"HaMokom"* is used.

8. I have had much trouble tracing the origin of this famous phrase of comfort. Although a similar prayer is offered when praying for a sick person and is a

talmudic prayer (see *Shabbos* 12b and *Shulchan Aruch, Yoreh De'ah* 335, 6), never-theless the mourner's phrase of comfort is not mentioned. Snatches of the phrase are mentioned in the *Shulchan Aruch, Yoreh De'ah* 379, in connection with the special grace after meals said, according to some customs, in the mourner's home, or by the law of comforting on *Shabbos*. As far as early sources are concerned, we only find the following: "*Baal nechamos yenachem eschem*"—"May the Master of com-fort comfort you" (*Kesubos* 8b); "*Hashochen babayis hazeh yenachemcha*"—"The One Who dwells in this house [the Temple] should comfort you" (*Pirkei d'Rabbi Eliezer,* chap. 17). In Rabbi Yitzchak Abohab, *Menoras HaMa'or* (Jerusalem: Mossad Horav Kook, 1961), p. 453, the version of the above citation in *Pirkei d'Rabbi Eliezer* is *HaMokom yenachemcho*. See also later the sources for the *minhag* of the Sephardim, which is based on a scriptural verse. Rabbi Tuchachinsky, author of *Gesher HaChaim*, one of the classic books on mourning, merely refers to it as *habrachah hamesoris*, the "traditional blessing," but cites no source (p. 210, 8). The earliest sources I have found are Rabbi Yehoshua Falk Katz, *Perishah* (gloss to *Tur*) (Lublin, 1635), in *Yoreh De'ah* 393, 3, with slight differences—"*Hashem yenachemcha im she'ar aveilei Tziyon*." (Rabbi Katz lived from 1540 to 1614), and Rabbi Yechiel Michal Epstein Ashkenazi, *Kitzur Shaloh* (Furth, 1693), p. 30a, shown to me by Rabbi Wolmark of Detroit, who only slightly changes two words (*im she'arei* instead of *besoch she'ar*). The Shaloh HaKodosh (*Shnei Luchos HaBris*), Rabbi Isaiah ben Avraham HaLevi Horowitz, lived between 1560 and 1630. See also *Breishis Rabbah,* 100, 14. According to this, the origin of the phrase is approximately just 400 years old.

9. *Kesubos* 8b.

10. Psalms 147:3.

11. Jeremiah 31:12.

12. Isaiah 54:7.

13. Hoseah 6:1.

14. *Breishis Rabbah* 84, 21; *Maseches Sofrim,* chap. 21.

15. Rabbi Eliyahu Eliezer Dessler, *Michtav m'Eliyahu* (Jerusalem, 1983), vol. 4, p. 342.

16. See Rabbi Moshe Savar, *Michlol HaMaamarim v'HaPisgamim* (Jerusalem: Mossad Harav Kook, 1961), bottom of p. 1631; *Devarim* 2, 14. See also Rabbi Eliezer Papo, *Peleh Yo'eitz* (Constantinople, 1825), vol. 2, *Nechamah,* p. 26a.

17. From Rabbi Sydney Greenberg, *A Treasury of Comfort* (North Hollywood, CA: Wilshire Book Company, 1975), attributed to Helen Keller.

18. See Yaffa Eliach, *Hasidic Tales of the Holocaust* (New York: Avon Books, 1982), pp. 188-189.

19. Refer also to Rabbi Schwab's interpretation of this phrase and the word *nichum* in general, p. xxvii, this volume.

20. See Rabbi Shimon Frankfurter, *Sefer HaChaim* (Amsterdam, 1703); Rabbi Yitzchak Baer, *Totza'os Chaim* (Rodelheim, 1832); Rabbi Tuchachinsky, *Gesher HaChaim,* p. 210, 8; Rabbi Moshe Stern, *Responsa Be'er Moshe* (New York, 1972), vol. 2, no. 107; Rabbi Label Katz, *Chesed Shel Emes* (New York, 1981), p. 116 n. 19; Rabbi Gavriel Zinner, *Nitei Gavriel,* p. 383 n. 3.

21. Rabbi Katz, *Chesed Shel Emes,* loc. cit.

22. *Imrei Emes Likutim,* p. 206.

23. See *Maavar Yabok, Sifsei Renanos,* chap. 19.

24. *Kol Bo* (author unknown) (Naples, 1590), *Hilchos Aveil,* 114, *Tinachamu min HaShamayim;* Rabbi Yaakov ben Asher, *Tur, Yoreh De'ah* 376; *Rambam, Yad HaChazakah, Hilchos Aveil,* chap. 14:2.

25. See Isaiah 66:13, *U'viYerushalayim tenuchamu.*

26. See Rabbi Aryeh Z. Ginzberg, *Responsa Divrei Chachomim* (New York, 1986), p. 227, citing HaGaon Rabbi Yaakov Kaminetzky.

27. Ibid., citing HaGaon Rabbi Moshe Feinstein. See note there from HaGaon Rabbi Moshe Bick. See Rabbi Yosef ben Moshe, *Leket Yosher* (Berlin, 1903-1904), *Yoreh De'ah,* p. 91, in the name of Rabbi Israel Isserlein, *Terumas HaDeshen* (Venice, 1519). See also Rabbi A. Horowitz, *Sefer Orchos Rabbeinu* (Bnei Brak, 1991), p. 313, concerning the Steipler Gaon. Incidentally, he mentions there that when the Steipler Gaon used to exit from the room, he faced the mourners.

28. Rabbi Yisroel Dovid Harfenes, *Responsa Vayevarech Dovid* (New York, 1989), vol. 2, sec. *Nechamas Sarah,* no. 8, so that the *aveil* is displaying his mourning at the time the visitors are comforting him. See Rabbi Shabsai ben Meir HaKohen, *Sifsei Kohen (Shach)* (gloss to *Shulchan Aruch*) (Cracow, 1646-1647), *Yoreh De'ah* 387. See Rabbi Shlomo ben Moshe, *Aveil HaShitim* (Jerusalem: Machon Yerushalayim, 1980), p. 91, 17.

29. See *Shulchan Aruch, Yoreh De'ah* 386:1, and *Shach;* Rabbi Malkiel Tennenbaum, *Responsa Divrei Malkiel* (Jerusalem, 1987), vol. 2, no. 93.

30. See above, pp. 75-76.

31. Rabbi Harfenes, *Responsa VaYevarech Dovid,* loc. cit.; Rabbi Aaron Felder, *Yesodei Semochos* (New York: CIS Publishers, 1992), p. 90, 4a. See Rabbi Yekutiel Greenwald, *Kol Bo al Aveilus* (New York: Feldheim, 1973), vol. 1, p. 298, citing Rabbi Tennenbaum, *Responsa Divrei Malkiel,* op. cit.

32. See Rabbi Felder, *Yesodei Semochos,* p. 101, 5, citing Rabbi Eliezer Valdenberg, *Even Yaakov* (Jerusalem, 1962), no. 13. There is not really an *obligation* to say it one time, but rather one is *permitted* to do so and it does not contravene the *Shulchan Aruch, Yoreh De'ah* 354, that says one cannot comfort two mourners at the same time, since one is using a common phrase to all mourners. See also Rabbi Yisrael Landau, *Responsa Beis Yisrael* (New York, 1976), *Yoreh De'ah,* no. 138.

33. Rabbi Zinner, *Nitei Gavriel,* p. 383, 3.

34. Ibid., op. cit., citing *Kovetz Mesorah,* vol. 5, p. 48.

35. Logical outcome of n. 32 above.

36. Rabbi Menachem Mendel Schneerson, the Lubavitcher Rebbe, in *Kuntras v'HaChai Yitten es Libo* (New York: Vaad Hanochos B'Lahak, 1988), p. 74, stresses that one should particularly say *Amein.* Rabbi Moshe Noah, *Nachamu Ami* (Petach Tikvah, 1978), p. 68, 11, and n. 12*, also cites HaGaon Rabbi Shlomo Zalman Auerbach that they should answer *Amein.*

37. Rabbi Aaron Felder, *Yesodei Semochos,* p. 101, 2a, quoting HaGaon Rabbi Moshe Feinstein, because it appears that by answering *Amein* one wants to mourn. Perhaps the explanation for this is similar to the reason offered by *Raavad* for not making a *berachah* when pain of others is involved (see chapter 2, n. 22). Similarly, it is the case in responding *Amein,* despite the fact that it refers to the aspect of comfort.

38. See Rabbi Yitzchak Hutner, *Pachad Yitzchak Igros u'Kesavim* (New York, 1981), p. 318; cf. also Rabbi Nissim Ashkenazi, *Responsa Maasei Avraham* (Smyrna, 1855), no. 60.

39. See Rabbi Jerome Fishman, *Understanding Bereavement and Grief* (New York: Ktav/Yeshiva University, 1977), p. 207.

40. *Sefer HaMinhagim, Minhagei Chabad* (New York: Kehot Publication Society, 1967), p. 77; cited also in Rabbi Noah, *Nachamu Ami*, p. 69, 14. See also *Midrash Rabbah, Esther* 8, 2.

41. Heard from Rabbi Gavriel Ginzberg, at a shivah house.

42. Rabbi Noah, *Nachamu Ami*, p. 68, 11, in name of HaGaon Rabbi Chaim Noah.

43. *Maavar Yabok, Sifsei Emes*, chap. 34. Also, see p. 146, this volume, for additional phrases added when mourners rise from shivah on the seventh day.

44. *Sefer HaMinhagim, Minhagei Chabad*, p. 77.

45. Rabbi Noah, *Nachamu Ami*, p. 68, 12.

46. *Sefer HaMinhagim, Minhagei Chabad*, loc. cit.; Rabbi Noah, *Nachamu Ami*, loc. cit. See also *Tur, Yoreh De'ah* 379, that in the special grace after meals they added, "*Goder pirtzos Yisrael, Hu yigdor hapirtzah hazos mei'aleinu u'mei'al aveil zeh lechaim u'leshalom.*"

47. See n. 40.

48. See Rabbi Chanoch Grossberg, *Chazon l'Moed* (Jerusalem, 1975), p. 55, 2. Rabbi Yitzchak Yosset, *Yalkut Yosef* (Jerusalem, 1989), vol. 7, p. 181. See below, n. 61.

49. See below, n. 61. See also Rabbi Yaakov Chaim Soffer, *Kaf HaChaim* (Jerusalem, 1963), *Orach Chaim,* 287.

50. See Dr. Joseph H. Hertz, *The Authorized Daily Prayer Book* (New York: Bloch, 1955), pp. 1094-1098.

51. *Kol Bo, Hilchos Aveil,* 114, p 88b. See also Rabbi Avraham Chaim Adadi, *Responsa Vayikra Avraham* (Livorno, 1865), *Kuntras Makom Shenahagu*, p. 126b, 16, concerning the minhag of washing the mourner, etc., all as a sign of instilling belief in resurrection of the dead.

52. *Sefer HaMinhagim, Minhagei Chabad,* p. 77; Rabbi Isaac Ushpol, *Darkei Chesed* (New York: 1975), p. 90, writes in n. 14 that he did not find a source for this. See also Rabbi Noah, *Nachamu Ami*, p. 69, 15, and n. 15, citing Rabbi Moshe Bergman, author of *Zibula Basraisa* (Jerusalem, 1931), heard from him and others, although this is not written in *Zibula Basraisa.*

Many years ago I wrote to the Lubavitcher Rebbe, enquiring the source for this custom, but did not merit a reply. When I was in Miami several years ago, I spoke to a member of the *Chevrah Kaddisha* (I have forgotten his name), who mentioned that he recalled this was done in Europe at the end of the taharah (the purification of the body). It would seem that this act symbolizes that this should be the finality of death.

53. This is the prevalent custom. I thought this may be connected with what is quoted by Rabbi Greenwald (*Kol Bo al Aveilus,* p. 280, 9): "Yosef ben Matisyahu in his book *Milchamos HaYehudim,* beginning of the second book, brings the minhag Yisrael that was prevalent in the times of the Temple—"When the shivah was over, the mourner made a big party for all the people, which was called '*lechem onim*';

this was an old accepted practice. In later days many became poor as a result of this, for many times they would expend all of their money in order to feed all of the comforters, not wishing to be considered as ones who desecrated the honor and loving memory of their departed fathers." See also there, p. 299 n. 42. Thus in order to spare the financial burden of a full meal, the custom is to provide light refreshments and a *lechaim*. This is very similar to the *minhag* of providing "*tikkun*" on the day of the *Yahrzeit*. See citation in Rabbi Yitzchak Weiss, *Responsa Minchas Yitzchok* (Jerusalem, 1976), vol. 6, no. 135, citing from *Chesed l'Avraham*. See also above, p. 59, the *minhag* of Sephardim.

54. *Kol Bo* (author unknown) (Naples, 1590), *Hilchos Aveil*, 114–this is what Rabbi Greenwald, *Kol Bo al Aveilus*, is probably referring to when he writes about the *minhag* to accompany the *neshamah* (p. 299, 55). Accordingly, he is not referring to walking around the block, but rather to going to the cemetery, for this is what the *Kol Bo* is talking about. If he is referring to walking around the block, there is no source from *Kol Bo*, as explained. See *Tur*, end of *Yoreh De'ah* 344; *Darkei Moshe, Yoreh De'ah* 393, 3; see Rabbi Yisrael Meir Kagan, *Mishnah Berurah* (Warsaw, 1892), *Orach Chaim* 696, 8; Rabbi Tuchachinsky, *Gesher HaChaim*, p. 306; Rabbi Noah, *Nachamu Ami*, p. 69, 19; Rabbi Grossbard, *Chazon l'Moed*, p. 55, 5, and others.

55. See Rabbi Ushpol, *Darkei Chesed*, p. 90, 11. In n. 13, ad loc., he writes that he has found no source for this *minhag*, "but that others write that this is because we are escorting the soul back to its place in the cemetery (called *bagleiten dee neshamah*)." As we know, the soul hovers back and forth during the *shivah* from the grave to the house–see p. 68 and note. Perhaps this is done because there are those who specifically advise against going to the cemetery during the first thirty days and some even beyond this. Therefore, we make the symbolic gesture of accompaniment. See also Rabbi Avrohom Leib Rosen, *Responsa Eisan Aryeh* (Jerusalem: Mossad HaRav Kook, 1976), no. 107, that we do not practice this *minhag* when the seventh day falls on *Shabbos*. In that case one should not follow the practice on *erev Shabbos* either, for mourning in private matters still applies on *Shabbos* and one may come to err in this respect were he or she to formally terminate the mourning in the above manner.

56. Rabbi Maurice Lamm, in *The Jewish Way in Death and Mourning* (New York: Jonathan David, 1969), p. 144, writes: "Many follow the custom of having all mourners walk together, for a short distance. This symbolizes the return to the society from which the *avel* has withdrawn." Similarly, *Mourning in Halachah* (New York: Mesorah, 1991), p. 277, states: "Some follow a custom of formally terminating the *shivah* by having the mourners walk outside together–or around the corner–*accompanied by the comforters* [emphasis mine]. Symbolically, this is explained as representing the mourner's re-emergence into society from which he had withdrawn during the *shivah* week. Others ascribe kabbalistic significance to this practice." In n. 3a there, the editors write: "While this custom is practiced in many communities, we have not found a written halachic source for this." Actually, Rabbi Goldberg himself does not cite this *minhag* in the original Hebrew work, *Pnei Baruch*.

In keeping with the aforementioned reason, it occurred to me to equate it with one of the reasons mentioned above in chapter 6 for the law of the *seudas havraah.* Since the *aveilim* may not wish to eat, we force them, for their good, to do so—see p. 46 and note. Similarly, the mourners may have no desire to reenter society, but for their good, we force them to do so. See also Rabbi Label Katz, *Chesed Shel Emes,* p. 133, 23.

57. See Rabbi Avraham Eliezer Hershowitz, *Otzar Kol Minhagei Yeshurun* (St. Louis, 1917), pp. 304-305, and *Shabbos* 32a. See also Yerushalmi, end of *Moed Kattan,* that at the end of the *shivah* the *satan* still wishes to harm the mourner. This custom is also mentioned by Rabbi Yitzchak Ze'ev Vendrovsky, *Minhagei Beis Yaakov,* no. 220, but no source is cited.

On a personal note, I recall that when I began writing about the laws of mourning, etc., I was encouraged to do so by my *rosh hayeshivah*, the Gaon Rabbi Yaakov Yitzchak Ruderman, *ztz'l.* He mentioned to me that on the day he arrived in America he was questioned by a mourner on this very custom, and he was unsure what to tell her, not being familiar with the sources. He used this as an example to impress upon me how most halachic questions asked by the masses probably concern the laws of mourning. Notwithstanding, this custom is not mentioned in the classic books on mourning and I have not heard of its wide practice (although I personally observed it when I arose from *shivah*).

58. Rabbi Herbert C. Dobrinsky, *A Treasury of Sephardic Laws and Customs* (New York: Ktav/Yeshiva University, 1986), p. 74.

59. Ibid., pp. 84-85.

60. Ibid. p. 92.

61. Ibid., p. 105.

CHAPTER 11

1. See p. 43, this volume.

2. See chapters 1 and 2.

3. Quoted by William B. Silverman and Kenneth M. Cinnamon, *When Mourning Comes* (Northvale, NJ: Jason Aronson, 1990), p. 34. I have searched unsuccessfully for the source of this well-known story. I did find it briefly mentioned without referring to Kings David and Solomon in Rabbi Yosef Chaim ben Eliyahu Moshe Chaim, *Ben Ish Chai* (Jerusalem, 1898), *Parshas Shoftim,* p. 109.

4. Simcha Raz, *A Tzaddik in Our Time* (Jerusalem: Feldheim, 1976), p. 175.

5. Rabbi Sidney Greenberg, *A Treasury of Comfort* (North Hollywood, CA: Wilshire Book Company, 1975), p. 121.

6. Cited in Selma Stern, *The Spirit Returneth* (Philadelphia: Jewish Publication Society, 1946).

7. Morris Adler, *A Treasury of Comfort,* pp. 202-203.

8. See *Shemos* 22:21-23; and all sources in reference to *tzedakah,* charity. See also Rabbi Binyamin Weiss, *Responsa Even Yekarah* (Drohobycz, 1893), vol. 2, *Mahadura* 3, no.130. See also *Kuntras VaYehi Binsoa'ah* (Gottlieb); *Kovetz Mesorah,* vol. 2, p. 55, cited in Rabbi Zinner, *Nitei Gavriel,* p. 367, 4.

9. See Bibliography for suggested readings on this subject.

Glossary

a'h: Acronym for *alav hashalom*—may he rest in peace.
Abba: Father.
Amein: Amen.
aninus: State of mourning before burial.
apikores: A disbeliever, heretic.
Ashkenazic: Relating to Ashkenazic Jews of German Jewry and their descendants in other countries.
Avos: See *Pirkei Avos*.
baalei batim: Congregants.
Bamidbar: Book of Numbers.
beis hamidrash: Study hall.
Beis HaMikdash: The Holy Temple.
ben: Son.
bensching: Recitation of the grace after meals.
berachah: Blessing.
bikkur cholim: Visiting the sick.
bittul Torah: Wasting time from Torah study.
Breishis: Book of Genesis.
bris: Circumcision.
Chasidic: Pertaining to *chasidim*, followers of a *rebbe*.
chesed: Acts of kindness.
chesed shel emes: Kindness of truth used when referring to acts of kindness performed for the deceased.

Chevrah Kaddisha: The Jewish burial society.

Chol HaMoed: The intermediate days of Pesach and Succos.

Chumash: The Torah (Five Books of Moses).

chuppah: Marriage ceremony under the wedding canopy.

derech eretz: Manners; courtesy.

Devarim: Book of Deuteronomy.

din Torah: A Jewish court case.

erev: Eve of.

eschem: You (pl. masc.).

eschen: You (pl. fem.).

Gehinnom: The netherworld; hell.

gematriya: The numerical value ascribed to Hebrew letters of the alphabet.

gemillus chesed: The performance of good deeds.

ger: Convert.

gilgul: A reincarnated soul.

goy: Literally, nation. Referring to non-Jews (one not of the Jewish nation).

halachah: A Jewish law, rule, or regulation; the Jewish system of religious law and way of life.

halachic: Adjective form of *halachah*.

halbashas tachrichin: Clothing the deceased with the shrouds.

HaShem: Literally, the Name. An appellation of God, whose holy name we do not pronounce in vain.

havdalah: Ceremony ushering out the Sabbath on Saturday night.

heichal: A heavenly sphere.

imma: Mother.

Iyov: Job.

kabbalistic: Adjective form of *kabbalah*. The mystical teachings of Judaism.

kaddish: Prayer recited by the mourner when a *minyan* is present in *shul*, at the cemetery, or on a *Yahrzeit*.

kadosh: A holy person.

kal vechomer: A fortiori. A rule of logic meaning "with yet stronger reasoning."

kein yehi rotzon: May it be His will.

keriah: The mourner's rending of his or her garment(s).

kiddush: Sanctification of the Sabbath over a cup of wine.

kittel: A tunic-like garment worn on certain occasions in one's lifetime (Yom Kippur, the *seder* nights of Passover) and part of the shrouds of the deceased.

kivyachol: Literally, if we were able (to utter such words). Used when ascribing a corporeal action to the Almighty.

Klal Yisrael: The Jewish nation.

Koheles: Ecclesiastes.

lechaim: Literally, to life. Drinking a toast to life.

lehavdil: To separate from the holy.

lashon hora: Gossip.

Maariv: Evening prayer service.

Maggid: A Jewish preacher.

malshin: An informer.

menachem aveil: The act of going to comfort mourners.

mezuman: Group of three or ten (or more) banding together for the recitation of the grace after meals.

midas hadin: God's attribute of stern and strict justice.

Midrash: The name of a collection of rabbinic interpretations extending from talmudic times to the tenth century, comprised of moral, philosophical, and homiletical expositions of the Torah and specific books of *Tanach*.

Minchah: Afternoon prayer service.

minhag: Jewish custom (pl.—*minhagim*).

minyan: A qourum of ten males.

Mishnah: Earliest codification of Jewish oral law preceding the Talmud.

Mishnayos. Plural form of *Mishnah*.

mitzvah: A commandment or a good deed (pl.—*mitzvos*).

molei rachamim: Memorial prayer.

motzi: Blessing over bread.

Motzo'ei Shabbos: Saturday night.

nachas: Pleasure, satisfaction.

neshamah. Soul.

Nevi'im: The Books of the Prophets.

nichum aveilim: Comforting mourners.

niftar: The deceased.

oscho: You (masc. sing.).

osoch: You (fem. sing.).

Parshah: Torah portion.

Pirkei Avos: Ethics of the Fathers. Also referred to as *Avos*.

pushke: Charity box.

refuah shleimah: A speedy recovery.

Rosh Chodesh: First day of the new Hebrew month.

Rosh HaYeshivah: The dean of a rabbinical seminary.

rosho: A wicked person who violates on purpose the laws of the Torah.

Sanhedrin: Jewish court of seventy-one judges.

Sephardic: Relating to Sephardic Jews whose ancestry originated in Spain or Portugal before 1492, and their descendants in other countries.

seudas havraah: The meal of condolence served upon the mourners' return from the cemetery or as soon as *shivah* begins.

Shacharis: Morning prayer service.

shammes: Synagogue sexton.

Shemos: Book of Exodus.

shemuah kerovah: News of death within thirty days of burial.

shemuah rechokah: News of death after thirty days from burial.

sheva brachos: The seven blessings of the seven days following the wedding.

shidduch: Matrimonial match.

shiur: Torah lesson or lecture.

shivah: The seven days of mourning.

shlita: Acronym for *sheyichyeh leshanim tovim vaaruchim*—may he live for many long and good years.

Shulchan Aruch: Rabbi Yosef Caro's authoritative Code of Jewish Law.

siddur: Jewish prayer book (pl.—*siddurim*).

simchah: A happy occasion.

taharah: Ritual cleansing and purification of the deceased before burial.

tallis: Jewish prayer shawl (pl.—*talleisim*).

Talmud: Compendium of interpretations of the Torah and the *Mishnah*, discussions, rulings, and moral teachings compiled by generations of scholars known as *Amoraim* in the land of Israel and Babylonia during the third to sixth centuries.

techiyas hameisim: Resurrection of the dead.

Tehillim: Psalms.

tefillin: Phylacteries.

tinok shenishbah: Literally, a child that was captured. Refers to one who never had the opportunity to learn the laws of the Torah and *Shulchan Aruch*.

Tishah B'Av: The mourning and fast day of the 9th day of the month of *Av*.

Torah: The Pentateuch; also denotes the entire body of divine Jewish teachings, commandments, and literature that are the entirety of divine law and ideology.

tzaddik: A righteous individual.

tzedakah: Charity.

tzidduk hadin: The burial service.

tznius: Modesty and propriety.

tzorus: Yiddish for troubles.

Urim VeTumim: The precious stones on the breastplate of the High Priest that used to light up and signal a reply to a question.

Vayikra: Book of Leviticus.

Yahrzeit: Jewish anniversary of death.

Yalkut: *Yalkut Shimoni*, a midrashic commentary.

yakra deshechiva: Honor of the dead.

yakra dechaya: Honor of the living.

yeshivah: School or seminary of Torah learning.

yichud: Forbidden seclusion between men and women.

Yom Tov: Jewish festival or holiday (pl.—*yomim tovim*).

Zohar: Kabbalistic writings of Rabbi Shimon bar Yochai.

z"l: Acronym for *zichro livrachah*, "may his memory be for a blessing."

ztz'l: Acronym for *zecher tzaddik livrachah*, "may the memory of the righteous be for a blessing."

Bibliography

BIBLIOGRAPHY BY TITLE

Note: Since many readers are more familiar with the title of the book than with the surname of the author, especially when it comes to Hebrew sources, what follows below is a complete alphabetical title index of all works quoted. After each title, the surname or first name of the author is shown, as it appears in the Bibliography, followed by the roman numeral of the section of the bibliography where the work is found. When no name is available, or where no name is mentioned, the work is listed in the Bibliography under the title of the book.

Abarbanel, Abarbanel, I-A.
Abudraham, Abudraham, IV.
Ach l'Tzarah, Greenwald, VI.
Ahavas Chesed, Kagan, VII.
Alei Shur, Wolbe, VII.
Ani Maamin, Eliav, VII.
Arba'ah Turim (or *Tur*), Yaakov, IV.
Aruch HaShulchan, Epstein, IV-A.
Authorized Daily Prayer Book, Hertz, VII.
Aveil HaShitim, Shlomo, VI.
Avnei Shoham, Tomashoff, V.
Avodah Zarah, Talmud Bavli, III.
Avos (or *Pirkei Avos*), Mishnah, III.
Avos d'Reb (*d'Rabbi*) *Nosson*, II.

Baal Hilchos Gedolos (or *BaHaG*), Kaira, IV.
Bach (or *Bayis Chadash*), Sirkis, IV.
BaHaG (or *Baal Hilchos Gedolos*), Kaira, IV.
Bamidbar (Numbers), I.
Bartenurah, Ovadyah, III-A.
Bava Basra, Talmud Bavli, III.
Bava Kamma, Talmud Bavli, III.
Bava Metzia, Talmud Bavli, III
Bayis Chadash (or *Bach*), Sirkis, IV.
Be'er HaGolah, Rivkes, IV.
Be'er Hetev, Ashkenazi, IV.
Be'er Hetev, Zechariah, IV.
Be'er Moshe, Epstein, I-B.
Be'er Moshe, Stern, V.
Be'er Sarim, Schlesinger, V.
Beis Dovid, Leiter, V.
Beis Dovid, Philosof, IV.
Beis HaBechirah (or *Meiri*), Menachen ber Shlomo Hameiri, III-A.
Beis HaRoeh, Florentine, IV.
Beis Hillel, Hillel, IV.
Beis Lechem Yehudah, Tzvi, IV.
Beis Oved (or *Siddur Beis Oved*), Ashkenazi, IV-A.
Beis Yisrael, Landau, V.
Beis Yosef, Caro, IV.
Ben Ish Chai, Yosef, IV-A.
Berachos, Talmud Bavli, III.
Berachos, Talmud Yerushalmi, III.
Bereavement, Parkes, IX.
B'Nesivei Chesed v'Emes, VI.
Binyamin Ze'ev, Binyamin, V.
Binyan Yehoshua, IV-A.
Birkei Yosef, Azulai, IV.
Biur HaGra, Elijah, IV.
Breishis (Genesis), I.
Breishis Rabbah, II.
B'Tzeil HaChochmah, Stern, V.
Chaim b'Yad, Palagi, V.
Chasam Sofer, Sofer, V.
Chayei Adam, Danzig(er), IV-A.
Chayei HaMussar, VII.
Chazon l'Mo'ed, Grossberg, VI.
Chelkas Yaakov, Breisch, V.
Chesed Shel Emes, Katz, VI.
Chikekei Lev, Palagi, V.
Chikrei Halachah, Wein, IV-A.
Chochmas Adam, Danzig(er), IV-A.

Chochmas Shlomo, Luria, IV.
Chofetz Chaim al HaTorah, Greineman, I-B.
The Complete Yizkor Handbook, Levine, VI.
Concern for the Living (or *Yakra DeChaya*), Press, VI.
Daas Chochmah u'Mussar, Levovitz, VII.
Daas Torah, Schwadron, IV-A.
Darkei Chaim v'Sholom, Gold, IV-A.
Darkei Chesed, Ushpol, VI.
Darkei HaChaim, Marber, VI.
Darkei Moshe, Isserles, IV.
Death, Grief, and Mourning, Gorer, IX.
Derech HaChaim (or *Siddur Derech HaChaim*), Lorberbaum, IV-A.
Derishah, Falk, IV.
Devarim (or *Deuteronomy*), I.
Devorei Emes, Donath, VI.
Divrei Chachomim, Ginzberg, V.
Divrei Malkiel, Tennenbaum, V.
Divrei Torah, Shapira, IV-A.
Dudaei HaSadeh, Deutsch, V.
Eichah Rabbah, II.
Einayim l'Mishpat, Arieli, III-B.
Eisan Aryeh, Rosen, V.
Eishel Avraham, Wharman, IV-A.
Eleh Shelo Nichne'u, Prager, VII.
Eliyah Rabbah, Shapira, IV.
Eruvin, Talmud Bavli, III.
Eser Tzichzachus, Berger, VII.
Even Yaakov, Valdenberg, VI.
Even Yekarah, Weiss, V.
Exodus (or *Shemos*), I.
Ezekiel, I.
The Faith and Doubt of Holocaust Survivors, VIII.
Gateway to Happiness, Pliskin, VIII.
Gedulas Yehonoson, Zunz, VII.
Genesis (or *Breishis*), I.
Gesher HaChaim, Tuchachinsky, VI.
Gevul Yehudah, Tzirelson, V.
Ginzei Yosef, Schwartz, V.
Gittin, Talmud Bavli, III.
Guidelines to Understanding the Traditions of Shivah, Paull, VI.
HaChofetz Chaim, Yoshor, VII.
Hadras Kodesh, Schwartz, VI.
HaElef Lecha Shlomo, Kluger, V.
Hagahos Maimoniyos, Meir, IV.
HaHistalkut HaNefesh, Mintz, VII
HaKuntras HaYechiali (*Beis Olomim*), Alfaya, VI.

Har Tzvi, Frank, V.

Hasidic Tales of the Holocaust, Eliach, VIII.

The Holocaust and Halakkah, Rosenbaum, VIII.

Horeb, Hirsch, VIII.

Hoshea (or Hosea), I.

How to Perform the Great Mitzvah of Bikkur Cholim, Levine, VI.

Ibn Ezra, Ibn Ezra, I-A.

Igros Moshe, Feinstein, V.

Imrei Emes, Likutim, Alter, VII.

In the Footsteps of the Maggid, Krohn, VIII.

Isaiah, I.

Iturei Torah, Greenberg, I-B.

Jeremiah, I.

The Jewish Way in Death and Mourning, Lamm, VI.

Job, I.

Judaism: Thought and Legend, Meisels, VII.

Kaf HaChaim, Soffer, IV-A.

Kenesses HaGedolah, Benveniste, IV.

Kesav Sofer, Sofer, V.

Kesef Mishneh, Caro, IV.

Kesubos, Talmud Bavli, III.

Kiddushin, Talmud Bavli, III.

Kisvei Eish, Stern, V.

Kitzur Shaloh, Epstein, IV.

Kitzur Shulchan Aruch, Ganzfried, IV-A.

Kochav MiYaakov, Kranz, I-B.

Kochavei Yitzchak, Sternhell, V.

Koheles (or Ecclesiastes), I.

Koheles Rabbah, II.

Kol Bo, IV.

Kol Bo al Avilus, Greenwald, VI.

Lechem HaPanim, Chaim, IV-A.

Lechem HaPanim, Kaufman, IV.

Lechem Mishneh, De Boton, IV.

Leket Yosher, Yosef, IV.

Lev Eliyahu, Lopian, VII.

Leviticus (or *Vayikra*), I.

Levush(im), Yaffe, IV.

Levushei Mordechai, Winkler, V.

Levushei Yom Tov, Teitelbaum, V.

Likutei Yaffe, Feldman, VI.

Love Your Neighbor, Pliskin, VIII.

Maasei Avraham, Ashkenazi, V.

Maavar Yabok, Aaron, VI.

Machazeh Avraham, Steinberg, V.

Machzor Vitry, Simchah, IV.

Maftei'ach HaTalmud, Guttman, IV-A.

Magen Avraham, Gombiner, IV.
The Maggid Speaks, Krohn, VII.
Maharam Rothenberg, Meir, V.
Maharil, Moelin, V.
Maharitz Chiyus, Chajes, III-B.
Mattei Moshe, Mos, IV.
Mechilta d'Rabbi Yishmael (or *Mechilta*), II.
Meishiv Halachah, Luria, V.
Mekor Chaim HaShaleim, HaLevi, IV-A.
Mekor Chesed, Margolis, IV-A.
Menachem Aveilim, Menachem, VI.
Menoras HaMa'or, Abohab, VII.
Meshech Chochmah, Meir, I-B.
Messilas Yeshurim, Luzzatto, VII.
Michah, I.
Michlol HaMaamarim v'HaPisgamim, Savar, VII.
Michtav m'Eliyahu, Dessler, VII.
Midrash, II.
Midrash Rabbah, II.
Midrash Shochar Tov, II.
Midrash Tanchuma, II.
Milei d'Avos, Tziltz, V.
Minchas Dovid, V.
Minchas Yitzchok, Weiss, V.
Minhagei Beis Yaakov, Vendrovsky, IV-A.
Misgeres HaShulchan, Kastilnovo, IV.
Mishmeres Sholom, Cherniak, VI.
Mishnah Berurah, Kagan, IV-A.
Mishnas Avraham, Price, IV.
Mishnas Binyamin, Zilberberg, V.
Mishnas Yaavetz, Zolty, V.
Mishneh Torah, Maimonides, IV.
Mishpat Tzedek, Melamed, V.
Moed Kattan, Talmud Bavli, III.
Mordechai, Ashkenazi, III-A.
Mourning and Remembrance (or *Yesodei Semochos*), Felder, VI.
Mourning in Halachah, Goldberg, VI.
Nachalas Avi, Frankel, V.
Nachamu Ami, Noah, VI.
Nedarim, Talmud Bavli, III.
Negid u'Metzaveh, Tzemach, VII.
Nichum Aveilim, Goodman, VI.
Nichum Aveilim, Greenbaum, VI.
Niddah, Talmud Bavli, III.
Nimukei Orach Chaim, Shapiro, IV-A.
Nimukei Yosef, Chaviva, III-A.
Nitei Gavriel, Zinner, VI.

Noam, Kasher, IV-A.
Noda b'Yehudah, Landau, V.
Noheg Katzon Yosef, Kosman, IV.
Numbers (or *Bamidbar*), I.
Ohel Yaakov, Kranz, I-B.
Oholei Yissachar, Frand, VI.
Or HaChaim, Atar, I-A.
Or Yisrael, Blauser, VII.
Or Zarua, Yitzchak, IV.
Orchos Chaim, Aharon, IV.
Orchos Chaim, Kahane, IV-A.
Otzar HaAgaddah, Gross, VII.
Otzar Kol Minhagei Yeshurun, Hershowitz, IV-A.
Pachad Yitzchak, Lampronti, IV.
Pachad Yitzchak, Igros u'Kesavim, Hutner, VII.
Panim Meiros, Eisenstadt, V.
Pe'ah, Talmud Bavli, III.
Pe'ah, Talmud Yerushalmi, III.
Pe'eir HaDor, Cohen, VII.
Peleh Yo'eitz, Papo, VII.
Perishah, Falk, IV.
Pesachim, Talmud Bavli, III.
Pesikta Rabbasi D'Rav Kahanah, II.
Pirkei d'Rabbi Eliezer, II.
Pischei Teshuvah, Eisenstadt, IV-A.
Pnei Baruch, Goldberg, VI.
Pnei Meivin, Fried, V.
Pri Megadim, Teomim, IV.
Psalms (or *Tehillim*), I.
Rabbeinu Yerucham, Yerucham, IV.
Rabbeinu Yonah, Gerondi, III-A.
Rabbi Akivah Eiger, Eiger, V.
Rabbinical Council of America Manual, Lipschutz, VII.
Radvaz, Zimrah, V.
Ramat Rachel, Valdenberg, VI.
Rambam, Maimonides, IV.
Ramban (or Nachmanides), Nachmanides, I-A.
Rashba, Aderes, V.
Rashi, Shlomo, I-A; III-A.
Rav Hillel Omer, Posek, V.
Reb Elchonon, Sorasky, VII.
Remoh, Isserles, IV.
Rif, Alfasi, III-A.
Ritva, Ashvili, III-A.
Rivevos Ephraim, Greenblatt, V.
Roke'ach, Rokeach, IV.
Rosh, Asher, IV.

Salmas Chaim, Sonnenfeld, V.
Samuel, I.
Sanhedrin, Talmud Bavli, III.
Sanhedrin, Talmud Yerushalmi, III.
Sdei Chemed, Medini, IV-A.
Sefer Chasidim, Yehudah, IV.
Sefer HaChaim, Frankfurter, VI.
Sefer HaChinuch, Aaron, IV.
Sefer HaGilgulim, Vital, VII.
Sefer HaMinhagim, Minhagei Chabad, IV-A.
Sefer HaMitzvos
Sefer HaPardes, Shlomo, IV.
Sefer HaYahrzeit, VI.
Sefer Mataamim, Lipitz, IV-A.
Sefer Mitzvos Kattan (or *SeMaK*), Yitzchak, IV.
Sefer Orchos Rabbeinu, Horowitz, VII.
Seridei Eish, Weinberg, V.
Shaarei Aharon, Rotter, VI.
Shaarei Teshuvah, Margolis, IV.
Shabbos, Talmud Bavli, III.
Shaloh HaKadosh (or *Shnei Luchos HaBris*), Horowitz, IV.
She'arim Metzuyanim b'Halachah, Braun, IV-A.
Sheiltos d'Rav Achai Gaon, Gaon, IV.
Shemiras HaLashon, Kagan, IV-A.
Shemos (Exodus), I.
Sheroshim b'Semochos, Freolich, VI.
Shevet HaLevi, Wosner, V.
Shevet Shimon, Sidan, VI.
Shevet Yehudah, Ayache, VI.
Shevus Yaakov, Reischer, V.
Shibolei HaLeket, Tzidkiah, IV.
Shir HaShirim Rabbah, II.
Shittah Mekubetzes, Ashkenazi, III-A.
Shivas Tziyon, Landau, V.
Shnei Luchos HaBris (or *Shaloh HaKadosh*), Horowitz, IV.
Shochar Tov, Midrash, II.
Sho'eil u'Meishiv, Nathanson, V.
Shulchan Aruch, Caro, IV.
Shulchan Govoha, Molko, IV.
Si'ach Sarfei Kodesh, Reketz, VII.
Sifra Devei Rav, II.
Sifrei Devei Rav, II.
Sifsei Kohen (or *Shach*), Shabsai, IV.
Sippurei Chasidim al HaTorah, Zevin, I-B.
Sofrim, Talmud Bavli, III.
Sotah, Talmud Bavli, III.
Succah, Talmud Bavli, III.

The Symptomatology and Management of Acute Grief, Lindenmann, IX.
Taamei HaMinhagim u'Mekorei HaDinim, Sperling, IV-A.
Taanis, Talmud Bavli, III.
Tanchuma, Midrash, II.
Tanna d'Bei Eliyahu, Midrash, II.
Tanya Rabbasi, Anav, IV.
Taz (or *Turei Zahav*), David, IV.
A Time to Mourn, Spiro, IX.
Tefillah KeHilchasah, Fuchs, IV-A.
Tehillim (Psalms), I.
Terumas HaDeshen, Isserlein, IV.
Teshuvah m'Ahavah, Fleckles, V.
Toldos Adam v'Chavah, (or *Rabbeinu Yerucham*), Yerucham, IV.
Toras HaAdam, Nachmanides, VI.
Tosfos, III-A.
Totza'os Chaim, Baer, VI.
A Treasury of Comfort, Greenberg, IX.
A Treasury of Sephardic Laws and Customs, Dobrinsky, VIII.
Tur (or *Arbaah Turim*), Yaakov, IV.
Turei Zahav (or *Taz*), David, IV.
Tuv Taam v'Daas, Kluger, V.
A Tzaddik in Our Times, Raz, VIII.
Tzapichis b'Devash, Pontremoli, V.
Tzitz Eliezer, Valdenberg, V.
Tziyon l'Nefesh Chayah (or *Tzlach*), Landau, III-B.
Understanding Bereavement and Grief, Nemzoff, IX.
VaYelaket Yosef, Schwartz, V.
VaYevarech Dovid, Harfenes, V.
Vayikra (or *Leviticus*), I.
Vayikra Avraham, Adadi, V.
Vayikra Rabbah, II.
Vayitzbor Yosef, Schwartz, V.
V'HaChai Yitten es Libo, VI.
We Bereaved, Keller, IX.
When Bad Things Happen to Good People, Kushner, IX.
When Mourning Comes, Silverman, IX.
When Sorrow Comes, Oursler, IX.
Yabia Omer, Yossef, V.
Yad Eliyahu, Rigoler, V.
Yaffe l'Lev, Palagi, V.
Yagdil Torah, Schneerson, V.
Yalkut Avraham, Lipshitz, IV-A.
Yalkut Lekach Tov, Byfus, I-B.
Yalkut Me'Am Loez, Culi, I-A.
Yalkut Lekach Tov, Pirkei Emunah u'Nechamah, Byfus, VII.
Yalkut Shimoni, II.
Yakra d'Chaya, Bernstein, VI.

Yakra d'Chaya, Rabi, VI.
Yakra d'Chaya (or *Concern for the Living*), Press, VI.
Yalkut Dos v'Din, Assaf, VI.
Yalkut Yossef, Yossef, VI.
Yam Shel Shlomo, Luria, III-A.
Yaskil Avdi, Hedayah, V.
Yedei Mosheh, II.
Yereim (or *Sefer Yereim*), Eliezer, IV.
Yesodei Semochos (or *Mourning and Remembrance*), Felder, VI.
Yom Kippur Machzor, VII.
Yosef Ometz, Hahn, IV.
Zechor l'Avraham, Alkelai, IV-A.
Zera Chaim, Sofer, VI.
Zera Emes, Yishmael, V
Zevach Mishpachah, Hollander, IV-A.
Zibula Basraisa, Bergman, VI.
Zichron Betzalel, Deblitzky, VI.
Zichron Meir al Aveilus, Levine, VI.
Zikoron l'Yom Acharon, VI.
Zohar, Bar Yochai, I-A.

BIBLIOGRAPHY SECTIONS

I. Bible
    I-A. Bible Commentaries—Early Sources
    I-B. Bible Commentaries—Later Sources
II. *Midrashim*
III. *Mishnah, Talmud Bavli, Talmud Yerushalmi*
    III-A. *Mishnah*-Talmud Commentaries—Early Sources
    III-B. *Mishnah*-Talmud Commentaries—Later Sources
IV. Codes, *Halachah, Mitzvos, Minhagim*—Early Sources
    IV-A. Codes, *Halachah, Mitzvos, Minhagim*—Later Sources
V. Responsa
VI. Books on Sickness, Death, and Mourning—Hebrew and Jewish Sources
VII. Extralegal Literature: Moralistic, Philosophic, and Mystic
VIII. English Sources—Jewish Subjects
IX. Grief and Mourning—Secular Sources
    IX-A. Additional Books on Grief and Bereavement
        Widows and Widowers
    IX-B. Death of a Child
    IX-C. Death of a Parent—Adults
    IX-D. Bereavement Bibliography for Parents and Children
        Books for Parents or Teachers
    IX-E. Books for Parents and Children
    IX-F. Books for Elementary School Children
    IX-G. Bibliography on Death and the Afterlife in Judaism

BIBLIOGRAPHY BY SUBJECT

All books are listed by surname of author, or by first name of author when surname is unavailable. If no name at all is available or the book is biblical, the work
is listed by title.

Since many of the Hebrew works quoted were published many years ago,
the first date represents the year the work was first printed; the second date is the
publishing date of the current edition used by the author (or a commonly used
edition). Wherever possible, some brief biographical information is included, such
as place where author resided, and date and place of birth and death. This biographical information appears in parentheses.

I. BIBLE

Mikraos Gedolos. New York: Gross Brothers, 1983. (Where publishing information is not specified, it can be found in the above editions of the
Mikraos Gedolos).

Breishis (Genesis)	*Yirmiyahu* (Jeremiah)
Shemos (Exodus)	*Yechezkel* (Ezekiel)
Vayikra (Leviticus)	*Hoshea* (Hosea)
Bamidbar (Numbers)	*Michah* (Micah)
Devarim (Deuteronomy)	*Tehillim* (Psalms)
Shmuel (2 Samuel)	*Iyov* (Job)
Yeshayahu (Isaiah)	*Koheles* (Ecclesiastes)

I-A. BIBLE COMMENTARIES (EARLY SOURCES)

(Where publishing information is not specified, it can be found in the above
editions of *Mikraos Gedolos*).

Abarbanel, Rabbi Don Yitzchak. (b. Lisbon, 1437; d. Venice, 1508). *Abarbanel*
    (Ezekiel). Pesaro, 1520; Jerusalem, 1957.

Atar, Rabbi Chaim Ibn. (1696–1743). *Or HaChaim*. Venice, 1744.

Bar Yochai, Rabbi Shimon. (2nd century). *Zohar*. Jerusalem: Mossad Harav Kook,
    1960.

Culi, Rabbi Yaakov. *Yalkut Me'Am Loez*. (b. 1689, d.1732), Constantinople, 1733
    (original manuscripts by Rabbi Culi); Jerusalem: Mossad Yad Ezrah, 1971
    (later volumes continued by Rabbi Yitzchak of Agriso and Rabbi Yitzchak
    Arguity).

Ibn Ezra, Rabbi Avraham. (b. Toledo, Spain, 1089; d. ca. 1164). *Ibn Ezra*.

Nachmanides, Rabbi Moshe ben Nachman. (b. Gerona, 1194; d. in Israel, 11 *Nissan*,
    1270). *Ramban*.

R' Shlomo ben Yitzchak. (b. Troyes, France, 1040; d. 29 Tammuz, 1105). *Rashi*.

I-B. BIBLE COMMENTARIES (LATER SOURCES)

Byfus, Rabbi Yaakov Yisrael HaKohen. *Yalkut Lekach Tov*. Kfar Chasidim: Tashbar
    HoRav, 1990.

Epstein, Rabbi Moshe Yechiel HaLevi. *B'er Moshe*. Jerusalem: HoIvri Publishing,
    1966.

Greenberg, Rabbi Aharon Yaakov. *Iturei Torah*. Tel Aviv: Yavneh, 1967.

Greineman, Rabbi Shmuel. *Chofetz Chaim al HaTorah*. Bnei Brak: n.d.

Kranz, Rabbi Yaakov Krantz. (Maggid of Dubnow—1741-1804). *Ohel Yaakov*. Josefow: 1830; Israel, n.d.

——. *Kochav MiYaakov*. (commentary to *Haftaras*). Warsaw, 1880.

R' Meir Simcha of Dvinsk. (1843-1926). *Meshech Chochmah*. Riga, 1927; Jerusalem, 1978.

II. MIDRASHIM

Avos d'Rebbi Nosson. (2nd century, C.E.).; Zolko, 1723; New York: Meoroth edition, 1959 (in back of Talmud Bavli tractate *Avos*).

Helin, Rabbi Yaakov Mosheh. *Yedei Mosheh*. Frankfurt an der Oder, 1692; Jerusalem, 1970.

Mechilta d'Rabbi Yishmael. (attributed to the tanna, Rabbi Yishmael, redacted ca 135 C.E.). Constantinople, 1515.

Midrash Rabbah. Venice, 1545; Vilna edition, reproduced in Jerusalem: Ortzel, 1961.
  Breishis Rabbah.
  Vayikra Rabbah.
  Shir HaShirim Rabbah.
  Eichah Rabbah.
  Koheles Rabbah.

Midrash Shochar Tov. Constantinople, 1512.

Midrash Tanchumah. (attributed to Rabbi Tanchuma bar Abbah). Constantinople: 1520-1522; Jerusalem: Lewin-Epstein, Ltd., 1964.

Pesikta Rabbasi d'Rav Kahannah. Prague, 1653-1655; Warsaw ed., 1893—reproduced in Jerusalem: Machon Chasam Sofer, 1969.

Pirkei d'Rabbi Eliezer. (attributed to the *tanna*, Rabbi Eliezer ben Hyrcanus, 1st century C.E.). Constantinople, 1514; Warsaw ed. reproduced in New York: Om Publishing Co., 1946.

Sifra Devei Rav. (*Midrash* on *Toras Kohanim*, attributed to Rabbi Chiya or Rav, 200-220 C.E.). Constantinople, 1530; Jerusalem, 1959.

Sifri Devei Rav. (as above). Venice, 1546.

Tanna d'Bei Eliyahu Rabbah/Zuttah. (attributed to Elijah the Prophet). Venice, 1598; Jerusalem, 1980.

Yalkut Shimoni. (midrashic anthology attributed to Rav Shimon HaDarshan of Frankfort, 13th century). New York: Pardes, 1944.
  Hoshea
  Mishlei
  Koheles

III. MISHNAH, TALMUD BAVLI, AND TALMUD YERUSHALMI

The *Mishnah* was redacted by Rabbi Judah Hanasi (the Prince), d. ca. 190 C.E. The *Talmud Yerushalmi* (Jerusalem Talmud) was redacted by Rabbi Yose ben Bun, ca. 350 C.E., or Rabbi Yochanan. The *Talmud Bavli* (Babylonian Talmud) was redacted by Rav Ashi (died ca. 427 C.E.), and Ravina II (died ca. 475 C.E.). The first edition of a tractate of the Talmud printed with Rashi's commentary and *Piskei Tosafos* was in Soncino, 1483-1484. The first complete edition with Rashi was printed in Venice, 1520–1523. Similarly the Talmud Yerushalmi was first printed in Venice, 1520-1524. Edition of *Talmud Bavli* used by author was issued in New York: M'Oroth Publishing Corp., 1959. Edition of *Talmud Yerushalmi* was issued in Jerusalem: El Hamekoroth, 1949.

Mishnah
  Avos (Pirkei Avos)
Talmud Bavli

Avodah Zarah	*Nedarim*
Bava Basra	*Niddah*
Bava Kamma	*Pe'ah*
Bava Metzia	*Pesachim*
Berachos	*Sanhedrin*
Eruvin	*Shabbos*
Gittin	*Sofrim*
Kesubos	*Sotah*
Kiddushin	*Succah*
Yevamos	*Taanis*
Moed Kattan	

Talmud Yerushalmi
  Berachos
  Peah
  Sanhedrin

III-A. COMMENTARIES ON MISHNAH AND TALMUD (EARLY SOURCES)

Where publishing data is not specified, the commentaries can be found in the back of the aforementioned edition of the Meoroth edition of the *Talmud Bavli* (New York: 1959).

Alfasi, Yitzchak. (b. Kila Chamad, Algeria, 1013; d. Lucena, Spain, 1103). *Rif.*

Asher ben Yechiel. (b. Germany, ca. 1250; d. Toledo, Spain, 15 *Mar Cheshvan*, 1327). *Rosh.*

Ashkenazi, Rabbi Bezalel ben Avraham. (b. Israel, ca. 1520; d. Jerusalem, ca. 1592). *Shittah Mekubetzes.* Metz: 1764; New York: Friedman-Kohn, n.d.

Ashkenazi, Rabbi Mordechai ben Hillel. (b. Germany, ca. 1240; d. Nuremberg, Germany, 22 *Av*, 1298). *Mordechai.* Riva de Trento: 5318; New York: Meoroth, 1959.

Ashvili, Ibn, Rabbi Yom Tov ben Avraham. (b. ca. 1270; d. Seville, Spain, ca. 1340). *Ritva.* New York: Otzar Haseforim, 1959.

Chaviva, Rabbi Yosef. (Spain, late 14th and early 15th centuries). *Nimukei Yosef.* Written in 1393. New York: Meoroth, 1959.

Gerondi, Rabbi Yonah. (b. Gerona, Spain, ca. 1180; d. Toledo, Spain, 8 *Mar Cheshvan*, 1263). *Rabbeinu Yonah.* Back of tractate *Berachos.*

Luria, Rabbi Shlomo (b. Brisk, ca. 1510; d. Lublin, 12 *Kislev*, 1573). *Yam Shel Shlomo. (Bava Kamma).* Prague, 1616; Bnei Brak, 1960.

R' Menachem ben Shlomo HaMeiri. (b. Provence, ca. 1249; d. Perpignan, Provence, ca. 1306). *Beis HaBechirah (Meiri).* Amsterdam, 5529; Jerusalem: Isaak S. Lange, 1968.

R' Shlomo ben Yitzchak. *Rashi.* See above in Bible Commentaries.

Tosfos. (12th to 14th century Tosafists, five generations of commentators, mainly in France and Germany).

III-B. MISHNAH, TALMUD COMMENTARIES (LATER SOURCES)
Arieli, Rabbi Yitzchak. *Einayim l'Mishpat.* Jerusalem: Holvri, 1971.
Chajes, Rabbi Tzvi Hirsch. (Ukraine, Poland, 1805-1855). *Maharitz Chiyus.*
Landau, Rabbi Ezekiel. (Prague, 1713-1793). *Tziyon l'Nefesh Chaya (Tzlach),* tractate *Pesachim.* New York: A. Y. Friedman, 1956.
Ovadyah Yarei of Bertinoro. (b. Italy, ca. 1440; d. Jerusalem, ca. 1516; commentary to Mishnah). *Bartenurah.* New York: Yochin U'Boaz edition, Zundel Berman, 1988.

IV. CODES, HALACHAH, MITZVOS, MINHAGIM, AND COMMENTARIES (EARLIER SOURCES)
R' Aaaron HaKohen of Lunel. (b. Narbonne, Provence; d. Majorca, Spain, c. 1325). *Orchos Chayim.* Florence, 1750; Berlin, 1899.
R' Aaron HaLevi of Barcelona. (so attributed—14th century Spain). *Sefer HaChinuch.* Jerusalem: Eshkol, n.d.
Abudraham, Rabbi David (ben Yosef). (Seville, Spain, late 13th-14th centuries). *Abudraham.* Lisbon, 1489; Jerusalem, Hotzoas Usha, 1959.
Anav, Rabbi Yechiel ben Yekusiel. (d. Rome, Italy, ca. 1300). *Tanya Rabbasi.* Mantua, 1514; New York, with commentary, *Pri Yeshurun,* by Gedaliah Felder, 1976.
Ashkenazi, Rabbi Yehudah, Dayan of Tiktin. (Poland, 18th century). *Be'er Hetev.* Gloss to *Shulchan Aruch, Yoreh De'ah.*
Ayache, Rabbi Yehuda. (1700-1761). *Matteh Yehudah.* Livorno, 1783; Jerusalem, 1971.
Azulai, Rabbi Yosef David. (1724-1806). *Birkei Yosef.* Livorno, 1774-1776; Jerusalem, n.d.
Benveniste, Rabbi Chaim. (b. Constantinople [Instanbul], Turkey, 1603; d. Izmir [Smyrna], Turkey, 17 Elul, 1673). *Knesses HaGedolah.* Leghorn, 1658; Jerusalem, 1966.
Caro, Rabbi Yosef. (b. Toledo, Spain, 1488; d. Safed, Israel, 13 Nissan, 1575). *Beis Yosef.* Venice-Sabbionetta, 1550-1559; Gloss to *Tur, Shulchan Aruch,* New York: Otzar Haseforim Turim Publishers, 1959.
——. *Kesef Mishneh.* Gloss to *Mishneh Torah.*
——. *Shulchan Aruch (Code of Jewish Law).* Venice, 1565; New York: Otzar Halacha, 1959.
David ben Samuel HaLevi. (b. Ludmir [Vladimir], Poland, 1586; d. Lemberg [Lvov], Poland, 26 Shevat, 1667). *Turei Zahav (Taz).* Lublin, 1646. Gloss to *Shulchan Aruch.*
De Boton, Rabbi Avraham. (b. Salonica, Turkey [Greece], 1545; d. there, 1588). *Lechem Mishneh.* Venice, 1609. Gloss to *Mishneh Torah.*
R' Eliezer of Metz. (Metz, France, ca. 1175). *(Sefer) Yereim.* Venice, 1565; New York, 1960 (with commentary, *Sowiw Lereow,* Rabbi Aaron Walkin, 1935).
R' Elijah, Gaon of Vilna. (1720-1797). *Biur HaGra.* Gloss to *Shulchan Aruch.*
Epstein, Rabbi Yechiel Michel. *Kitzur Shaloh.* (an abridgement of *Shnei Luchos HaBris*). Fiorda, 1693; Warsaw, 1879. See *Shnei Luchos HaBris.*

Falk, Rabbi Yehoshua (Katz). (b. ca. 1540; d. Lemberg, Poland [Lvov, Russia], 19 Nissan, 1614). *Derishah*. Lublin, 1635; Gloss to *Tur, Shulchan Aruch*. See *Tur*.

——. *Perishah*. Gloss to *Tur*.

Florentine, Rabbi Shmuel. *Beis HoRoeh*. Salonica, 1758.

Gaon, Rav Achai. (ca. 750 C.E.). *Sheiltos d'Rav Achai Gaon*. Venice, 1546; Vilna ed., Jerusalem: Mossad HoRav Kook, 1967.

Gombiner, Rabbi Avraham Abele. (b. Gombin, Poland, ca. 1634; d. Kalish, Poland, Tishrei 1682). *Magen Avraham*. Dyhernfurth, 1692. Gloss to *Shulchan Aruch*.

Hahn, Rabbi Yosef Yuspa Nordlinger. (b. Frankfurt am Main, ca. 1570, d. there 9 Nissan, 1637). *Yosef Ometz*. Frankfurt am Main, 1723; Jerusalem, 1965.

R' Hillel ben Naftali Hertz. (b. Brisk, Lithuania, 1615; d. Zolkiew, Poland, 22 Teves, 1690). *Beis Hillel*. Dyhernfurth, 1691. Gloss to *Shulchan Aruch*.

Horowitz, Rabbi Isaiah ben Avraham HaLevi. (b. Prague [?], Bohemia [Czechoslovakia], ca. 1560; d. Tiberias, Israel, 11 Nissan, 1630). *Shnei Luchos HaBris (ShaLoH HaKodosh)*. Amsterdam, 1649; Jerusalem, 1960.

Isserlein, Rabbi Israel. (b. Regensburg, Germany, ca. 1390; d. Wiener Neustadt, Austria, 1460). *Terumas HaDeshen*. Venice, 1519; Warsaw ed., 1882, reprinted, Bnei Brak, 1971.

Isserles, Rabbi Moses. (b. Cracow, Poland, 1530; d. there, 18 Iyar, 1572). *Darkei Moshe*.

——. *Remoh*. *Yoreh De'ah*, Sulzbach, 1692; *Orach Chaim*, Fuerth, 1760. Gloss to *Shulchan Aruch*.

Kaira, Rabbi Shimon. (ca. 760). *Baal Hilchos Gedolos, BaHaG* (a compilation of many halachic decisions of Rabbi Yehudai Gaon, and of the *Sheiltos*). Venice, 1548; Jerusalem, 1972.

Kastilnovo (Castelnuovo), Rabbi Menachem Azariah Meir. *Misgeres HaShulchan*. Livorno, 1840.

Kaufman (Koifman), Rabbi Moshe Yekusiel. (son-in-law of Rabbi Gombiner). *Lechem HaPanim*. Hanau, 1716. Gloss to *Shulchan Aruch*.

Kol Bo. Author unknown. Naples, 1590; Jerusalem, n.d.

Kosman (Segal), Rabbi Yosef Yospa of Frankfurt. *Noheg Katzon Yosef*. Hanau, 1718; Tel Aviv, 1969.

Lampronti, Rabbi Yitzchak Chizkiyah. (b. 1679; d. Ferrara, Italy, 1756). *Pachad Yitzchak*. Encyclopedia, 10 vols. Venice-Levorno, 1750-1840; Bnei Brak, n.d.

Luria, Rabbi Shlomo Luria (Maharshal). (b. Brisk, Poland, ca. 1510; d. Lublin, Poland, 12 Kislev, 1573). *Chochmas Shlomo*. Lublin, 1559-1568. Gloss to Talmud.

Maimonides, Rabbi Moshe ben Maimon (RaMbaM). (b. Cordova, Spain, 1135; d. Cairo, Egypt, 20 Teves, 1204). *Mishneh Torah (Yad HaChazakah)*. Rome, ca. 1480; New York: Hotzoas Rambam, 1956.

——. *Sefer HaMitzvos*. Constantinople, 1510; Warsaw, 1871; Jerusalem: Pardes Publishers, n.d.

Margolis, Rabbi Chaim Mordechai. (Rabbi of Dubno; d. at Dunajowce, 1818; brother of Ephraim Zalman Margolis). *Shaarei Teshuvah*. Dubno, 1820. Gloss to *Shulchan Aruch*.

R' Meir HaKohen. (13th century). *Hagahos Maimoniyos*. Gloss to *Mishneh Torah*.

Molko, Rabbi Yosef. *Shulchan Govoha*. Salonica, 1756; Jerusalem: n.d.

Mos (Mat), Rabbi Moshe of Przemysl. (b. Przemysl, Poland, ca. 1540; d. Apta [Opatow], Poland, 1606). *Matteh Moshe*. Cracow, 1591; Warsaw ed., 1876; reprinted in Israel, n.d.

Philosof, Rabbi Yosef ben David. *Beis Dovid*. Salonica, 1740-1747.

Rivkes, Rabbi Moshe. (b. Prague, Bohemia [Czechoslovakia]; d. Vilna, Lithuania, 4 *Elul*, 1671). *Be'er HaGolah*. Amsterdam, 1662-1666. Gloss to *Shulchan Aruch*.

Rokeach, Rabbi Elazar of Worms. (b. Mainz, Germany, ca. 1160; d. there ca. 1238). *(Sefer Ha-)Roke'ach*. Fano, 1505; Warsaw, 1840.

R' Shabsai ben Meir HaKohen. (b. Vilna, 1622; d. Holleschau, Moravia [Czechoslovakia], 1 *Adar* I, 1663). *Sifsei Kohen (Shach)*. Cracow, 1646-1647. Gloss to *Shulchan Aruch*.

Shapira (Spira), Rabbi Eliyah. (d. 8 *Nissan*, 1712). *Eliyah Rabbah*. Sulzbuch, 1752; Jerusalem, 1982.

R' Shlomo ben Yitzchak. See *Rashi* above in Bible Commentaries. *Sefer HaPardes*. Constantinople, 1802; Budapest ed.: 1924, reprinted Bnei Brak, 1980.

R' Simchah of Vitry. (d. Vitry, France, 1105). *Machzor Vitry*. Berlin, 1889-1897; Jerusalem, n.d.

Sirkis, Yoel. (b. Lublin, Poland, ca. 1561; d. Cracow, 20 *Adar*, 1640). *Bayis Chadash (Bach)*. Gloss to *Tur*.

Teomim, Yosef. (b. Lemberg, 1727; d. Frankfurt an der Oder, 1793). *Pri Megadim (Mishbetzos Zahav* and *Fishel Avraham)*. Frankfurt am Main, 1785-1787; Gloss to *Shulchan Aruch*.

R' Tzidkiyah ben Avraham HaRofei. (b. Italy, ca. 1230; d. Rome, ca. 1300). *Shibolei HaLeket*. Venice, 1546; Jerusalem, 1976.

R' Tzvi Hirsch ben Rabbi Azriel of Vilna. *Beis Lechem Yehudah*. Zolkiew, 1733. Gloss to *Shulchan Aruch*.

R' Yaakov ben Asher. (b. Germany, ca. 1275; d. Toledo, Spain, ca. 1340). *Tur (Arbaah Turim)*. Pieve de Sachi, 1475; New York: Otzar Hasefarim Turim, 1959.

Yaffe, Rabbi Mordechai. (b. Prague, Bohemia [Czechoslovakia], 1535; d. Posen, Poland, 3 *Adar* II, 1612). *Levush(im)*. Lublin, 1590; Prague, 1604; Jerusalem, n.d.

R' Yehudah ben Samuel HaChasid. (b. Speyer, Germany, ca. 1150; d. Regensburg, Germany, 13 *Adar*, 1217). *Sefer Chasidim*. Bologna, 1538; Jerusalem: Mossad HoRav Kook, 1957.

R' Yerucham ben Meshulam. (b. Provence, France, ca. 1280; d. Toledo, Spain, ca. 1350). *Toldos Adam v'Chavah (Rabbeinu Yerucham)*. Constantinople, 1516; Venice ed.: 1553, reprinted in Israel, 1976.

R' Yitzchak of Corbeil. (d. Corbeil, France, 28 *Iyar*, 1280). *Sefer Mitzvos Kattan (SMaK)*. Constantinople: 1510; Satmar: 1935.

R' Yitzchak of Vienna. (b. Bohemia, ca. 1190; d. Vienna, Austria, ca. 1260). *Or Zorua*. Zhitomir, 1862; Jerusalem, 1867; Jerusalem, n.d.

R' Yosef ben Moshe. (b. Hochstadt, Bavaria [Germany], ca. 1420; d. 1490). *Leket Yosher*. Berlin, 1903-1904; Jerusalem, 1964.

R' Zechariah Mendel of Belz. *Be'er Hetev*. Gloss to *Shulchan Aruch, Yoreh De'ah*.

IV-A. CODES, HALACHAH, MITZVOS, MINHAGIM, AND COMMENTARIES (LATER SOURCES)

Alkalai, Rabbi Avraham ben Shmuel. (Turkey). *Zechor l'Avraham*. Salonica: 1798; Muncacz ed., 1895, reprinted Bnei Brak: Yahadus, n.d.

Ashkenazi, Rabbi Yehudah Shmuel. *(Siddur) Beis Oved*. Lvorno, 1843.

Braun, Rabbi Solomon. *Shearim Metzuyanim b'Halachah*. Jerusalem/New York: Feldheim, 1970.

R' Chaim Yehudah HaKohen (Halbesberg). *Lechem HaPanim*. Jerusalem: Eshkol, 1954. Gloss to *Kitzur Shulchan Aruch*.

Danzig(er), Rabbi Abraham ben Yechiel Michal. (1748-1820). *Chayei Adam*. Vilna, 1810; with commentary of *Nishmas Adam*, New York, 1974.

——. *Chochmas Adam*. Vilna, 1814; with commentary of *Binas Adam*, Jerusalem, 1960.

Eisenstadt, Rabbi Avraham Tzvi Hirsch. (1812-1868). *Pischei Teshuvah*. Gloss to *Shulchan Aruch*.

Epstein, Rabbi Yechiel Michel. (1829-1908). *Aruch HaShulchan*. Warsaw, 1898; Pietrikow, 1908; New York, n.d.

Fuchs, Rabbi Yitzchak Yaakov. *Tefillah KeHilchasah*. Jerusalem, 1989.

Ganzfried, Rabbi Solomon. (1806-1886). *Kitzur Shulchan Aruch*. Lvov, 1860; with commentary *Ir David*, by Rabbi David Feldman, Manchester, England/ New York, 1948.

Gold, Rabbi Yechiel Michal. *Darkei Chaim v'Sholom*. (customs of the Munkaczer Rebbe, Rabbi Chaim Elazar Shapiro). Muncacz, 1940; Jerusalem, 1970.

Guttman, Rabbi Michael HaKohen. *Maftei'ach HaTalmud*. Czongrad, 1906.

HaLevi, Rabbi Chaim Dovid. *Mekor Chaim HaShaleim*. (5 volumes). Tel Aviv, 1967-1974.

Hershowitz, Rabbi Avraham Eliezer. *Otzar Kol Minhagei Yeshurun*. St. Louis, 1917; Jerusalem, 1970.

Hollander, Rabbi Chaim Tzvi (ed.). *Zevach Mishpachah*. Chicago, 1976.

Kagan, Rabbi Yisrael Meir HaKohen (Chofetz Chaim). (1839-1933). *Mishnah Berurah*. Warsaw, 1892-1898; Jerusalem: Vaad HaYeshivos, 1963.

——. *Shemiras HaLoshon*. (in *Kol Kisvei Chofetz Chaim HaSoleim*). New York: A. Y. Friedman, 1952.

Kahane, Rabbi Nachman. *Orchos Chayim (Spinka)*. Siget, 1898; Jerusalem, 1983.

Kasher, Rabbi Moshe Shlomo (Director). *Noam*, vol. 16. Jerusalem: Torah Sheleimah Institute, 1973.

Lipitz, Rabbi Yitzchak. *Sefer Mataamim*. Warsaw, 1889; Jerusalem, n.d.

Lipshitz, Rabbi Abraham. *Yalkut Avraham*. Muncacz, 1931; New York, 1969.

Lorberbaum, Rabbi Yaakov. (1760-1832). *(Siddur) Derech HaChaim*. Berlin, 1860.

Margolis, Rabbi Reuven. *Mekor Chesed*. Jerusalem: Mossad HaRav Kook, 1957. Gloss to *Sefer Chasidim*.

Medini, Rabbi Chayim Chizkiyahu. (1832-1904). *Sdei Chemed*. 10 vols. Warsaw-Pietrokov, 1890-1891, 1911-1912; New York: A. Y. Friedman, 1967.

Schwadron, Rabbi Sholom Mordechai HaKohen. (1835–1911). *Da'as Torah (Yoreh De'ah)*. Jerusalem: Machon Daas Torah, 1980.

Shapira, Rabbi Chaim Elazar. (Munkaczer Rebbe). (d. 1937). *Nimukei Orach Chaim*. Tyrnau, 1930; Jerusalem, 1984.

——. *Divrei Torah*. Munkacz: 1922; Bratislav, 1930; New York, 1955.
Sefer HaMinhagim, Minhagei Chabad. New York: Kehot Publication Society, 1967.
Soffer, Rabbi Yaakov Chaim. (Baghdad-Jerusalem, 1870-1939). *Kaf HaChaim*. Jerusalem, 1963.
Sperling, Rabbi Avraham Yitzchak. *Taamei HaMinhagim u'Mekorei HaDinim*. Lvov, 1896; Jerusalem: Eshkol, 1957.
Vandrovsky, Rabbi Yitzchak Ze'ev. *Minhagei Beis Yaakov*. New York, 1910.
Wein, Rabbi Berel. *Chikrei Halachah*. Jerusalem: Mossad Harav Kook, 1976.
Wharman, Rabbi Abraham Dovid of Buczacz. *Eishel Avraham*. Lvov, 1893; Buczacz, 1906.
R' Yosef Chaim (Al-Chakkam) ben Eliyahu Moshe Chaim. (ca. 1833-1909). *Ben Ish Chai*. Jerusalem, 1898.

V. RESPONSA
Adadi, Rabbi Avraham Chaim. *Vayikra Avraham*. Livorno, 1865; Jerusalem, 1983.
Aderes, Rabbi Shlomo ibn. (b. Barcelona, Spain, 1235; d. there, 1310). *Rashba*. Bologna, 1539; Bnei Brak, 1958.
Ashkenazi, Rabbi Nissim Avraham. *Maasei Avraham*. Symrna (Izmir), 1855.
R' Binyamin ben Mattisyahu (d. 1540) *Binyamin Ze'ev*. Vol. 1. Venice, 1539; Jerusalem, 1988.
Breisch, Rabbi Mordechai J. *Chelkas Yaakov*. Vol. 2. London. 1959. Vol. 3. Bnei Brak, 1966.
Deutsch, Rabbi Eliezer Chaim. *Dudaei HaSadeh*. Szeini, Satmar: 1929.
Eiger, Rabbi Akivah of Posen. (1761-1837). *Rabbi Akivah Eiger*. Vienna, 1889; New York, 1945.
Eisenstadt, Rabbi Meir. (b. 1670; d. Eisenstadt, Hungary, June 6, 1744). *Panim Meiros*. Amsterdam, 1715; Jerusalem, n.d
Feinstein, Rabbi Moses. (1895-1986). *Igros Moshe*. 7 vols. New York, 1959; Bnei Brak, 1981.
Fleckles, Rabbi Eliezer. (b. Prague, August 26, 1754; d. there April 27, 1826). *Teshuvah m'Ahavah*. Vol. 3. Prague, 1821; Jerusalem, 1970.
Frank, Rabbi Tzvi Pesach. *Har Tzvi, Yoreh De'ah*. Jerusalem, 1964.
Frankel, Rabbi Eliyahu Teomim. *Nachalas Avi*. Bulgaria, 1937; New York, 1980.
Fried, Rabbi Nesanel HaKohen. *Pnei Meivin*. Munkacz, 1913-1914; New York, 1971.
Ginzberg, Rabbi Aryeh Z. *Divrei Chachomim*. New York, 1986.
Greenblatt, Rabbi Ephraim. *Rivevos Ephraim*. Vol. 3. New York, 1980.
Harfenes, Rabbi Yisrael Dovid. *VaYevarech Dovid*. Vol. 2. New York, 1989.
Hedayah, Rabbi Ovadiah. *Yaskil Avdi*. Vol. 6. 2nd ed. Jerusalem, 1983.
Kluger, Rabbi Shlomo. (b. Komarow, Russian [Poland], 1783; d. Brody, June 9, 1869). *HaElef Lecha Shlomo*. Lvov, 1910; Bulgaria, 1931.
——. *Tuv Taam v'Daas*, sec. 3, vol. 2. Podgorze, 1900; Jerusalem, n.d.
Landau, Rabbi Ezekiel (Segal). (b. Opatow, October 8, 1713; d. Prague, April 29, 1793), *Noda b'Yehudah*. Prague, 1776-1811; New York, 1958.
Landau, Rabbi Shmuel (Segal). (son of Rabbi Ezekiel; d. October 31, 1834). *Shivas Tziyon*. Prague, 1787; New York, 1966.
Landau, Rabbi Yisrael Avraham Alter. *Beis Yisrael, Yoreh De'ah*. New York, 1976.

Leiter, Rabbi Ze'ev Wolf. *Beis Dovid*. Vienna, 1932.

Luria, Rabbi Chaim Pinchas. *Meishiv Halachah*. Lodz, 1922.

R' Meir of Rothenberg. (b. Worms, Germany, ca. 1215; d. Alsace, France, 19 *Iyar*, 1293). *Maharam Rothenberg*. Cremona, 1557; Jerusalem: Mossad HoRav Kook, 1960.

Melamed, Rabbi Meir. *Mishpat Tzedek*. Salonica, 1617; Jerusalem, 1990.

Moellin, Rabbi Yaakov Moellin. (b. Mainz, Germany, ca. 1365; d. Worms, Germany, 21 Elul, 1427). *Maharil*. Venice, 1549; Cracow ed. 1881, reprinted New York: 1974.

Nathanson, Rabbi Yosef Shaul HaLevi. (b. Berzan, 1808; d. Lemberg, March 4, 1875). *Shoeil u'Meishiv*. 13 vols. Lvov, 1869-1890; New York, 1954.

Palagi, Rabbi Chaim. (b. Smyrna, 1788; d. there 1869). *Chaim b'Yad*. Smyrna, 1873.

——. *Chikekai Lev*. Vol. 1. Salonica, 1840-1849; Jerusalem, n.d.

Palagi, Rabbi Yitzchak. *Yaffe LeLev*. Smyrna, 1872; Jerusalem, 1978.

Pontremoli, Rabbi Chiya. (d. Smyrna, 1832). *Tzapichis b'Devash*. Salonica, 1848.

Posek, Rabbi Hillel. *Rav Hillel Omer*. Tel Aviv, 1957.

Reischer, Rabbi Yaakov. (b. Prague; d. Metz, 10 *Teves*, 1733). *Shevus Yaakov*. 3 vols. Lvov, 1861; Jerusalem, 1972.

Rigoler, Rabbi Eliyahu of Kalish. *Yad Eliyahu*. Warsaw, 1900; Jerusalem, 1969.

Rosen, Rabbi Abraham Leib. *Eisan Aryeh*. Jerusalem: Mossad HaRav Kook, 1976.

Schlesinger, Rabbi Avraham Yafe. *Be'er Sarim*. Vol. 3. Jerusalem, 1986.

Schneerson, Rabbi Menachem Mendel. *Yagdil Torah*. New York, 1981.

Schwartz, Rabbi Josef. *Ginzei Yosef*. Oradea (Grosswardein), 1930.

——, ed. *Vayelaket Yosef*. Munkacz, 1899-1917.

——. *VaYitzbor Yosef*. Oradea (Grosswardein), 1936.

Sofer (Schreiber), Rabbi Abraham Shmuel Binyamin. (1815-1871). *Kesav Sofer, Yoreh De'ah*. Pressburg, 1879; Jerusalem, 1984.

Sofer (Schreiber), Rabbi Moshe. (b. Frankfurt am Main, September 14, 1763; d. Pressburg, October 3, 1839). *Chasam Sofer, Yoreh De'ah*. New York, 1958.

Sonnenfeld, Rabbi Yosef Chaim. (1849-1932). *Salmas Chaim, Yoreh De'ah*. Bnei Brak, 1982.

Steinberg, Rabbi Abraham Menachem HaLevi. *Machazeh Avraham*. 3 vols. New York, 1964, 1972; Jerusalem, 1988.

Stern, Rabbi Abraham. *Kisvei Eish*. Vol. 1. Jerusalem, 1964.

Stern, Rabbi Bezalel. *b'Tzeil HaChochmah*. Vol. 2. Jerusalem, 1967.

Stern, Rabbi Moshe. *Be'er Moshe*. 8 vols. New York, 1973-1987.

Sternhell, Rabbi Isaac. *Kochavei Yitzchak*. Vol. 1. New York, 1969.

Teitelbaum, Rabbi Chananya Yom Tov Lippa. *Levushei Yom Tov*. New York, 1970.

Tennenbaum, Rabbi Malkiel Tzvi HaLevi. (d. 1910). *Divrei Malkiel*. Vols. 2, 3. Jerusalem, 1987.

Tomashoff, Rabbi Moshe Binyamin. *Avnei Shoham*. Vol. 4. New York, 1947.

Tziltz, Rabbis Moshe Leib and Tziltz, Shmuel. *Milei d'Avos*. Tel Aviv, 1972.

Tzirelson, Rabbi Yehudah Leib. (d. 1941). *Gevul Yehudah*. Pietrikow: 1906.

Valdenberg, Rabbi Eliezer Yehudah. *Tzitz Eliezer*. 19 vols. Jerusalem, 1947-1992.

Weinberg, Rabbi Yechiel Yaakov. *Seridei Eish* Vol. 2. 2nd printing. Jerusalem: Mossad HaRav Kook, 1977.

Weiss, Rabbi Binyamin Aryeh HaKohen. *Even Yekarah*. Vol. 1. Lemberg, 1894

Weiss, Rabbi Yitzchak Yaakov. *Minchas Yitzchok*. Vols. 2 and 4. London, 1958, 1967.

Winkler, Rabbi Mordechai Leib. *Levushei Mordechai*. Vol. 2, *Yoreh De'ah*. Budapest, 1917-1924; New York, n.d.

Wosner, Rabbi Shmuel HaLevi. *Shevet HaLevi*. Vols. 2 and 3. New York, 1981.

R' Yishmael ben Avraham Yitzchak HaKohen. (1724-1811). *Zera Emes, Yoreh De'ah*. Livorno, 1796.

Yossef, Rabbi Ovadyah. *Yabia Omer*. 6 vols. Jerusalem, 1954-1976; 2nd ed., 1986.

Zilberberg, Rabbi Avraham Binyamin. *Mishnas Binyamin*. New York, 1948.

Zimrah, Rabbi David ibn. (b. Spain, ca. 1480; d. Safed, 1573). *Radvaz*. 7 vols. Warsaw, 1883; New York, 1967.

Zolty, Rabbi Yaakov Bezalel. *Mishnas Yaavetz*. Jerusalem, 1984.

VI. ON SICKNESS, DEATH, AND MOURNING
(HEBREW AND JEWISH SOURCES)

R' Aaron Berechiah of Modena. (d. Italy, 26 *Tammuz*, 1639). *Maavar Yabok*. Mantua, 1626; Vilna ed., 1896, reprinted Jerusalem, n.d.

Alfiyah, Rabbi Yitzchak. *HaKuntras HaYechiali (Beis Olomim)*. Jerusalem, 1928, 1975.

Assaf, Rabbi Dovid. *Yalkut Das v'Din*. Palestine, 1944.

Ayache, Rabbi Yehudah. (1700-1761). *Shevet Yehudah*. Levorno, 1783; Jerusalem, 1970.

Baer, Rabbi Yitzchak (Seligman). (b. Mosbach, September 18, 1825; d. Biebrich-on-the-Rhine, March 1897). *Totzaos Chaim*. Rodelheim, 1832.

Bergman, Rabbi Moshe. *Zibula Basraisa*. Jerusalem, 1931.

Bernstein, Rabbi Chaim. *Yakra d'Chaya*. 2nd ed., Bnei Brak, 1979.

B'Nesivei Chesed v'Emes, Annual of the Chevrah Kaddisha of Tel Aviv, year 5753. Dr. Yitzchak Alfasi, editor.

Cherniak, Rabbi Sholom Shachna. *Mishmeres Sholom*. Warsaw, 1928-1930; Jerusalem, n.d.

Deblitzky, Rabbi Sharya. *Zichron Betzalel*. Bnei Brak, 1977.

Donath, Rabbi Moshe Eliezer. *Devorei Emes*. Berdiczew, 1931.

Felder, Rabbi Aaron. *Yesodei Semachos (Mourning and Remembrance)*. New York: CIS Publishers, 1992.

Feldman, Rabbi Israel. *Likutei Yaffe*. New York, 1974.

Frand, Rabbi Yissachar. *Oholei Yissachar*. Baltimore, 1986.

Frankfurter, Rabbi Shimon. (b. Schwerin, Germany; d. Amsterdam, December 9, 1712). *Sefer HaChaim*. Amsterdam, 1703 (1716 as *Sefer HaChaim*).

Freolich, Rabbi Avraham Yisrael. *Sherashim b'Semachos*. Jerusalem, 1980.

Goldberg, Rabbi Chaim Binyamin. *Pnei Baruch*. Jerusalem, 1986.

———. *Mourning in Halachah*. New York: Mesorah, 1991.

Goodman, Michelle. *Nichum Avelim: Comforting the Mourners*. Toronto: Benjamin Family Foundation, 1987.

Greenbaum, Naftali. *Nichum Aveilim*. Jerusalem: Yetzirah, n.d.

Greenwald, Yekutiel Yehuda. *Ach l'Tzora*. St. Louis, 1939.

———. *Kol Bo al Aveilus*. New York: Feldheim, 1973.

Grossberg, Rabbi Chanoch Zundel. *Chazon l'Moed*. Jerusalem, 1975.

Katz, Rabbi Label Katz. *Chesed Shel Emes*. New York, 1981.

Lamm, Rabbi Maurice. *The Jewish Way in Death and Mourning*. New York: Jonathan David, 1969.

Levine, Rabbi Aaron. *How to Perform the Great Mitzvah of Bikkur Cholim*. Toronto: Zichron Meir, 1987.

———. *The Complete Yizkor Handbook*. Toronto: Zichron Meir, 1987.

———. *Zichron Meir al Aveilus*. Toronto: Zichron Meir, 1985.

Marber, Rabbi Gershon Ephraim. *Darkei HaChaim*. Lublin, 1927; Jerusalem, 1974.

Menachem ben Rabbi Shimon Mordechai of Adrianopoli. *Menachem Aveilim*. Symrna, 1880; New York, 1978.

Nachmanides, Rabbi Moshe ben Nachman. (See Bible Commentaries above). *Toras HaAdam*. Constantinople, 1519; in *Kisvei Ramban*, Jerusalem: Mossad Harav Kook, 1964.

Noah, Rabbi Moshe Tzvi. *Nachamu Ami*. Petach Tikvah, 1978.

Paull, Simcha Steven. *Guidelines to Understanding the Traditions of Shiva*. Toronto: The Benjamin Family Foundation, 1987.

Press, Rabbi Chaim. *Yakra d'Chaya: Concern for the Living*. Jerusalem: Targum/ Feldheim, 1990.

Rabi, Rabbis Nissim, and Rabi, Chaim. *Yakra d'Chaya*. Jerusalem: Nesiv Binyamin, 1980.

Rotter, Rabbi Aharon Yeshaya. *Shaarei Aharon*. Bnei Brak, 1968.

Schneerson, Rabbi Menachem Mendel. *v'HaChai Yitten es Libo*. New York: Vaad Hanochos B'Lahak, 1988.

Schwartz, Rabbi Yosef HaKohen. *Hadras Kodesh*. Oradea, 1930.

Sidan, Rabbi Shimon. *Shevet Shimon*. Pressburg, 1884.

R' Shlomo ben Moshe of Chelma. (d. Salonica, 1778). *Kuntras Aveil HaShitim*. Jerusalem: Machon Yerushalayim, 1980.

Sofer, Rabbi Yaakov Chaim. *Zera Chaim*. Jerusalem, 1988.

Tuchachinsky, Rabbi Yechiel Michel. *Gesher HaChaim*. Jerusalem, 1947.

Ushpol, Rabbi Isaac B. *Darkei Chesed*. New York, 1975.

Valdenberg, Rabbi Eliezer Yehudah. *Even Yaakov*. Jerusalem, 1962. Also printed in vol. 5 of *Responsa Tzitz Eliezer*, Jerusalem, 1985.

———. *Ramat Rachel*. Printed in vol. 8 of *Responsa Tzitz Eliezer*, Jerusalem, 1984; also in vol. 5 of *Tzitz Eliezer*, Jerusalem, 1985.

Wikler, Meir. "The Psychodynamics of Grief and Mourning." *Jewish Observer* 18:2 (January 1985): 20-21.

Yossef, Rabbi Yitzchak. *Yalkut Yossef*. Vol. 7. (Rulings of Rabbi Ovadiah Yossef). Jerusalem, 1989.

Zikoron l'Yom Acharon, Seder Maavar Yabok. Prague, 1828.

Zinner, Rabbi Gavriel. *Nitei Gavriel*. New York, 1993.

VII. EXTRALEGAL LITERATURE: MORALISTIC, PHILOSOPHIC, AND MYSTIC

Abohab, Rabbi Yitzchak I. (Spain, ca. 1300). *Menoras HaMaor*. Turkey, 1514; Vilna, 1857; reprinted New York, n.d.

Alter, Rabbi Binyamin Menachem. *Imrei Emes Likkutim*. Jerusalem, 1988.

Berger, Rabbi Yisrael. *Eser Tzichtzachus*. Pietrikow, 1910.

Blauser, Rabbi Yitzchak. (1837-1907). *Or Yisrael*. Vilna, 1900.

Byfus, Rabbi Yisrael. *Yalkut Lekach Tov, Pirkei Emunah u'Nechamah*. Kfar Chassidim: Tashbar HoRav, 1993.

Chayei HaMussar. Bnei Brak: Hotzoas Chochmah U'Mussar, 1963.

Cohen, Rabbi Shlomo. *P'eir Hador*. (Biography of the Chazon Ish—1878-1953). Bnei Brak: Netzach, 1970.

Dessler, Rabbi Eliyahu Eliezer. (1891-1954). *Michtav m'Eliyahu*. Vol. 4. Jerusalem, 1983.

Eliav, Mordekhai. *Ani Ma'amin*. Jerusalem: Mossad Harav Kook, 1965.

Gross, Rabbi Moshe Dovid. *Otzar HaAggadah*. Jerusalem: Mossad Harav Kook, 1977.

Hertz, Rabbi Dr. Joseph H. *Authorized Daily Prayer Book*. New York: Bloch, 1955.

Horowitz, Rabbi Avraham. *Sefer Orchos Rabbeinu, Baal HaKehilas Yaakov* (Steipler Gaon). Bnei Brak, 1991.

Hutner, Rabbi Yitzchak. *Pachad Yitzchak, Igros u'Kesavim*. New York, 1981.

Kagan, Rabbi Yisrael Meir HaKohen (Chofetz Chaim). (1839-1933). *Ahavas Chesed*. Warsaw, 1888; in *Kol Kisvei Chofetz Chaim*, New York: A. Y. Friedman, 1952.

Levovitz, Rabbi Yerucham. (1874-1936). *Daas Chochmah u'Mussar*. Vol. 3. New York, 1969.

Lipschutz, Rabbi Jules. *Rabbinical Council of America Manual*. New York, RCA, 1978.

Lopian, Rabbi Eliyahu Lopian. (1876-1970). *Lev Eliyahu*. Vol. 1. Jerusalem, 1972.

Luzzatto, Rabbi Moshe Chaim. (1707-1746). *Messilas Yesharim (Path of the Just)*. English ed., Jerusalem: Feldheim, 1966.

Meisels, Meir. *Judaism: Thought and Legend*. Kfar Chabad, n.d.

Mintz, Binyamin. *(Sefer) HaHistalkus (HaNefesh)*. Tel Aviv, 1930.

Papo, Rabbi Eliezer. (b. Sarajevo, Bosnia; d. 1824). *Peleh Yo'etz*. Constantinople, 1825; Tel Aviv, Sinai Publishing, 1966.

Prager, Moshe. *Eleh She'lo Nichne'u*. Bnei Brak: Netzach, 1963.

Reketz, Rabbi Yoetz. *Siach Sarfei Kodesh*. Vol. 3. Lodz, 1931; Jerusalem, n.d.

Savar, Rabbi Moshe. *Michlol HaMaamarim v'HaPisgamim*. Jerusalem: Mossad Harav Kook, 1961.

Sorasky, Aaron. (adapted from Hebrew). *Reb Elchonon*. New York: Mesorah, 1982.

Tzemach, Rabbi Yaakov Chaim. *Negid u'Metzaveh*. Constantinople, 1726; Jerusalem, 1967.

Tzunz, Dovid Leib. *Gedulas Yehonoson*. Jerusalem, 1968.

Vital, Rabbi Chayim. (b. Safed, 1543; d. Damascus, May 6, 1620). *Sefer HaGilgulim*. Frankfurt am Main, 1684; Jerusalem, 1967.

Wolbe, Rabbi Shlomo. *Alei Shur*. Be'er Yaakov, 1968.

Yom Kippur Machzor. New York: Hebrew Publishing Company, n.d.

Yoshor, Rabbi Moshe. *HaChofetz Chaim (Chayav u'Paalo)*. Tel Aviv: Netzach Publishers, 1958.

VIII. ENGLISH SOURCES—JEWISH SUBJECTS

Brenner, Reeve Robert. *The Faith and Doubt of Holocaust Survivors*. New York: Free Press, 1980.

Dobrinsky, Rabbi Herbert C. *A Treasury of Sephardic Laws and Customs*. New York: Ktav/Yeshiva University Press, 1986.

Eliach, Yaffa. *Hasidic Tales of the Holocaust*. New York: Avon Books, 1982.

Hirsch, Rabbi Samson Raphael. (1808-1888, Germany). *Horeb*. Trans. Dayan I. Grunfeld. London: Soncino Press, 1962.

Krohn, Rabbi Paysach J. *The Maggid Speaks*. New York: Mesorah, 1987.

——. *In the Footsteps of the Maggid*. New York: Mesorah, 1992.

Pliskin, Rabbi Zelig. *Love Your Neighbor*. New York: Aish HaTorah Publications, 1977.

——. *Gateway to Happiness*. Jerusalem: Aish HaTorah Publications, 1983.

Raz, Simcha. *A Tzaddik in Our Time*. Jerusalem: Feldheim, 1976.

Rosenbaum, Irving J. *The Holocaust and Halakhah*. New York: Ktav, 1976.

IX. GRIEF AND MOURNING—SECULAR SOURCES

Gorer, Geoffrey. *Death, Grief, and Mourning in Contemporary Britain*. London: Cresset, 1965.

Greenberg, Rabbi Sydney. *A Treasury of Comfort*. North Hollywood, CA: Wilshire Book Company, 1975.

Kushner, Harold S. *When Bad Things Happen to Good People*. New York: Schocken, 1981.

Lindenmann, Eric. *The Symptomatology and Management of Acute Grief*. American *Journal of Psychiatry* 101 (September 1944): 141-148.

Nemzoff, Sol L. In *Understanding Bereavement and Grief*, ed. Norman Linzer, pp. 32-36. New York: Yeshiva University Press, 1977.

Oursler, Grace Perkins, and Armstrong, April. *When Sorrow Comes*. New York: Doubleday, 1950.

Parkes, Colin Murray. *Bereavement*. New York: International University Press, 1965.

Silverman, William B., and Cinnamon, Kenneth M. *When Mourning Comes*. Northvale, NJ: Jason Aronson, 1990.

Spiro, Jack D. *A Time to Mourn*. New York: Bloch, 1967, 1985.

Weiner, Alfred. In *Understanding Bereavement and Grief*, ed. Norman Linier, pp. 37-44. New York: Yeshiva University Press, 1977.

IX-A. ADDITIONAL BOOKS ON GRIEF AND BEREAVEMENT

The rest of this bibliography was supplied to me by Dr. Michelle B. Goodman, a grief specialist and therapist in Toronto, Canada. The reader must be aware that these are secular sources and are recorded here for those who do not have available to them the traditional sources of guidance, or who are experiencing problematic grief and wish to read the studies on general psychology of grief.

Brooks, Anne M. *The Grieving Time: A Year's Account of Recovery from Loss*. New York: Harmony Books, 1985.

Caine, Lynn. *Being a Widow*. Markham, Ontario: Penguin Books, 1990.

Campbell, Scott, and Silverman, Phyllis. *Widower: When Men Are Left Alone*. New York: Prentice Hall, 1987.

Davis Ginsburg, Genevieve. *To Live Again: Rebuilding Your Life After You've Become a Widow*. Toronto: Bantam, 1987.

Di Giulio, Robert C. *Beyond Widowhood: From Bereavement to Emergence and Hope.* New York: The Free Press, 1989.

IX-B. DEATH OF A CHILD
Fair Donnely, Katherine. *Recovering from the Loss of a Child.* New York: MacMillan, 1982.
Schiff Sarnoff, Harriet. *The Bereaved Parent.* New York: Penguin, 1977.

IX-C. DEATH OF A PARENT—ADULTS
Angel, Marc D. *The Orphaned Adult—Confronting the Death of a Parent.* New York: Human Sciences Press, 1987.
Myers, Edward. *When Parents Die: A Guide for Adults.* New York: Viking, 1986.
Schiff Sarnoff, Harriet. *Living through Mourning: Finding Comfort and Hope When a Loved One Has Died.* Donnelley & Sons Co., 1986.

IX-D. BEREAVEMENT BIBLIOGRAPHY FOR PARENTS AND CHILDREN
Furman, Earl. *A Child's Parent Dies—Studies in Childhood Bereavement.* New Haven: Yale University Press, 1974.
Gordon, Audrey K., and Klass, Dennis. *They Need to Know: How to Teach Children about Death.* Englewood Cliffs, NJ: Prentice-Hall, 1979.
Grollman, Earl. *Explaining Death to Children.* Boston: Beacon Press, 1969.
Jackson, Edgar N. *Telling a Child about Death.* New York: Channel Press, 1965.
Klopfenstein, Janette. *Tell Me about Death, Mommy: A Young Widow's Advice on How to Help Children Understand Death.* Scottdale, PA: Herald Press, 1977.
Knowles, D. W., and Reeves, N. *But Won't Granny Need Her Socks?: Dealing Effectively with Children's Concerns about Death and Dying.* Dubuque: Kendall/Hunt Publishing, 1983.
Kübler-Ross, Elisabeth. *On Children and Death.* New York: Macmillan Books, 1983.
Rudolph, Marguerite. *Should the Children Know?: Encounters with Death in the Lives of Children.* New York: Schocken, 1978.
Schaefer, Dan, and Lyons, Christine. *How Do We Tell the Children?* New York: Newmarket Press, 1986.
Schneiderman, Gerald. *Coping with Death in the Family.* Toronto: NC Press, 1985.
Wolfeltz, Alan. *Helping Children Cope with Grief.* Muncie, IN: Accelerated Development, 1983.

IX-E. BOOKS FOR PARENTS AND CHILDREN
Buscaglia, Leo. *The Fall of Freddie the Leaf.* New York: Holt, Rinehart & Wilson, 1982.
Gardner, Richard A. *The Boys & Girls Book about One Parent Families.* New York: Putnam, 1978.
Grollman, Earl. *Talking about Death: A Dialogue between Parent and Child.* Boston: Beacon Press, 1970.
Jewett, C. *Helping Children Cope with Separation and Loss.* Cambridge, MA: Harvard Common Press, 1982.
LeShan, Eda. *Learning to Say Goodbye When a Parent Dies.* New York: Avon Books, 1978.

Mellonie, Bryan. *Lifetimes: The Beautiful Way to Explain Death to Children*. New York: Bantam Books, 1983.

Stein, Sarah Bonnett. *About Dying: An Open Family Book for Parents and Children Together*. New York: Walker, 1974.

IX-F. BOOKS FOR ELEMENTARY SCHOOL CHILDREN
Adkins, Michael C. *Orknon Was My Friend*. Image, 1984.

Clardy, Andrea F. *Dusty Was My Friend*. New York: Human Sciences Press, 1984.

Geller, Norman. *Talk to God . . . I'll Get the Message*. Lewiston, ME: Norman Geller, 1983.

Goodman, Michelle M. *Vanishing Cookies: Doing OK When a Parent Has Cancer*. Toronto: Benjamin Family Foundation, 1990.

Grollman, Sharon. *Shira*. New York: Doubleday Press, 1988.

Hazen, Barbara Shook. *Why Did Grandpa Die?* Racine, WI: Western Publishing, 1985.

Krements, Jill. *How It Feels When a Parent Dies*. New York: Alfred A. Knopf, 1981.

Lee, Virginia. *The Magic Moth*. New York: Seabury Press, 1972.

Pomerantz, Barbara. *Bubby, Me, and Memories*. New York: UAHC, 1983.

Rofes, E. *The Kids Book about Death and Dying*. Boston: Little, Brown, 1985.

Spero, Moshe H. *Zeydeh*. Lawrence, NY: Simcha Publishing, 1984.

Varley, Susan. *Badger's Parting Gifts*. New York: Lothrop, Lee & Shepard Books, 1984.

Viorst, Judith. *The Tenth Good Thing about Barney*. Hartford: Atheneum, 1971.

IX-G. BIBLIOGRAPHY ON DEATH AND THE AFTERLIFE IN JUDAISM
Chavel, Charles B., trans. *Ramban—The Gate of Reward*. New York: Shilo Publishing, 1983.

Rosner, Fred, trans. *Moses Maimonides' Treatise on Resurrection*. New York: Ktav, 1982.

Scholem, Gershom. *Kabbalah [Essays on "Gilgul;" "Eschatology;" "Man and His Soul"]*. New York: New American Library, 1976.

Winkler, Gershon. *The Soul of the Matter*. New York: Judaica Press, 1982.

Index

Dedications

וְהַמַּשְׂכִּלִים יַזְהִרוּ כְּזֹהַר הָרָקִיעַ
וּמַצְדִּיקֵי הָרַבִּים כַּכּוֹכָבִים לְעוֹלָם וָעֶד:
(דניאל יב ג)

ברצוני להביע את מיטב תודותי לכל אלו שתרמו מהונם ובנדבת לבם אפשרו
את הוצאתו לאור של ספר זה במתכונת הדורה ומשוכללת.

יתן ד' ויתברכו הם ומשפחותיהם ממקור הברכות לרוב בריאות, אושר וכבוד,
ולאורך ימים ושנים.

יהא ספר זה לזכות ולעילוי נשמת כל אותם הנפטרים שלזכרם הוקדשו
והונצחו התרומות בעין יפה וביד נדיבה ע"י קרוביהם משפחותיהם וידידיהם.
המחבר

The author wishes to express his hearfelt appreciation to all of the
sponsors who have made possible the publication of this Sefer.

May Hashem Yisbarach bless them and their families with His
bounty of blessings for long life, good health and much happiness.

May this book truly be a merit for all of their dearly beloved ones,
to whom they have dedicated honor or memorial sponsorships.

לעלוי נשמת
ר' שואל ב"ר מרדכי יוסף סיגלער ז"ל
נלב"ע ער"ח אדר ב' תשמ"ט--לזכר היאהרצייט החמישי
זכרון עולם לקדושי השואה
אחיו ואחותיו של ר' שואל ע"ה למעלה מששים נפש

ר' חיים ב"ר מרדכי יוסף ע"ה ומשפחתו

ר' אברהם משה ב"ר מרדכי יוסף ע"ה ומשפחתו

ר' ישעיה וואלף זאב ב"ר מרדכי יוסף ע"ה ומשפחתו

מרת רבקה בת ר' מרדכי יוסף ע"ה ומשפחתה

מרת שרה בת ר' מרדכי יוסף ע"ה ומשפחתה

מרת שינדל בת ר' מרדכי יוסף ע"ה ומשפחתה

מרת עלקא בת ר' מרדכי יוסף ע"ה ומשפחתה

ה' ינקום דמם

ולז"נ מרת באשא בת ר' מרדכי יוסף ע"ה

ולז"נ אביו של ר' שואל
ר' מרדכי יוסף ב"ר חיים שטאדטמויער ע"ה
נפטר ט' מרחשון תרע"ה

ולז"נ אמו של ר' שואל
מרת דינה לאה בת ר' שואל ציגלער (סיגלער) ע"ה
נפטרה י"ב שבט תרצ"ד

ולז"נ הורי מרת צביה שתחי' אשת ר' שואל
ר' משה ב"ר אריה זאב הלוי סג"ל ע"ה
נפטר ח"י אדר א' תשל"ג
וזוגתו העניא בת ר' יהודה צבי לבית גאלדענבערג ע"ה
מפטרה ו' כסלו תשי"ח

תנצב"ה

מוקדש ע"י
אשתו מרת **צביה** תחי', טורונטו
בניו ר' מרדכי יוסף ויהודית אסתר סיגלער
ומשפחתם נ"י, טורונטו
דינה לאה ואוריאל שפיגלמאן
ומשפחתם נ"י, לאס אנג'לס

נר תמיד

הוקדש

לעלוי נשמת

מוהר״ר **שמעיהו** בן מוהר״ר **דוד** ז״ל

נפטר א׳ דשבועות תשל״ה

ומרת **רבקה** בת מוהר״ר **אברהם** ז״ל

נפטרה י״ט שבט תש״ן

נר תמיד

לעי"נ

ר' יוסף ב"ר אברהם ז"ל

סילבר

מאת בנו אברהם אבא נ"י

ורעיתו בתי-ה פייגא

ומשפחתם

Dedicated in Memory of

MR. JOSEPH SILVER ז"ל

תנצב"ה

by

his son **Avraham**

and

The Silver Family

נר תמיד

Dedicated by the Author
לעי"נ

ר' יוסף טננבוים ז"ל

MR. JOSEPH TANENBAUM ז"ל
נפטר כ' מרחשון תשנ"ג

who dedicated the forthcoming English edition of
Zichron Meir Al Aveilus
in memory of his beloved parents

ר' אברהם ב"ר יוסף ז"ל
ABRAHAM TANENBAUM ע"ה
נפטר ב' דראש השנה תשי"ח

וזוגתו מרת **ציפה שרה בת ר' יצחק אייזיק** ע"ה
CHIPA SARAH TANENBAUM ע"ה
נפטרה י"ט תמוז תשי"ו

and to the memory of

מרת **פיגא בת ר' אברהם יעקב** ע"ה
MRS. FAYE TANENBAUM ע"ה
נפטרה כ"ו אלול תשנ"ב

תנצב"ה

נר תמיד

Dedicated

לזכר נשמת

החבר ר' **ברוך מרדכי בן כלב** ז"ל

נפטר ח' טבת תשמ"ח

חיה רץ כצבי וגבור כארי בעבודת בוראו

In Loving Memory

of

MR. BENJAMIN M. GARFUNKEL ז"ל

HIS DEDICATION AND DEVOTION
TO TORAH AND MITZVOS
HAS INFLUENCED SAVANNAH JEWRY
FOR DECADES

תנצב"ה

By

THE GARFUNKEL FAMILY
Savannah, Georgia

DEDICATED IN HONOUR OF MY PARENTS

לעלוי נשמת

To the further merit of:

MY FATHER

ר' משה בן זאב הלוי ז"ל

MR. MANFRED E. HART

whose kindness and patience continue to uplift and inspire

תנצב"ה

---

and

תבדל לחיים טובים וארוכים

MY MOTHER

מרת פנינה בת ר' יצחק תחי'

MRS. PENINA HART

who gently and compassionately, through all time and circumstances accomplishes the miracle of true sustained faith in, and an embracing protection of, all who love her and are loved by her.

From this union of Love and Truth came Love and Truth

In Memory of the Marder Family
Zlotschov, Poland

לז״נ

ר׳ אורי ב״ר מאיר הלוי ז״ל -- נהרג על קידוש השם א׳ סיון תש״ג-1943
וזוג׳ מרת חנה בת ר׳ שלמה ע״ה -- נהרגה על קידוש ה׳ יום א׳ דשבועות תש״ג-1943
ר׳ אריה צבי ב״ר שלמה הלוי ז״ל -- נפטר ט׳ באב תרפ״ח-1927
וזוגתו מרת שיינדל בת ר׳ שמואל ע״ה -- נפטרה א׳ טבת תרצ״ט-1938
ר׳ שלמה ב״ר אריה צבי הלוי ז״ל -- נהרג על קידוש ה׳ כ״ו אדר ב׳ תש״ג-1943
וזוגתו מרת חוה בת ר׳ אורי הלוי -- נפטרה ט״ו כסלו תשמ״ו-1985
ר׳ מאיר שמואל ב״ר שלמה הלוי ז״ל -- נהרג על קידוש ה׳ כ״ה אייר תש״ג-1943
ר׳ משה ליב ב״ר שלמה הלוי ז״ל -- נהרג על קידוש ה׳ כ״ה אייר תש״ג-1943
ר׳ יחיאל מיכאל ב״ר שלמה הלוי ז״ל -- נהרג על קידוש ה׳ כ״ו אדר ב׳ תש״ג-943
תנצב״ה

הונצח ע״י

מרת טשארנע איידל בת ר׳ שלמה הלוי שמערץ - מארדער תחי׳
ר׳ אריה צבי ב״ר שלמה הלוי מארדער נ״י
וזוגתו מרת חיה שולמית בת ר׳ אליהו מארדער צוועטשקענבואם תחי׳

In Memory of the Zwetschkenbaum and Loewith Families
Trzesn, Galicia

לז״נ

ר׳ יעקב יצחק ז״ל ממשפחת Zwetschkenbaum
וזוגתו מרת חיה ע״ה ממשפחת Kestenbaum
ר׳ צבי ז״ל ממשפחת Loewith
וזוגתו מרת שושנה ע״ה ממשפחת Schnurmacher
ר׳ אליהו ב״ר יעקב יצחק ז״ל נפטר י״ב אב תשכ״ח-1968
האשה ביילא בת ר׳ יעקב יצחק ע״ה
ר׳ ישראל ב״ר יעקב יצחק ז״ל
האשה מינדל בת ר׳ יעקב יצחק ע״ה
ר׳ אהרן ב״ר יעקב יצחק ז״ל
האשה גיטל בת ר׳ יעקב יצחק ע״ה
האשה איטע בת ר׳ יעקב יצחק ע״ה
ר׳ מרדכי ב״ר צבי ז״ל
האשה מרים בת ר׳ צבי ע״ה
האשה חנה בת ר׳ צבי ע״ה
ר׳ אדאלף ב״ר צבי ז״ל
תנצב״ה

הונצח ע״י

האשה שרה רייזל בת ר׳ צבי צוועטשקענבואם - לעוויט תחי׳
ר׳ יוסף ב״ר צבי לעוויט נ״י
וזוגתו מרת מינקא בת ר׳ אריה לעוויט - עיבלס תחי׳

נר תמיד

נר תמיד

הוקדש לעי"נ בנינו היקר

הרב נטע שלום ז"ל
נפטר ט' ניסן תשמ"ו

Dedicated in Loving Memory of
our beloved son

NOTA SHOLEM ז"ל

תנצב"ה

by
Anshel and Penina Rosenblum

Dedicated in Loving Memory of

ר' יחיאל אלטר ב"ר אברהם שפיגעל ז"ל
נפטר ט"ו אלול תשמ"ז

ואשתו

מרת קלארא שרה בת ר' אברהם (צוקרמאן) ז"ל
נפטרה כ"ז אלול תשנ"ב

תנצב"ה

by
Mr. & Mrs. Sidney Eisen

נר תמיד

הוקדש

לזכרון הקדושים

שנהרגו על קידוש השם

בימי השואה

ה׳ ינקום דמם

ע״י

ר׳ אפרים רייכמאן ומשפחתו שיחיו

לכבוד הורי היקרים

הרב ר׳ **שלמה יעקב** שליט״א
ב״ר יהודה אריה ז״ל
דייוויס

ורעיתו מרת **אסתר בלומה** תחי׳
בת הרב שרגא משה ז״ל

ע״י

ר׳ יוסף חיים דייוויס ומשפחתו

Chicago, Illinois

In Honor of
the Author
and his dear family

Thanking them for the
beautiful way in which
they touched our lives.

Cookie, Harry & Harvey
Yellin

Ester & Freddie Rabhan
& Family

Savannah, Georgia

הוקדש לז"נ
אבי מורי

ר' **ברוך**
ב"ר **פלטיאל** הכהן **סלום** ז"ל

ע"ה **MR. BRUCE SLOME**

נפטר א' דראש חדש אדר תשנ"א

תנצב"ה

ע"י
ר' משה סלום
ומשפחתו

Dedicated in Loving Memory of

ר' אברהם אבא ב"ר צבי ז"ל
MR. ABISH BERGEL ע"ה
נפטר כ"א אייר תשמ"ז

וזוג' מרת פייגע יטע ע"ה
בת ר' זרח ע"ה
MRS. FAYGA BERGEL ע"ה
נפטרה כ"א שבט תשמ"ג

תנצב"ה

by their children
Hy נ"י and Helen תחי'
and grandchildren
Shawna תחי' , Elisa תחי',
Ari נ"י, and Ilan נ"י

נדבה לזכר נשמותיהם של

מרת רוזיא
בת ר' שמחה הכהן פריעד ז"ל
נפטרה י"ח אלול תשנ"א

ר' יצחק ב"ר משה קפטן ז"ל
נפטר ו' אדר ב' תשמ"א

וזוגתו בילא צירל
בת ר' יהושע אשר ז"ל
נפטרה כ"ט תמוז תשמ"ז
תנצב"ה

ע"י
ר' יוסף פריעד ומשפחתו

הונצח לז"נ

ר' יצחק מאיר ז"ל
ב"ר ישראל יחיאל ז"ל
קאראלניק

נפטר ח' אייר תשל"א

וזוגתו מרת אלטא טאבא ע"ה
בת ר' משה אהרן ז"ל

נפטרה כ"ז תשרי תשל"ב

תנצב"ה

ע"י
בניהם ובנותיהם

הונצח לז"נ
ר' דוב דוד ב"ר אברהם חנוך ז"ל
וזוגתו מרת דאברא בת ר' דוד **ע"ה**
תנצב"ה
ע"י
ר' הרשיל טעננבוים נ"י

Dedicated in Loving Memory of
ר' צבי הירש ב"ר בנימין ע"ה
ע"ה **MR. HAROLD ARONSON**
כ"ז אב תשכ"ט Aug. 11, 1969
ומרת פריווא בת ר' אריה ליב ע"ה
ע"ה **MRS. PAULINE ARONSON**
כ"ח כסלו תשנ"ב Dec. 4, 1991
and families
תנצב"ה

הונצח ע"י
האחים מוהר"ר יוחנן נ"י
ומו"ר ר"ר יוסף נ"י רובין
לעיי"נ הוריהם
הר"ר עזריאל איכל ב"ר נפתלי ז"ל
וזוגתו מרת חנה רוזא בת ר' **יוסף** ע"ה
תנצב"ה

הונצח לז"נ
ר' יהודא ב"ר שמחה דוד ז"ל

וזוגתו
מרת פעסיא רבקה
בת ר' ישראל גרשון ז"ל

תנצב"ה

הונצח לז"נ

ר' זאב ב"ר אריה יהודה ז"ל
האפשטאדטער

נפטר י"ט מרחשון תשמ"ב

תנצב"ה

לז"נ
הרב חיים מאיר ב"ר יהודה ליב ז"ל
פנטל
ורעיתו מרת אילה הינדא בת
הרב אברהם ז"ל

RABBI MEYER & AYALAH PANTEL
by their children
ZOLTY, PANTEL,
& SILVERMAN FAMILIES

הונצח לז"נ הורינו היקרים

ר' מרדכי יהודה פריעדבערג ז"ל
ומרת רעכיל בת ר' שמואל מרדכי ע"ה
ר' יונה ב"ר משה צוידיערער היי"ד
ומרת שרה בת ר' מאיר היי"ד
תנצב"ה

ע"י ר' פרץ נ"י
ומרת פרידא פריעדבערג תחי'

מזכרת נצח
מר' שמעון ווערנער נ"י
ורעיתו מרת שרה אסתר תחי'
לעילוי נשמות
אביו ר' **נתן ב"ר שמעון** ז"ל-נפ' י"ד שבט תרצ"ז
אמו מרת **מירל** בת ר' **שמואל** ע"ה-
נפ' כ"ד חשון תשי"ב
אביה ר' **שמואל** ב"ר **יונה** ז"ל-נפ' ב' ניסן תשל"ד
אמה מרת **טילא רבקה** בת ר' **ירמיהו** ע"ה-נפ'
כ"ד ניסן תשמ"ג
תנצב"ה

Dedicated in Loving Memory of
ר' מרדכי ב"ר בנימין הלוי ע"ה
ע"ה MR. MAX MOVSOVITZ
ומרת רחל לאה בת ר' שלמה אליעזר ע"ה
ע"ה MRS. LENA MOVSOVITZ
ר' שמואל ב"ר משה ע"ה
ע"ה MR. SAM KARSMAN
ומרת ריזל ב"ר משה ע"ה
ע"ה MRS. ROSE KARSMAN
תנצב"ה

In Loving Memory of
MR. SOL COOPER ע"ה
&
MRS. RACHEL COOPER ע"ה
תנצב"ה
by
Edwin & Aviva Cooper
& Family
Savannah, Georgia

About the Author

Rabbi Aaron Levine has distinguished himself in the field of Jewish education, with twenty-five years' experience. He has served as dean and *menahel* of schools in Savannah, Georgia, Deal, New Jersey, and Toronto, Canada, where he is presently dean-elect of the Eitz Chaim Schools, a network of three branches comprising approximately 1,200 students. He is a recipient of the coveted Torah Umesorah Principal of the Year award. Rabbi Levine holds a master's degree in education, a doctorate in talmudic law, and a doctorate in Judaica. He has written extensively on Jewish mourning and bereavement, and the first volume of his encyclopedic work *Zichron Meir* has received wide acclaim. He also lectures in the field of Jewish laws and customs and is a regular contributor to the "Rabbinical Reflections" column of the *Canadian Jewish News*. He and his wife, Chanie (née Nussbaum), reside in Toronto. They have three sons and a new daughter-in-law.